SILENCED VOICES

Publication of this volume has been made possible, in part, through the generous support and enduring vision of Warren G. Moon and through the support of Randolph-Macon College.

# SILENCED VOICES

*The Poetics of Speech in Ovid*

Bartolo A. Natoli

THE UNIVERSITY OF WISCONSIN PRESS

The University of Wisconsin Press
728 State Street, Suite 443
Madison, Wisconsin 53706
uwpress.wisc.edu

Gray's Inn House, 127 Clerkenwell Road
London EC1R 5DB, United Kingdom
eurospanbookstore.com

Copyright © 2017
The Board of Regents of the University of Wisconsin System
All rights reserved. Except in the case of brief quotations embedded in critical articles and reviews, no part of this publication may be reproduced, stored in a retrieval system, transmitted in any format or by any means—digital, electronic, mechanical, photocopying, recording, or otherwise—or conveyed via the internet or a website without written permission of the University of Wisconsin Press. Rights inquiries should be directed to rights@uwpress.wisc.edu.

Printed in the United States of America
This book may be available in a digital edition.

Library of Congress Cataloging-in-Publication Data

Names: Natoli, Bartolo, author.
Title: Silenced voices : the poetics of speech in Ovid / Bartolo A. Natoli.
Other titles: Wisconsin studies in classics.
Description: Madison, Wisconsin: The University of Wisconsin Press, [2017] | Series: Wisconsin studies in classics | Includes bibliographical references and index.
Identifiers: LCCN 2016049007 | ISBN 9780299312107 (cloth : alk. paper)
Subjects: LCSH: Ovid, 43 B.C.-17 A.D. or 18 A.D.—Criticism and interpretation.
Classification: LCC PA6537 .N38 2017 | DDC 871/.01—dc23
LC record available at https://lccn.loc.gov/2016049007

ISBN 9780299312145 (pbk. : alk. paper)

MEO UXORI ET FILIIS,
CUM GRATIIS AMOREQUE

# Contents

| | | |
|---|---|---|
| | *Acknowledgments* | ix |
| | *Introduction* | 3 |
| 1 | Speech and Speech Loss in Ancient Rome | 17 |
| 2 | Speech Loss in the *Metamorphoses* | 33 |
| 3 | Speech Loss in the Exile Literature | 80 |
| 4 | Speech Loss and Memory in the Exile Literature | 140 |
| | *Notes* | 183 |
| | *Works Cited* | 211 |
| | *Appendix*: Instances of Speech Loss in the *Metamorphoses* | 221 |
| | *Index* | 223 |
| | *Index Locorum* | 225 |

# *Acknowledgments*

This book has its roots in a 2008 graduate seminar on Ovid at the University of Texas at Austin, conducted by Professor Karl Galinsky. During that seminar, I was allowed to explore the brilliance of the *Metamorphoses* as well as to foster a love for all the works of Ovid. In regard to speech loss in particular, I was fortunate enough to be encouraged to present a small project on the reception of the topic of speech loss in the *Metamorphosis* of Franz Kafka. This project sparked a desire to delve further into the Ovidian conception of speech loss and set me on a nearly decade-long journey of research and reflection. Therefore, I first must thank Karl for introducing me to the Ovidian corpus and for his encouragement and expertise in the field.

There are many other individuals whom I should thank for their insights and efforts. I thank Alessandro Barchiesi for his guidance in framing my argument and for his help during the infantile stages of this manuscript. I also thank Laurel Fulkerson, Rabun Taylor, L. Michael White, and Stephen Hinds for their discerning eyes and kind words that aided the revision—and, indeed, reconstructions!—of my argument. Moreover, I thank the entire Classics departments at the University of Richmond and Boston University for their generosity in allowing me to present earlier versions of my research and to learn from the insightful comments of those who attended those presentations. To Mark Payne, in particular, I give thanks for insight into the place of speechlessness and animality in ancient Rome.

As I revised the manuscript, I was lucky to have the unswerving support of my colleagues at Randolph-Macon College, particularly Gregory Daugherty, whose steadfast support afforded me the opportunity to work on the manuscript amid other departmental duties. Moreover, I thank Randolph-Macon as a whole for awarding me a Walter Williams Craigie Grant to fund the completion of this manuscript. I am deeply indebted to the college's generosity.

At the University of Wisconsin Press, I was lucky to be the beneficiary of a tremendous team of editors, all of whom helped me fine-tune the argument of this manuscript into its current form. I especially thank Raphael Kadushin and Amber Rose for their tireless efforts and for their patience with my endless e-mails. Likewise, Sheila McMahon and Barb Wojhoski were invaluable in the final preparations of the manuscript. The editors of the Wisconsin Studies in Classics were also a boon throughout the publication process with their laser-like focus on potential hurdles that needed to be addressed. Therefore, I give special thanks to these outstanding editors: Laura McClure, Mark Stansbury-O'Donnell, and Matthew Roller. Even more thanks are owed to the numerous anonymous readers who helped push me to make my argument stronger and sounder. Any shortcomings that remain in the manuscript are due to either my own stubbornness or oversight.

Finally, I thank my family, without whom this entire project would not have been possible. To my wife, Morgan, I am indebted for her unwavering confidence and patience throughout the many versions of this work. To my mother, Anne, I give thanks for listening to the constant successes and failures that came along with this project. And last, I thank my children, Luca and Mira, for uplifting me with their joy and curiosity for life, attributes I have attempted to make use of in this work.

# SILENCED VOICES

# Introduction

> To hide in this way was to be stripped of all self-respect. To be told to hide was a humiliation. Maybe, he thought, to live like this would be worse than death.
>
> Then there was the publishing front, where he could take nothing for granted in spite of all his work. Publication itself was still an issue. It was not certain that he could continue in the life he had chosen, not certain that he would always find willing hands to print and distribute his work.
>
> —SALMAN RUSHDIE, *Joseph Anton*

THE QUOTATIONS THAT OPEN THIS CHAPTER, taken from Salman Rushdie's recently published autobiographical account of his time spent as an exile, *Joseph Anton: A Memoir*, represent only some of the most recent iterations of the experience of exile. Rushdie, placed under a fatwa in 1989 by Ayatollah Ruhollah Khomeini for perceived insults against Islam in his *The Satanic Verses*, was forced both into hiding and into the adoption of a pseudonym: Joseph Anton. For the intensely proud and social author, the exile he describes is crushing. His identity as individual and, more importantly, as author was effectively erased: no longer could he hope to publish books or to converse with his society (both professional and personal). He had to be erased from his society, was forced to be forgotten, was made to "play dead" simply to save himself and his loved ones from the constant death threats resulting from the fatwa.

In addition to the obvious similarities (which will be discussed later) with that of Roman literature's most famous exile, Ovid, Rushdie's account also speaks to the larger fascination with and proliferation of exile literature in modernity, for exile has been "one of the most productive literary topics in twentieth century literature" (Gaertner 2007, 1). Perhaps the two developments most to blame for this increase in interest are (1) globalization and (2) the shift of the meaning of artist and production in both the modern and the postmodern sense. To the first point, the ability of electronic mass media to "collapse space and time barriers in human communication [and] to enable people to communicate on a global scale" has greatly aided in the proliferation of writings from the "fringes" of society or from an "exiled" writer back to his or her native land (Boldor 2005n1). Such emphasis features prominently in writings from the diaspora of expatriates, such as Thomas Mann, Vladimir Nabokov, or Joseph Brodsky.[1] As for the second point, shifting notions of artist and production have led to the use of the rhetoric of displacement, exile, and otherness to describe the authorial condition. Alexandru Boldor (2005) sums up how this idea played out in terms of the modern and the postmodern, stating: "Modernism relied on displacement being rooted in the idea that 'traditional' forms of art, literature, social organization and daily life had become outdated, and that it was therefore essential to sweep them aside and reinvent culture—obviously, a vision diverging from 'normal' social trends. Postmodernism took these ideas even further, with its focus upon the personal, regional, etc., in short, on the *alternative*" (5n4). Related to this movement is the adoption of exile as a common metaphor for alienation in intellectual literature, as the intelligentsia of modernity and postmodernity frequently sought to define their own position in humanity or the human condition in general as exilic or outcast (e.g., Friedrich Nietzsche, Jean-Paul Sartre, Theodor Adorno, Nabokov).

### Exile Literature and Classical Studies

Against this background, the interest and discussion of exile has moved into the Classics and has resulted in a tremendous growth in scholarship on exile and, in particular, on the three most prominent writers who went into exile, the *exulum trias*[2] of Cicero, Ovid, and Seneca the Younger.[3] Apart from the historical study of Ernst Ludwig Grasmück (1978), there have been three major voices in the discussion of exile from a literary angle: Ernst Doblhofer (1987), Jo-Marie Claassen (1999, 2008), and Jan Felix Gaertner (2005, 2007). Doblhofer, perhaps influenced by contemporary studies of exile literature from modernity, discusses the ancient exilic corpus from a psychological angle. He develops the concept of the exilic state as a sickness, an "*Exilkrankheit*," that is the universal response to being forced into exile. As evidence of this *Exilkrankheit*, Doblhofer points to the striking similarities between modern and ancient exile literature that help to create an almost identical depiction of exile. The major similarities of exile literature that Doblhofer notes are particular topoi, such as the exile's closeness to death, his identification with heroic figures, and his loss of the ability to speak in his native language (1987, 67–69, 261–73).

Claassen, in both her 1999 and 2008 discussions of exile, builds out from the sociohistorical foundations of Grasmück and the psychological arguments of Doblhofer and offers a new schema for organizing and analyzing ancient exilic literature based on grammatical person (e.g., first, second, third).[4] The shift of schema from the traditional, organizing "genre" of exilic literature aims at analyzing the variety of "modes of presentation" within that genre and at the different styles utilized by the exiled author to attain such *variatio* (Claassen 1999, 15). Through such an analysis of style and *variatio*, Claassen aims at identifying the "feelings of the writer" (1999, 15).[5]

The last of the three treatments of ancient exile is that of Gaertner (2007). In contrast to Claassen and Doblhofer, Gaertner eschews psychological evaluations of the authors of exile literature and instead focuses on the topoi used by those authors:

> If there is a tradition of typical complaints about and consolations for exile one cannot assume a direct and simple relation between the psychological condition of exile and the literature written by exiles, but one has to take into account that (a) authors may perceive and present their experience of exile according to pre-existing literary and cultural paradigms, that (b) they may merely style themselves or others as (typical) exiles, and that (c) being an exile obviously presupposes that the banished person accepts the role of an exile imposed by circumstances. (2007, 4–5)

Gaertner goes on to challenge the basic assumptions of genre made by Claassen and Doblhofer, who both seem to have applied modern notions of genre to ancient exilic texts in order to produce an organized, almost chronological schema, or at the least seem to have neglected the question altogether. In place of the modern conception of genre, Gaertner postulates an "ancient discourse on exile" that was almost a topos unto itself (2007, 4). Whenever exile came up as a topic in a literary work, certain topoi of exile could be employed by the artist and comprehended by the audience irrespective of the performance context or medium of production. For example, when Ovid describes his exile in terms of linguistic and cultural isolation, he need not be describing a psychological reality for Ovid the author or be alluding to a topos from a "genre of exilic literature," but he could be tapping into a cultural store of topoi of the exilic situation just as a sixth-century *iambos* of Solon had done (fr. 36 West).[6]

## Exile Literature and Ovidian Studies

Ovid has seemingly been at the center of this type of scholarly debate over the accessibility of an exilic author's emotional state or the veracity of his narrative about his state. Until the last half of the twentieth century, many of the statements

Ovid makes in his exile literature were taken as absolute fact through the so-called historicistic approach. L. P. Wilkinson, for example, accepted as true Ovid's statements of inferiority and conversion from a free spirit to a devotee of emperor worship. There is even the anecdote that Sir Ronald Syme carried with him a photograph of an iced-over Black Sea beach that definitively proved that the Ovidian descriptions of Tomis as a wintry wasteland were based in fact (Claassen 2008, 5). The predominance of the historicists began to wane in 1965, with the publication of E. J. Kenney's article "The Poetry of Ovid's Exile," which brought to the fore the style and poetics of Ovidian exile literature, throwing into doubt Ovid's assertions that his poetry had declined in quality. In the last two decades of the twentieth century, scholarship, perhaps taking its cue from Kenney's article, began to focus more directly on the poetics of the exile literature, downplaying the historicist tendencies of the previous generations of scholarship by questioning the veracity of Ovid's statements of poetic decline, developing theories of *variatio* and organization, and drawing connections and allusions to other genres and literary works.[7] Such an increase in scholarly interest has, in the last decade, resulted in a seemingly constant stream of new commentaries and monographs on all the exile literature (see works cited for a listing).

Yet, for all the increase in scholarly attention on the truthfulness of Ovid's depiction of himself and his situation, a passage in the *Tristia* seems to have gone unnoticed or, at least, underanalyzed.[8] At the end of the programmatic first poem of *Tristia* 1, Ovid gives explicit instructions to his book of poetry about how his poems from exile should be compared with the rest of his poetic corpus:

> aspicies illic positos ex ordine fratres,
>     quos studium cunctos euigilauit idem.
> cetera turba palam titulos ostendet apertos,
>     et sua detecta nomina fronte geret;
> tres procul obscura latitantes parte uidebis:
>     hi quia, quod nemo nescit, amare docent;
> hos tu uel fugias, uel, si satis oris habebis,
>     Oedipodas facito Telegonosque uoces.
> deque tribus, moneo, si qua est tibi cura parentis,
>     ne quemquam, quamuis ipse docebit, ames.
> sunt quoque mutatae, ter quinque uolumina, formae,
>     nuper ab exequiis carmina rapta meis.
> his mando dicas, inter mutata referri
>     *fortunae vultum* corpora posse *meae,*

namque ea dissimilis subito est effecta priori,
  flendaque nunc, aliquo tempore laeta fuit.
    (*Tr.* 1.1.107–22)

[You will see there [in the bookshelf] your brothers placed in order, all of whom the same zeal composed. The rest of the crowd shows their open covers publicly and bear their names with the cover turned aside; but three you will see far off, hiding in a dark part of the shelf because these taught that which no one is ignorant of: how to love. Either flee these or, if you have enough voice, speak in Oedipal or Telegonal strains. About these three I warn you, if you care for your parent at all, so that you won't love one, although it itself will teach you. Also there are changed bodies—thrice five volumes—songs recently snatched from my ashes. To these I ask you to say that the appearance of my fortune is able to be counted among the changed bodies, for the fortune has suddenly been made different from before: now it is lamentable, but was in another time happy.[9]]

Two major aspects of this passage are striking, both of which may have import for the debate over Ovidian "truthfulness" and, more broadly, for the manner in which Ovid conceptualized the poetic aim of his exile literature: (1) the emphasis on *vultus fortunae meae* as the main topic of his exile poetry and (2) the relationship between that *vultus fortunae meae* and the characters (i.e., *mutata corpora*) of the *Metamorphoses*.

To get at the reason why Ovid emphasized *vultus fortunae meae*, one must first start with what the phrase itself means, in particular why Ovid chose to give his fortune a *vultus*.[10] The term *vultus* is used frequently by Ovid; a *Thesaurus Linguae Latinae* (*TLL*) search shows that it appears 261 times throughout his poetic corpus. Moreover, as would be expected, the term is particularly prevalent in the *Metamorphoses*, in which it is used 121 times. In the *Metamorphoses*, *vultus* routinely appears in Ovidian depictions of change to emphasize the metamorphosis of the outward appearance of the character. The example of Lycaon from *Metamorphoses* 1 serves as an example of this emphasis on outward change:

in villos abeunt vestes, in crura lacerti:
fit lupus et veteris servat vestigia formae;
canities eadem est, eadem violentia *vultus*,
idem oculi lucent, eadem feritatis imago est.
  (*Met.* 1.236–39)

[Clothes change into hair, arms into legs: he becomes a wolf and preserves the vestiges of his old form; there is the same gray hair, the same violence of expression, the same eyes gleam: there is the same image of savagery.]

Here Ovid depicts the outward transformation of Lycaon, commenting on his gray hair, eyes, and overall outward appearance. The inclusion of *vultus* with *canities* and *oculi* strengthens its identification with outward appearance.

Likewise, the metamorphosis of Actæon in *Metamorphoses* 3 points to the same emphasis:

ut vero *vultus* et cornua vidit in unda,
"me miserum!" dicturus erat: vox nulla secuta est!
ingemuit: vox illa fuit, lacrimaeque per ora
non sua fluxerunt; mens tantum pristina mansit.
     (*Met.* 3.200–203)

[Truly, when he saw his appearance and horns in the water, he was about to say, "Woe is me!" but no voice followed. He groaned: that was his voice, and tears flowed down a face not his own; yet his mind remained as before.]

As in the example of Lycaon, the use of *vultus* in the depiction of Actæon is one based on outward appearance. Actæon looks into the water and sees his *vultus*, as that *vultus* now comes with antlers.

Yet these two examples also point to another aspect of *vultus* in the *Metamorphoses*: although the *vultus* of a character is changed, the underlying essence of the character remains unchanged.[11] For Lycaon, although his *vultus* is now that of a wolf, he still maintains the savage personality he had as a man.[12] Likewise, Actæon, although his *vultus* changes from a man's to a deer's, retains his inner identity (*mens tantum pristina mansit*).

If one brings this relationship between *vultus* and outside appearance into the context of *Tristia* 1.1, the truthfulness of Ovid's self-portrayal is thrown into doubt. By making *vultus fortunae meae* the main consideration of his exile literature, Ovid seems to point to the fact that his exile literature presents a *vultus*, an outward appearance, that is subject to change and that hides beneath it whatever truth there may be.[13] Ovid's self-depiction is simply a facade, a poetic covering that conceals the unchanged quintessential substance of the poet. There seems to be no psychological truth to be had here; the exile literature is merely creating a poetic depiction.

The use of *vultus* in the exile literature also points to a similar emphasis on outward appearance.¹⁴ In particular, the mention of *vultus* in *Tristia* 1.7 seems apropos here:

Si quis habes nostri similes in imagine *vultus*,
    deme meis hederas, Bacchica serta, comis.
ista decent laetos felicia signa poetas:
    temporibus non est apta corona meis.
        (*Tr.* 1.7.1–4)

[If any of you has similar *vultus* to mine in an *imago*, take down the ivy, the bacchic wreath, from my hair. Those fortunate signs are fitting for happy poets: crowns are not suitable for my times.]

In this poem, *vultus* is combined with *imago* to describe a ring with Ovid's portrait or perhaps a bust of Ovid in somebody's library.¹⁵ Both of these possibilities point to the fact that the *vultus* here is an artistic representation, a fictional portrayal of the "real" Ovid. Moreover, as Stephen Hinds has pointed out, this mention of *vultus* is closely linked with our programmatic use in *Tristia* 1.1, as not only is the same term employed, but both contexts are linked with the *Metamorphoses*; in his mention of *vultus* and *imago* in *Tristia* 1.7, Ovid suggests that his audience turn not to this physical *imago* but to a *maior imago* (1.7.11), the *Metamorphoses*, to remember him.¹⁶ This recalls the close relationship between *vultus* and the *mutata corpora* of the *Metamorphoses* in 1.1. It stands to reason, therefore, that the connotation of *vultus* in 1.7 strengthens the reading of 1.1 as a programmatic statement that Ovid's *vultus*, the very thing Ovid's *parvus liber* was meant to describe, was not a historical portrait but rather a fictional persona.

In addition, when the *fortunae meae* portion of the phrase is added, Ovid is further removed from consideration. Not only is Ovid indicating that his exile literature deals not with reality but with a changing outward appearance, but he also states that this changing appearance belongs to his *fortuna* and not to him.¹⁷ Indeed, throughout the *Tristia*, Ovid keeps coming back to the trope of his changing fortune. In *Tristia* 1.5, he reflects back on times when he enjoyed a fortune that had a *vultu sereno*. Likewise, in *Tristia* 5.8, Ovid warns an enemy not to rejoice too much in Ovid's exile, as fortune is naturally ever-changing (*sed modo laeta venit, vultus modo sumit acerbos, / et tantum constans in levitate sua est,* 17–18).

Therefore, because of the distance Ovid creates between himself and the content of the exile literature, Claassen and Doblhofer's attempts at ascertaining Ovid's true feelings or analyzing his psychological reality become somewhat less persuasive. For a description of exile true to reality was seemingly not Ovid's stated purpose. Nevertheless, that does not mean that Claassen and Doblhofer's readings of Ovid's authorial intent should not be pursued. After all, Ovid made the conscious, authorial decision to describe his exile literature as a facade or outward appearance.

This, in fact, brings us to the second aspect of this passage: the connection between *vultus* and the *mutata corpora* of the *Metamorphoses*. Ovid gives his *parvus liber* explicit instructions to tell his fellow books that the appearance of Ovid's fortune should be counted among the changed bodies of the *Metamorphoses*. This small phrase has led scholars to believe that some part of Ovid's depiction of his *vultus* resembled that of a character(s) of the *Metamorphoses*. Nearly all these scholars have equated the exilic Ovid with a character from the *Metamorphoses* that closely resembles him.

Samuel Huskey, in particular, has shown the similarities drawn by Ovid between his depiction as an exile and the portrayal of multiple characters from the *Metamorphoses*. For example, Huskey (2001a) has found striking similarities between Ovid's self-depiction and that of Philomela from *Metamorphoses* 6 and has pointed to the fact that both were taken away to a barbarous land against their will and were robbed of the ability to speak.[18] For Huskey, in Philomela Ovid found "an effective model for the depiction of his exilic persona." Likewise, he has argued for similarities between Ovid's self-depiction of himself and that of Jason (*Metamorphoses* 7) (Huskey 2001b), Palinurus (*Metamorphoses* 14) (2009), and Palamedes (*Metamorphoses* 13) (2001a).

In addition to Huskey's efforts, several scholars have drawn multiple similarities between Ovid's self-depiction and his portrayal of artists in the *Metamorphoses*. Judith Hallett (2009) has shown the similarities between Ovid in *Tristia* 4.10 and Pygmalion in *Metamorphoses* 10, as both are described as partaking in the same artistic process in the creation of art in their respective media of poetry and sculpture. Likewise, Stephen Hinds (2006) and Allison Sharrock (1994, 168–74) have both drawn attention to the links between the exilic Ovid and the great inventor Daedalus from *Metamorphoses* 8, both of whom were supreme artificers in exile across the sea and were attempting to return to their homeland through their powers of creation.

However, although all these connections between Ovid's self-depiction in the *Tristia* and particular characters in the *Metamorphoses* have some degree of validity and have added much to how Ovid's exilic poetry has been read, analyzing the relationship between Ovid's exilic self-depiction and the *Metamorphoses* in terms of which characters Ovid resembles does not exhaust the ways in which one can compare the texts. One can also look thematically at how Ovid's self-depiction compares to the *Metamorphoses*. In essence, when analyzing Ovid's relationship to his *mutata corpora*, one can shift the focus from individual *corpora* to the method behind how they become *mutata*.

One manner in which this can be done is to examine the ways in which characters in the *Metamorphoses* become *mutata* and to compare their methods of change to the manners in which Ovid chooses to create his self-depiction in the exile literature. If one analyzes the connection between Ovid's self-depiction and his stories of change in the *Metamorphoses*, a pattern does arise that pervades both the entirety of the *Metamorphoses* and the exile literature: the loss of speech and subsequent removal from society that befalls a character when she or he is transformed.

Scholars have long identified speech loss as a key aspect of characters' transformations in the *Metamorphoses*.[19] In fact, speech loss occurs in nearly 20 percent of all the tales included in the *Metamorphoses*, regardless of whether a particular character is the focal point.[20] Characters that have been transformed into rocks, trees, or animals cease to speak in their human voice. As a result, these characters become isolated from their community because they are no longer able to communicate with its members. However, as was mentioned in the example of Actæon, the underlying identity of the character remains intact, heightening the character's sense of isolation and disconnection and increasing the overall pathos of the story of his or her transformation. While the continual awareness of their situation heightens the character's sense of isolation, it also allows the opportunity for the characters to work free of their solitary situations through the use of their remaining human faculties. Thus, in the *Metamorphoses*, some of the transformed characters are able to reconnect with their lost communities through the creation of written representations by which they communicate their true identities to members of their communities.

The situation just described shares a great many similarities with Ovid's depiction of himself in exile, and scholarship on the exile literature has likewise tracked Ovidian mentions of speech loss in his self-depiction. Throughout the exile literature, Ovid portrays himself as suffering from a sudden loss of voice that manifests itself in various ways ranging from a loss of the ability to speak Latin fluently, to a failing ability to create poetry, to the complete loss of a voice of any kind.[21] Such a focus on speech loss has led to a number of discussions of the trope, all of which have come to extremely divergent conclusions.

Doblhofer, for example, has identified speech loss as a symptom of Ovid's *Exilkrankheit* and argues that such mentions of speech loss were part of the universal psyche of the exile, regardless of time and space, and were not limited to Ovid. Gaertner, commenting on the same instances of speech loss in the exile literature, concludes that they were mere tropes of a type of Greco-Roman exile literature that Ovid was employing for poetic aims; they spoke to no part of Ovid's psyche nor were they unique to Ovid, although he may have been the first to use them to create a corpus of exile poetry. Those same aspects of speech loss were also analyzed most recently by Benjamin Stevens, who argues that Ovid's continued focus on speech loss was indicative of his "deeply ambivalent" attitude toward the composition of poetry in exile and its possible reception "both because of its deepening compromise by the local languages and . . . because of the lack of a competent audience" (2009, 180). These three views of speech loss in the exile literature create three different pictures of Ovid: is Ovid truly depressed and devastated by his exile enough to paint a true portrait of himself as voiceless, as Doblhofer would have it; is Ovid playing a literary game, as he often did, by combining tropes from existing exile literature together to create a fictional exilic persona, as Gaertner suggests; or, has Ovid—or his exilic persona—simply given up due to his lack of audience in Tomis, as argued by Stevens?

However, none of these approaches takes into account Ovid's assertion that the *vultus fortunae meae* is to be added among the *mutata corpora*, as none seek to ground their approaches in the *Metamorphoses*. Doblhofer omits Ovid's assertion that his self-depiction is merely a *vultus*, an outward appearance such as those of the transformed in the *Metamorphoses*. Stevens downplays Ovid's portrayal of speech loss in exile literature because he treats it as a trope limited to the exile literature and not one present in the *Metamorphoses* as well; as a result, Stevens concludes that Ovid is ambivalent toward poetry, when, in fact, the exact opposite may be true: by using the trope of speech loss that is seen in the *Metamorphoses*, Ovid is being exceedingly literary and expects his audience to recognize that his exilic persona has become like the transformed characters of the *Metamorphoses*—Ovid has become the poetry itself, or the book, in the terminology of Philip Hardie and Carole Newlands.[22] Unlike Stevens and Doblhofer, Gaertner argues that Ovid is creating a poetic persona and is using speech loss as a literary trope; however, he links that trope to the larger group of exilic texts and not to the *Metamorphoses*.

Yet over the past two decades, in addition to these studies of speech loss both in the *Metamorphoses* and in the exile literature, other scholars have begun to compare the manner in which speech loss is deployed in both. The work of Judith de Luce and Elizabeth Forbis has been particularly illuminating.

De Luce, following the lead of Leo Curran, has examined instances of speech loss in the *Metamorphoses* and argued that such a loss symbolized the dehumanization of a character.[23] In particular, she focuses on speech loss in stories of rape, showing how the motif was used more frequently in tales of rape than in any other context.[24] As a side note to her study, de Luce suggests that Ovid's focus on his own speech loss in the exile literature perhaps looked back to his characterization of dehumanized characters in the *Metamorphoses* and symbolized his own dehumanization at the hands of Augustus (1992, 317–18). However, she leaves the discussion at that point and defers to other scholars, such as Forbis.[25]

Forbis perhaps represents the fullest exploration of the connection of speech loss in the *Metamorphoses* with that in the exile literature. To Forbis, Ovid consciously included self-allusive instances of speech loss in the exile literature as a means to protest Augustus's treatment of him and to highlight the injustice of his precarious situation.[26] She argues that Ovid compares himself to stories such as that of Actæon (*Metamorphoses* 3) and of the Swan and the Raven (*Metamorphoses* 2) in an effort to emphasize his innocence and the harshness of his punishment because he never spoke harsh words against Augustus. Likewise, Forbis draws a close connection between Ovid's self-representation in the exile literature and Io and Philomela in the *Metamorphoses*, as those stories emphasize the isolation experienced by these characters. From these examples, she concludes that the voicelessness expressed by Ovid in the exile literature expresses an overall helplessness felt by the poet, as he realized that "his poetry cannot convince Augustus to recall him . . . he might as well be trapped inside the bark of a tree or within an animal's form for all the good his poems can accomplish" (1997, 259). All Ovid could hope for is that his *Metamorphoses* would live on and overcome the voicelessness suffered by the poet in exile.

Yet, for all of the valid points and arguments made by de Luce and Forbis, both also seem to start from the premise that the Ovid who felt his poetry was worthless and expressed his feelings of isolation and sorrow was the *historical* Ovid.[27] However, as I have discussed, Ovid clearly mentions that what he is depicting in the exile literature is his *vultus*, an appearance or persona, but not a historical portrayal. In addition to running the risk of unquestioned acceptance of Ovid's pose of decline, the argument that Ovid both considered his poetry worthless and accepted helplessly his exile in Tomis also becomes difficult to square with the fact Ovid also continually extols his poetic immortality in that same exile literature, or the fact that he even wrote poetry at all:[28] if he truly felt his poetry was helpless, why would he even have written it?

## The Scope of This Work

This book seeks to reevaluate earlier discussions of speech loss, starting from a different premise, namely, that Ovid is not attempting to portray a historical account but is instead creating an exilic persona. That exilic persona is, as has been shown by these scholars, bound up in the idea of speech loss. Therefore, I will argue that the presence of speech loss is not a psychological trait, as argued by Doblhofer, or only part of a wider discursive trope, as Gaertner suggests, but an allusion to a pattern that Ovid himself set up in the tales of transformation within his *Metamorphoses*.

This approach to speech loss solves many of the problems that trouble the other discussions of speech loss in the exile literature. First, by treating Ovid in the exile literature as a persona and not as the historical poet, this book avoids the contradictions present in Forbis, de Luce, and Stevens, all of whom favor a reading of the worthlessness of poetry, while accepting that that very poetry accomplished the goal it set out to meet: the memorialization of Ovid. Second, by identifying the trope of speech loss as a pattern created by Ovid in his *Metamorphoses* and reemployed by him in the exile literature, this book can reach beyond the exilic persona of Ovid to the historical Ovid in a manner that the approaches of Gaertner, Claassen, and Doblhofer do not, for the fact that Ovid alludes to a trope that *he himself* created allows for a greater analysis of authorial intent (i.e., a form of psychoanalysis), while still acknowledging that Ovid's pattern of speech loss had its genesis in the tropes of earlier exile literature.

This book approaches the topic of speech loss in Ovid, as it were, from the bottom up: starting first with a general background of conceptions of speech loss in first-century BCE Rome, then moving to the identification and analysis of both Ovid's pattern of speech loss in the *Metamorphoses* and its later iteration in the exile literature, finally moving to a deeper discussion of authorial intent and what forces might have driven Ovid to create and employ such a pattern. These steps are taken over the span of four chapters.

In chapter 1, I set the foundation for the entire discussion of speech loss in Ovid by analyzing the conception of speech loss in first-century BCE Roman thought. Using modern socio-cognitive theories of schemata and cognitive poetics, the analysis uncovers a schema of speech loss, along with its corresponding scripts. To that end, I trace the contexts in which the terms for speechlessness, particularly *mutus*, are used in first-century BCE Roman texts. The results indicate that speechlessness in that time period was bound up with concepts of the nonhuman, isolation, and emotionality, all of which Ovid chooses as foundational to his pattern of speech loss.

Chapter 2 sets out the pattern for speech loss that is the basis for Ovid's depiction of both his characters and himself. The chapter begins with what has been said about speech and speech loss in the *Metamorphoses*. Commentators such as William S. Anderson (1985), Franz Bömer (1969–86), and Alessandro Barchiesi (2001) have duly noted that characters who have transformed into rocks, trees, or animals cease to speak in their human voice. Yet most of the scholarship on speech loss in the *Metamorphoses* has concluded that characters lose their ability to speak because their human voice is transformed along with their forms. In this chapter I argue that speech loss in the *Metamorphoses* can be interpreted through the schematic model created in chapter 1 (i.e., speech loss as associated with the nonhuman and emotional) as a cessation of the ability to be human and an isolation from community. Stories from the *Metamorphoses* are examined as evidence of this interpretation, most notably the tales of Lycaon, Actæon, and Callisto. From here, I argue that, although the removal from society is a reality for these characters, Ovid builds a method of communal reintegration through the completion of another human act: artistic creation. The stories of Philomela and Io are analyzed to show this point, as these two characters regain their status in community through artistic creation.

In chapter 3, having set the theoretical frameworks of the book and the pattern of speech loss, artistic creation, and community in the *Metamorphoses*, I turn to how Ovid applies this model to his exilic persona in the exile literature. The chapter builds on the work of Spentzou (2003), Forbis (1997), de Luce (1993), and Stephens (2009), all of which have examined speech loss as an aspect of how Ovid depicts his transformation in exile, arguing that Ovid portrays himself as one of his transformed characters in order to engage with the model of speech loss and community, a model by which he can describe his reintegration into his community. However, as mentioned earlier, this chapter departs from these handlings of the exile literature by emphasizing that the Ovid of the exile literature is a persona and not the historical poet. As evidence of Ovid's interaction with his previous pattern of speech loss, this chapter provides close readings and interpretations of passages from the exile poetry, especially the opening sequence of poems from *Tristia* 1, which depict Ovid's journey from Rome to Tomis, the fictitious depictions of Tomis throughout the exilic project, and Ovid's focus on the written word as a communicative means in place of his lost speech.

In chapter 4, I turn to a discussion of authorial intent and consider the question of why Ovid attempts to portray himself in such a manner and what he gains—or hopes to gain—from doing so. It is in this section that the methodological framework of memory studies can prove to be enlightening. As has been shown by the work of Gareth Williams (1994), Hinds (1985), and Betty Rose Nagle (1980), Ovid manipulates his audience by engaging in what has been called a "pose of decline" or what Williams (1994) has fashioned as the "poetics of exile." This chapter builds on these previous discussions by casting Ovid's depiction of his exile in terms of memory. Using and modifying the terminology provided by Maurice Halbwachs (1925) and Jan Assmann (1992), I argue that Ovid engages with multiple aspects of Roman cultural memory to create an account of his exile that he wanted to be disseminated. Instead of reporting a "truthful" story of his exile based in individual memory, Ovid recalls his past engagement in a literary community and creates a literary patina out of Roman stereotypes and expectations of the generic tropes of absence and friendship in epistolography. Through these means, Ovid can, in essence, rewrite his own exile, creating a literary tale of a pose of decline based in cultural memory. In so doing, Ovid creates an artistic creation of his exile that he hopes will reintegrate him into Roman community by reconnecting him to Roman memory.

*chapter 1*

# Speech and Speech Loss in Ancient Rome

BEFORE TURNING TO THE OVIDIAN DEPICTION of speech loss and its subsequent effects in the *Metamorphoses* and exile literature, it will be helpful to frame the Ovidian depiction within the larger discourse of speech loss in Ovid's Rome. Therefore, in this section I will attempt to unpack some of the ways in which Ovid's contemporaries were discussing speechlessness in order to gain a deeper understanding of what exactly came to mind when one was speechless. To accomplish this, I will turn to the modern concept of schema theory, a method of conceptualizing how human beings conceive and make meaning of a situation, and one that has become a major part of the field of cognitive poetics. By piecing together the schemata that were activated when Ovid's contemporaries discussed speech loss, we can identify the contexts in which the topic of speech loss was most likely to occur and other concepts with which speech loss was closely associated. This background, consequently, will act as a foil to subsequent discussions in chapters 2 and 3 on how Ovid interacted with and innovated within this schematic model. In particular, I will focus on the schemata activated by the Latin word *mutus*, a common method of expressing this speechlessness in Ovid and in Latin more generally, although not the only one.[1] Still, an analysis of *mutus* provides us with an adequate number of instances to allow us to gain an understanding of the concept without the study being too large and cumbersome to glean anything useful.

What we will find through an analysis of *mutus* is that the concept of speechlessness involved much more than the simple removal of the physical ability to speak; the real loss was of the social variety. In antiquity, speech was regarded as a uniquely human linguistic ability.[2] Whereas animals had a type of communication, a method of communicating through inarticulate sounds denoting pain or pleasure, humankind developed their language into speech, an articulated form of communication that was able to recall and discuss matters removed from the present time and place, to produce new sounds and meanings for new objects and ideas, and to describe abstract ideas devoid of any physical manifestation. Along with this articulated speech came the rational ability to organize the linguistic and physical world into community. In fact, for the Greeks, the related concepts of speech and rational thought were bound up in the term λόγος. The clearest statement of this notion is found in Aristotle's *Politics*:[3]

> Λόγον δὲ μόνον ἄνθρωπος ἔχει τῶν ζῴων· ἡ μὲν οὖν φωνὴ τοῦ λυπηροῦ καὶ ἡδέος ἐστὶ σημεῖον, διὸ καὶ τοῖς ἄλλοις ὑπάρχει ζῴοις (μέχρι γὰρ τούτου ἡ φύσις αὐτῶν ἐλήλυθε, τοῦ ἔχειν αἴσθησιν λυπηροῦ καὶ ἡδέος καὶ ταῦτα σημαίνειν ἀλλήλοις), ὁ δὲ λόγος ἐπὶ τῷ δηλοῦν ἐστι τὸ συμφέρον καὶ τὸ βλαβερόν, ὥστε καὶ τὸ δίκαιον καὶ τὸ ἄδικον· τοῦτο γὰρ πρὸς τὰ ἄλλα ζῷα τοῖς ἀνθρώποις ἴδιον, τὸ μόνον ἀγαθοῦ καὶ κακοῦ καὶ δικαίου καὶ ἀδίκου καὶ τῶν ἄλλων αἴσθησιν ἔχειν· ἡ δὲ τούτων κοινωνία ποιεῖ οἰκίαν καὶ πόλιν. (*Pol.* 1253a.9–19)

> [For nature, as we say, makes nothing in vain, and man is the only animal who possesses speech (*logos*). The *voice* (*phônê*), to be sure, signifies pain and pleasure and therefore is found in other animals... but *speech* is for expressing the useful and the harmful, and therefore also the just and the unjust. For this is the peculiar characteristic of man in contrast to the other animals, that he alone has perception of good and evil, and just and unjust and the other such qualities, and the participation in these things makes a household *and* a city-state (*polis*). (Heath 2005, 10)]

The λόγος that Aristotle describes differs from the communication of animals (φωνή) in that it (1) is articulated and able to convey multiple meanings, some of which are abstract, and (2) serves as the foundation for human community itself (οἰκίαν καὶ πόλιν).[4] Through speech humankind is able to build community and develop cultural customs and ideals such as conceptions of good/evil and just/unjust. Such an ability makes the human being a ζῷον λόγικον, a rational animal; all other ζῷα are ἄλογικα. Likewise, Vitruvius, in his *De Architectura*, makes the same connection between the development of speech and the formation of community:

> In eo hominum congressu cum profundebantur aliter e spiritu voces, cotidiana consuetudine vocabula, ut optigerant, constituerunt. Deinde significando res saepius in usu ex eventu fari fortuito coeperunt et ita sermones inter se procreaverunt. (*De Arch.* 2.1.1)

[In the association of men, *voces* began to pour forth somewhat from the spirit, the vocabulary of daily custom, as they happened and became customary; then by identifying things used more frequently, they began to talk about them at random occurrences and in such a fashion conversations sprung forth among them.]

In the Vitruvian passage, the term *voces* is equated with the Aristotelian φωνή: these are inarticulate sounds that make up an extremely limited form of communication. These *voces* were then replaced by a speech and language: deliberate speech in the form of *vocabula*.[5] With these *vocabula*, human beings could take part in *sermones*, conversations that eventually led to the creation of houses and, subsequently, other disciplines (see Aristotle's creation of οἰκίαν καὶ πόλιν through λόγος).[6]

On the other hand, members of humanity who had any type of speech impairment (i.e., an impairment of the vocal ability to produce articulate speech) were consistently depicted as located on the peripheries of society and in a sort of primitive state between human and beast. In his *Indica*, the fourth-century BCE historian Ctesias describes the Κυνοκεφάλοι, a people with the bodies of men and the heads of dogs who live at the fringes of the known world.[7] The Κυνοκεφάλοι have no verbal speech but bark as dogs in order to communicate with one another (φωνὴν δὲ διαλέγονται οὐδεμίαν ἀλλ' ὠρύονται ὥσπερ κύνες, καὶ οὕτω συνιᾶσιν αὐτῶν τὴν φωνήν).[8] Although they are unable to communicate with their human neighbors, the Indians, they are still able to comprehend the human language of the Indians and attempt to communicate with them through physical gesture. Their liminal position between man/beast and speech/speech loss places them on the fringes of society, isolated from civilization.

Like the Κυνοκεφάλοι, another group suffering from impaired speech on the fringes of civilization is the Ἰχθυοφάγοι of the sixth-century ethnographer Agatharchides.[9] These people also lived on the fringes of the known world and lacked speech, communicating only through nods, inarticulate sounds, and imitative gestures.[10] Moreover, the Ἰχθυοφάγοι only communicate about their day-to-day lives and mundane occurrences, never expressing their individual feelings or doing anything leading to individual identity within the group.[11] In both of these cases, because the Ἰχθυοφάγοι and the Κυνοκεφάλοι are without speech, they are also without individual identity as human and are placed at the fringes of society in a middle state between human and beast.

The following schematic analysis of the term *mutus*—the preferred term for the type of inarticulate sound of animals—shows that this conception of speech as human, rational, and communal was still prevalent in the Roman literature of the first century BCE through the time of Ovid's death. The term is frequently used either to describe inarticulate beings with neither speech nor reason, namely, animals, or to emphasize the difference between the adjective's antecedent and humanity. Furthermore, the term also occurs often in the description of emotional situations, fitting locations for the curtailment of reason.

Therefore, the presence of *mutus* in the Roman literature appears to have brought to mind a schema in which the most salient features are speechlessness, the nonhuman, and emotionality. To illustrate this point more clearly, I will first turn to a brief background of schema theory and then to the actual instances of *mutus* in first-century BCE Rome in order to analyze the cognitive features underlying each instance.

## Schema Theory: A Brief Introduction

Since schema theory is still slowly making its way into Classical studies, it may be best to provide a brief introduction to it and its relation to literary analysis in particular.[12] The notion of schema theory dates back to the beginning of the twentieth century[13] and to the educational psychologist Piaget,[14] who himself termed the concept. Throughout the subsequent century, other educational psychologists, such as Bartlett[15] and Andersen,[16] expanded the use of the theory. At its root, schema theory postulates that all knowledge is organized into units called schemata and that these schemata "mediate between stimuli received by the sense organs and behavioral responses" (Casson 1983, 430). Each separate schema is a device for representing knowledge of a concept, along with specifications for relating it to a network of connections that seem to hold all components of that particular concept. Individuals acquire schemata through their experiences, and as they have more experiences, they refine, correct, and restructure their schemata. For example, if one has a particularly frightening experience the first time one encounters a dog, then one's "dog schema" will associate with itself emotions such as fear, worry, and anxiety as well as the physical characteristics of that particular dog. As one meets other dogs, perhaps of other breeds and dispositions, one restructures one's "dog schema" to include these modifications; no longer are all dogs considered frightening, but only the ones like the original, hostile dog. This process of renegotiation and modification is continuous and is activated every time one encounters something relating to dogs.

Over the past decade, schema theory has been employed to analyze literary texts as well as a part of what has come to be known as cognitive poetics.[17] Based on the foundations gained from schema theory that individuals are constantly (re)constructing information to (re)negotiate their reality, cognitive poetics suggests that "meaning is not something that resides in a text, but is rather something that is constructed by the recipient in his or her encounter with the text" (Lundhaug 2006, 19). When an individual comes to a particular reading, that person brings to it his or her own conscious and unconscious biases. Likewise, when an author composes a text, the author embeds in that text certain traces of individual or cultural schemata (Stockwell 2002, 3–4). For example, one might not think much is to be gleaned, if one were to hear these phrases:

"I'm running out of time"
"I have plenty of time."
"I don't have enough time for that."

Although each of these phrases communicates the amount of time available to an individual, it also belies the pieces of a "time schema" for modern Americans, namely, that time is conceived of as a tangible commodity of which one can have various amounts of possession (i.e., time is something that can be "had"). So however improbable it may have seemed at first, the "time schema" is closely associated with tangibility and possession.

Recently, such methodological use of cognitive poetics has begun to be seen in the Classics as well, particularly in the work of Robert Kaster and Andrew Riggsby. Kaster (2005, 4) uses schema theory to "understand at least some of the interplay between the emotions and the ethics of the Roman upper classes in the late Republic and early Empire." In particular, he focuses on the meanings embedded within texts, those not stated outright or allusively but subconsciously. By focusing on the schemata surrounding certain emotions in Roman texts (e.g., *amor, pudor, paenitentia, verecudia*), Kaster attempts to sidestep modern conceptions of love, shame, regret, and worried regard and all their modern associations in order to uncover the *Roman* schemata of these terms and the associations that the *Romans* made with them. Likewise, Riggsby (2006) has attempted to analyze Caesar's *De Bello Gallico* in terms of space, ethnography, and *virtus* through schema theory.[18] He also suggests manners in which questions of genre and self-presentation can be approached through schema theory, analyzing cultural notions and discourses to uncover whether the work would have been perceived by a Roman audience as apologetic.

Both of these approaches to ancient literature through cognitive poetics and schema theory have much to offer our current investigation of the Roman concept of speech loss. By analyzing the contexts in which terms for speech loss are employed (just as terms for emotion or genre), we can remain focused on Roman conceptions and not on modern notions of speech loss. Instead of starting from modern conceptions of speech loss as a physical handicap, as isolating, or as involving, at points, heightened emotion (e.g., "I was left speechless by the enormity of the situation"), we can identify what Romans seem to have associated most closely with speech loss and let that serve as the background for understanding the social context in which Ovid wrote about speech loss and schemata that he *expected* to be activated in his audience.

## Presentation of Data

Having explained the basic method I use to explore speech loss in Ovid's Rome, I turn now to the term that will be at the heart of my schematic analysis: *mutus*. The *Oxford Latin Dictionary*'s (*OLD*) definition of *mutus* confirms the reason why that term is appropriate for my analysis:

> *Mutus, a, um*; Gr. μύτις, μυάω; cf. Lat. mussare, *dumb, mute*. Lit. *that does not speak, silent*.—Of creatures who do not possess the faculty of speech, and can utter only inarticulate sounds

That definition highlights the fact that *mutus* was the typical Latin term to describe those who did not possess articulate speech and, consequently, lacked the humanity that came along with it. As such, an analysis of *mutus* and the contexts in which it was employed locates my analysis in texts that are discussing the themes of speech and speech loss, either implicitly or explicitly. Moreover, an analysis of such discussions can identify the conceptions of speech that were active in Ovid's Rome and with which he was likely to have interacted.

The number of instances of *mutus* also provides a large and diverse group of texts for analysis. According to the *Thesaurus Linguae Latinae* (*TLL*), there are 478 instances of the term in extant Latin Literature, 94 of which occurred in the time period from the beginning of the first century BCE to Ovid's death in 18 CE. The use of *mutus* in this period is the focus of my analysis, for by chronological proximity, the literature of this period provides a more accurate conception of speech and speech loss in Ovid's Rome.

A schematic analysis of these 94 instances of *mutus* confirms the basic definition of the *OLD* but adds more nuance to our understanding of *mutus* because it focuses more on the context in which the term was employed and ideas with which it was consistently associated (figure 1). A review of the results of the analysis concludes that *mutus* was consistently associated with two major concepts, the second of which had two distinct subcategories.

The first major concept with which *mutus* was associated was a strictly grammatical one and need not concern us for long. In texts dealing with the art of rhetoric, linguistics, or phonology, *mutus* was used to describe a silent consonant.[19] Quintilian and Servius, though later, exemplify this conception of *mutus*:[20]

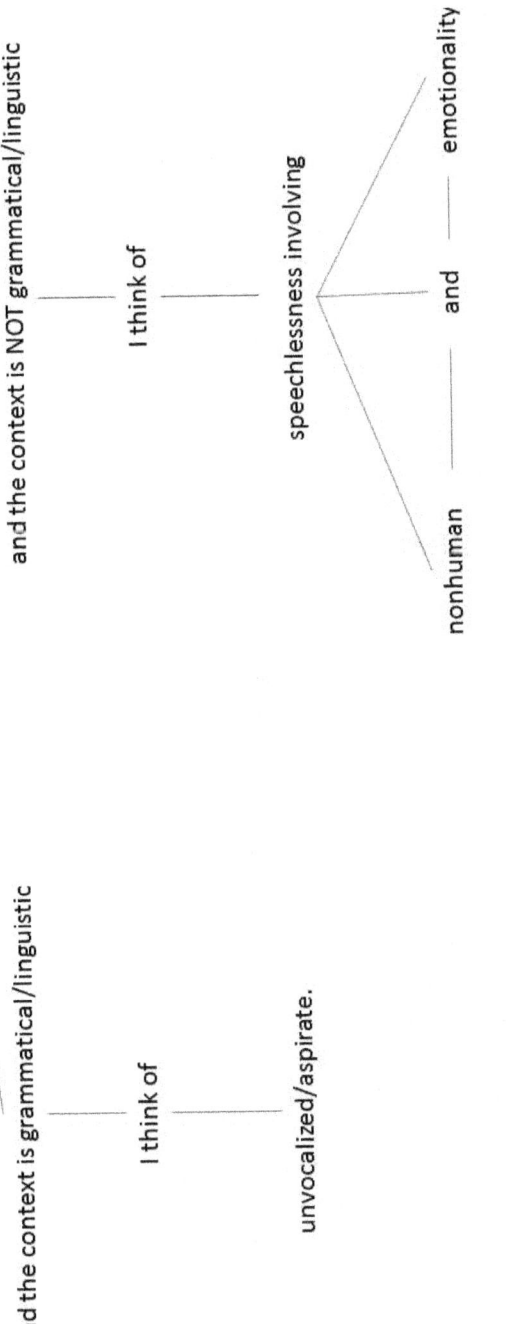

FIGURE 1. The *mutus* schema and its corresponding scripts.

Ne quis igitur tamquam parva fastidiat grammatices elementa, non quia magnae sit operae consonantes a vocalibus discernere ipsasque eas in *semivocalium numerum mutarumque* partiri, sed quia interiora velut sacri huius adeuntibus apparebit multa rerum subtilitas, quae non modo acuere ingenia puerilia, sed exercere altissimam quoque eruditionem ac scientiam possit. (Quint. *Inst.* 1.4.6)

[Let no man, therefore, look down on the elements of grammar as small matters, not because it requires great labor to distinguish consonants from vowels and to divide them into the proper number of semivowels and mutes, but because, to those entering the recesses, as it were, of this temple there will appear much subtlety on points, which may not only sharpen the wits of boys, but may exercise even the deepest erudition and knowledge.]

PERAGRO per habet accentum; nam "a" longa quidem est, sed non solida positione; *muta* enim et liquida quotiens ponuntur metrum iuvant, non accentum. (*Serv. Dan.* 1.384)

["Peragro" has an accent on "per"; for the "a" is indeed long, but not in a solid position; for mutes and liquids aid the meter as often as they are put down, not the accent.]

In both of these instances, *mutus* carries no underlying schematic conceptions, as the context in which it is used is limited to the technical and literal levels. No underlying assumptions or associations of *mutus* with identity are present.

The second major conception of *mutus*, however, does not concern grammar or linguistics but is associated with speech loss and is filled with underlying meanings that can be teased out through a schematic analysis. Beyond the general definition of "lacking speech" provided by the OLD, an analysis of the contexts in which this conception is used reveals two other subcategories of speech loss associated with *mutus*: (1) nonhuman and (2) emotionality.

The first of these subcategories, the nonhuman, is the association that the OLD addresses with its definition. In these contexts, *mutus* is consistently associated with nonhuman entities: animals and inanimate objects. In many of these instances, *mutus* is employed to draw a stark distinction between the human and the nonhuman and consequently is often found in stories of the evolution of human beings and the animals. Horace, Lucretius, and Catullus provide prime examples of this subcategory of *mutus*:

cum prorepserunt primis animalia terris,
*mutum* et turpe pecus, glandem atque cubilia propter
unguibus et pugnis, dein fustibus, atque ita porro
pugnabant armis quae post fabricaverat usus,
donec verba quibus voces sensusque notarent
nominaque invenere; dehinc absistere bello,
oppida coepeunt munire, et ponere leges,
ne quis fur esset, neu latro, neu quis adultery.
    (Hor. *Sat.* 1.3.99–106)

[When animals crawled forth on the first land, a mute and dirty race, they fought over food and shelter with nails and fists, then with sticks, and thereafter with arms, which, later, skill had created, until they found nouns and verbs with which they denoted their feelings; henceforth they abstained from war, began to build cities, and put down laws, that one should not be a thief, nor a robber, nor one an adulterer.]

postremo quid in hac mirabile tantoperest re,
si genus humanum, cui vox et lingua vigeret,
pro vario sensu varia res voce notaret,
cum pecudes *mutae*, cum denique saecla ferarum
dissimilis soleant voces variasque ciere,
cum metus aut dolor est et cum iam gaudia gliscunt?

. . .

Ergo si varii sensus animalia cogunt,
*muta* tamen cum sint, varias emittere voces,
quanto mortalis magis aequumst tum potuisse
dissimilis alia atque alia res voce notare.
    (Lucr. 5.1056–61, 1087–90)

[Finally, what is so very amazing in this business, if the human race, whose voice and tongue are more developed, denote things with a various voice for a various sense, while the mute flocks, indeed, while the types of beasts are accustomed to utter different and various voices, when fear or grief is present or even when now joys swell?

. . .

Therefore, if various senses impel animals, mute though they are, to produce various sounds, how much more equal it is then for mortals to be able to denote different things with one sound or another.]

> Multas per gentes et multa per aequora uectus
>     aduenio has miseras, frater, ad inferias,
> ut te postremo donarem munere mortis
>     et *mutam* nequiquam alloquerer *cinerem*.
> quandoquidem fortuna mihi tete abstulit ipsum.
>     heu miser indigne frater adempte mihi,
> nunc tamen interea haec, prisco quae more parentum
>     tradita sunt tristi munere ad inferias,
> accipe fraterno multum manantia fletu,
>     atque in perpetuum, frater, aue atque uale.
>         (Catull. 101)

[Passing through many peoples and many seas I come to these miserable funeral rites, so that I might bestow upon you the last gifts of the dead and I might console mute ash in vain. Alas, poor brother, unfairly taken from me, now, however, these things, which have been handed down by the ancient custom of ancestors as a sad gift for funeral rites, accept, drenched much with a brother's tears, and forever, brother, greetings and farewell.]

In the first two of these passages, Horace and Lucretius use *mutus* to describe similar antecedents. Lucretius uses *mutus* to emphasize the major physiological distinction between human and beast. He describes animals as *mutus* and used to uttering only random sounds (*dissimilis soleant voces variasque ciere*; *varias emitter voces*) to exhibit sensations of pain or pleasure. Humans, on the other hand, are capable of articulating sounds and communicating through speech (*vox et lingua vigeret*) their individual feelings and responses to circumstances.[21] The verb *notaret*, which is used to describe an ability that humans have and animals lack, has further undertones of the creation of law and community that fall along the lines of Aristotle's conception of λόγος as the dual foundation of speech and community for mankind (see the discussion earlier in this chapter).

For Horace, who most likely modeled his passage on the Lucretian description of the evolution of human and beast,[22] the term is reserved to describe primitive *animalia*, a *turpe pecus*. This group lived in a primitive existence until they found an articulate means through which they could express themselves (*donec verba quibus voces sensusque notarent nominaque invenere*). After they developed language, they were able to found cities, to create laws, and to live in community in much the same manner that Aristotle described (see the discussion earlier in this chapter). What distinguished primitive animals from humankind, therefore, was the ability to speak, and the use of *mutus* to describe primitive human beings (along with the deliberate use of *animalia*) serves to highlight the distinction.[23]

Whereas the Lucretian and Horatian passages use *mutus* to describe the distinction between man and beast in evolutionary terms, the third passage from Catullus is of a different sort. In this poem, Catullus composes a memorial for his deceased brother in the form of a Hellenistic grave epigram. Here *mutus* is used to depict not an animal but Catullus's brother, who has recently deceased and been cremated. The distinction made between the brothers in the poem is clearly portrayed in terms of speech: Catullus comes to his brother's grave to speak with him, but his brother, being dead, is unable to reply. Yet by using *mutus* here, Catullus imbues the passage with more meaning and pathos than mere "speechless," as, through his use of the term, he indicates that his brother is no longer human, no longer in existence.[24] He is dead and cut off from the human community. No matter how much Catullus attempts to converse with him in the typical human fashion, he does so in vain. This Catullan passage, therefore, expands the use of *mutus* from the basic definition provided by the *OLD*: *mutus* not only is used to describe nonhuman animals but also humans who have ceased to be human. More properly, then, *mutus* was associated with all nonhuman entities, not simply animals.

A last passage drives home this association of *mutus* with the nonhuman in general, while providing a bit of a divergent view. In the *Res Rusticae*, Varro distinguishes between the types of instruments that the Roman *agricola* had at his disposal:

quas res alii dividunt in duas partes, in homines et adminicula hominum, sine quibus rebus colere non possunt; alii in tres partes, instrumenti genus vocale et semivocale et mutum, *vocale*, in quo sunt servi, *semivocale*, in quo sunt boves, *mutum*, in quo sunt plaustra. (*Rust.* 1.17.1.7)

[Some divide these things [i.e., types of instruments] into two groups: into men and man's tools, without which they cannot farm; others into three groups: the articulate kind of instrument, the inarticulate, and the mute. The articulate group consists of slaves, the inarticulate of cattle, and the mute of plows.]

Instead of dividing man and beast into two groups based on speech, Varro complicates the situation. Whereas all other instances of *mutus* as speech loss associate the term with the inarticulate sounds of animals, Varro employs it to describe an inanimate object, a plow. Animals, here cattle, are described not as *mutus* but as *semivocalis*. Yet even though the term is different from what is used in other authors, for present purposes, the general concept remains the same: humans are distinguished from animals by articulate speech. In fact, Varro may come closest to truly conceptualizing that difference, choosing to differentiate inarticulate from articulate speech through the terms *vocale* and *semivocale* instead of *mutus* and various adjectives depicting speech.

The second subcategory of speechlessness broadens the schematic associations of *mutus* from the basic definition of the term provided by the *OLD*. This subcategory of speechlessness revolves around the concept of emotionality, and individuals who are described as *mutus* in this subcategory are depicted as such due to excessive emotions (e.g., speechless from fear, pleasure). The reason for such an association can be best explained by the Aristotelian dual conception of λόγος. For Aristotle, λόγος was the foundation both of speech and of community because the articulate speech developed by humans was linked to rational thought, which, in turn, allowed civilization to form. Consequently, since the articulate speech of humans is closely related to rational thought, the removal of articulate speech as described by *mutus* is linked to the inhibition of rational thought created by emotion. Aristotle also explicitly makes the point that an animal only makes a sound in order to indicate emotions such as pleasure or pain (ἡ μὲν οὖν φωνὴ τοῦ λυπηροῦ καὶ ἡδέος ἐστὶ σημεῖον). Emotions, in fact, were seen to be the governing principles that guided the animal world, as animals acted by nature (*apo physeos*) and not by reason. In Latin literature, one of the main methods in which *mutus*'s association with emotion is expressed is the phrase *mutus metu*, literally "speechless because of fear."[25] The following three passages exemplify this use of *mutus*:

> cui simul infula virgineos circumdata comptus
> ex utrque pari malarum parte profusast,
> et maestum simul ante aras adstare parentem
> sensit et hunc propter ferrum celare ministros
> aspectuque suo lacrimas effundere civis,
> *muta metu* terram genibus summissa petebat.
>     (Lucr. 1.87–92)

[Once the ribbon, bound about her virgin headbands,
has poured in equal length down each of her cheeks,
and once she saw her sad father standing before the altars
and by him, the attendants hiding the knife
and the citizens pouring forth tears at the sight of her,
mute with fear, she, falling on her knees, sought the ground.]

ac velut ingenti Sila summove Taburno
cum duo conversis inimica in proelia tauri
frontibus incurrunt, pavidi cessere magistri
stat pecus omne *metu mutum, mussantque* iuvencae
quis nemori imperitet, quem tota armenta sequantur.
    (Verg. *Aen.* 12.715–19)

[And just as when on great Sila or highest Taburnus
two bulls attack with their brows turned to hostile battle,
the frightened masters withdraw, the whole flock stands
mute with fear, and the young bulls are mum on who should rule the
flock, whom the whole herds should follow.]

coniugis ad timidas aliquis male sedulus aures
    auditos memori rettulit ore sonos.
Procris, ut accepit nomen, quasi paelicis, Aurae,
    excidit et subito *muta dolore* fuit.
palluit, ut serae lectis de vite racemis
    pallescunt frondes, quas nova laesit hiems,
quaeque suos curvant matura Cydonia ramos
    cornaque adhuc nostris non satis apta cibis.
ut rediit animus, tenues a pectore vestes
    rumpit et indignas sauciat ungue genas,
nec mora, per medias passis *furibunda* capillis
    evolat, ut thyrso concita Baccha, vias.
Ut prope perventum, comites in valle relinquit,
    Ipsa nemus tacito clam pede fortis init.
Quid tibi mentis erat, cum sic male sana lateres,
    Procri? quis adtoniti pectoris ardor erat?
    (Ov. *Ars Am.* 3.699–714)

[To the timid ears of his wife, some busy-body brought back sounds, having been overheard, with a mindful mouth. Procris, when she received the name of Aura, as if of a rival, fainted and was suddenly mute with grief. She turned pale, as the late leaves from the picked clusters of vine pale, which the new winter injures, and as ripe quinces curve their branches, and as berries still not quite fit for our food. When her spirit returned, she plucked the thin garments from her breast and wounded her innocent cheeks with the nail; without delay, she, frenzied, flies out through the middle of the streets with her hair streaming down, as a bacchant, incited by the thyrsus. As she came near, she leaves her companions in the valley, and herself boldly enters the grove in secret with a quiet foot. What was your mind, Procris, when thus you, insane, laid in wait? What burning of your thunderstruck heart was there?]

The first of these passages is Lucretius's narration of the sacrifice of Iphigenia at Aulis. Iphigenia, having been brought to the altar to be sacrificed, is described as terrified to the point of speechlessness. The emotions aroused by the desperate situation temporarily inhibit Iphigenia's ability to speak. Moreover, Lucretius, with his focus on the girl's inability to speak, may be looking back to the Aeschylean version, in which the maiden is gagged with a bit (χαλινός) in order to stop her from crying out a curse against her father's house (κατασχεῖν φθόγγον ἀραῖον οἴκοις) (Aesch. *Ag.* 231–38). Beyond his depiction of the clear inhibition of speech brought on by emotion, Lucretius also may be acknowledging the prevalent ending to this myth through his choice of *mutus* to describe speechlessness. In most versions of the myth, Iphigenia is snatched away by Artemis at the point of slaughter and replaced with an animal. Lucretius may be hinting at the eventual animal sacrifice in place of Iphigenia by using *mutus*, which, as we have seen, is the typical term for depicting the speechlessness of animals. Even if going that far is too uncomfortable, the mere sacrificial situation (i.e., the replacement of a traditional animal sacrifice with a human victim) would most likely have brought animal imagery to mind, making *mutus* an appropriate descriptor of the victim's speechlessness.

In the second passage, Virgil describes the immediate situation preceding the final battle between Aeneas and Turnus, as the rest of the soldiers from both sides stand and watch in silent amazement. Here Virgil uses *mutus* to portray simultaneously the emotional response of the soldiers and to create an extended, intratextual simile that conflates humans with animals. First, the emotions of the soldiers are highlighted as the reason why they were *muti metu*: the fear of the huge size of Turnus and Aeneas (*pavidi, metu*), the groan of the earth created by their size, and the uncertainty of the future facing them under the victorious warrior (*quis nemori imperitet, quem tota armenta sequantur*). Second, the use of *mutus* fits with the deliberate use of animal imagery to describe the combatants: Turnus and Aeneas are likened to bulls (*tauri*) that come together into battle; the remaining soldiers are portrayed as the flock (*pecus, iuvencae*) standing in awed silence; the soldiers are only able to maintain silence or to moo as cattle would (*mutum, mussant*).²⁶ The consistent ambiguity between cattle and humans here is reminiscent of the famous cattle at the future site of the Roman forum in *Aeneid* 8:²⁷ in that scene, the cattle serve as a link between Rome's present and past; here Aeneas and Turnus, the warriors who will become the ancestors of the new Roman people, battle for control of those cattle. The use of *mutus* thus fits the context well, simultaneously bringing to the fore associations not only of speechlessness but also of the nonhuman and emotionality.

In the third passage, Ovid tells the tale of Cephalus and Procris and portrays the grief of Procris upon falsely hearing that Cephalus has betrayed her with another woman. Procris, having heard the name of her perceived rival, Aura, is described as speechless with grief (*muta dolore*). Ovid's use of *mutus* to define her countenance is appropriate because it fits the associations with emotion and lack of reason. She exhibits all the outward signs of emotion: she turns pale (*palluit*), she faints (*excidit*), and she loses the ability to speak. In addition to her initial emotional response, Procris then begins to act in tremendously irrational ways: she tears the garments from her body, runs through the streets in a total frenzy (*furibunda*), and is likened to a bacchant. The comparison drawn between Procris and the bacchants furthers the point that she is intensely emotional and devoid of reason and amplifies Ovid's use of *mutus* as her descriptor in two ways. First, the bacchic cult was one closely associated with the rejection of reason in favor of an emotional, ecstatic connection with the divinity.²⁸ Second, since the Bacchanalian Conspiracy of 186 BCE, the cult was considered—at least in part—a threat to Roman rule inasmuch as it went against the traditional dominant Roman cultural practices and endangered the foundations on which the community was built.²⁹ In short, the bacchanalian cult threatened to topple the community that, in Aristotelian terms, λόγος (speech/reason) allowed humans to create. Describing one acting like a bacchant as *muta* and devoid of λόγος, is, therefore, entirely appropriate.

Beyond the associations with emotion that *mutus* activated here, those with the nonhuman are also brought to bear through Procris's actions: after she tears through the streets, she leaves her companions and flees into the woods, hunting Cephalus as an animal would and retaining her silence (*comites in valle relinquit, ipsa nemus tacito clam pede fortis init*, 711–12). Therefore, Ovid's use of the word *muta* to describe Procris's reaction to the news of supposed adultery highlights the associations that the word had with the nonhuman and emotionality.

She is quite literally struck dumb by grief and, from that moment, engages in most irrational behavior. Her emotions get the better of her, and she acts like an animal, responding simply to impulse and emotion.

As can be seen through the passages cited above, ancient conceptions of speechlessness maintained currency in the literature of Ovid's time, and we should expect him to be familiar and interact with them. Speech was seen as a fundamental aspect of rational, communal humanity; any loss of that ability moved one into the realm of the nonhuman, as animals and inanimate objects were considered devoid of reason and unable to create community. In the passages examined above, this conception of speech loss was traced into a schematic model through the term *mutus*, the traditional manner of describing the lack of articulate speech. Along with the presence of speechlessness, we have seen that the salient associations of such a lack of articulate speech were the nonhuman and emotionality.

It is against this background of speech loss that we must read the nonhuman and emotional elements in the pattern of speech loss developed by Ovid in the *Metamorphoses* and manipulated by him in the exile literature. Throughout the stories of change in the *Metamorphoses*, characters are often changed into animals, and their emotions at such a change are explored in order to heighten the pathos of the scene. Likewise, in the exile literature Ovid continually depicts his movement toward barbarism and does so through emotional outbursts. However, what this schematic background does not account for, and what makes Ovid's pattern of speech loss unique, is the inclusion of the written medium as a means of renegotiating one's emotions, regaining one's voice, and returning to one's human community. It is to this pattern of speech loss, therefore, that we will now turn.

*chapter 2*

## Speech Loss in the *Metamorphoses*

> Gregor was shocked when he heard his answering voice, which surely seemed to be his earlier one; yet into this voice a somewhat oppressive, painful squeaking had mixed itself, as from below, a squeaking that only left his words completely comprehensible in the first moment, then distorting them in reverberation in such a manner that one couldn't tell if one had heard them correctly.
>
> —Franz Kafka, *The Metamorphosis*

In Franz Kafka's *Metamorphosis*, the protagonist, Gregor Samsa, wakes up to find that he has been magically and inexplicably transformed into an enormous insect. The passage quoted at the beginning of this chapter is from early in the story. Gregor has not seen himself but has begun to suspect that something is different, for he is unable to speak in his normal voice. Although he can clearly identify that it is, in fact, his voice, it is mixed with a painful squeaking that distorts his spoken words into an almost unintelligible reverberation. Soon afterward, Gregor discovers that his voice is distorted because his former faculty of human articulation has been replaced by a new insectean buzzing.

The transformation of Gregor that begins with his realization of his new voice emphasizes some of the major themes of the *Metamorphosis* and, indeed, of all of Kafka's works: alienation, the absurdity of life, and the disconnect between mind and body. The main method employed by Kafka to achieve the expression of these concepts is the nature of Gregor's transformation. The pathos and absurdity at which Kafka was aiming only work because Gregor's transformation is not complete: although his physical appearance has taken on a completely new and alien form, his human mind remains intact. It is Gregor's anguish at the realization of his transformation that provides the opportunity for Kafka to explore issues of alienation, absurdity, and disconnection. Had Gregor entirely become an insect, he would never have been conscious of that fact.

This type of incomplete transformation, however, was not an entirely Kafkan innovation but perhaps had its roots in Ovid's tales of metamorphosis. The prevailing notion of the Ovidian conception of incomplete transformation is the concept of "wavering identity" first introduced by Hermann Fränkel and expanded on by subsequent scholars.[1] This concept is present in nearly all of Ovid's tales of metamorphosis: when a character is transformed, she or he is only changed physically; the character, however, retains the human ability to rationalize and to comprehend. In the Aristotelian terms from the previous chapter, a transformed character loses only one half of his or her λόγος: although the change in physical form has removed the character's ability to produce articulate speech, the character's ability to rationalize and construct identity remains intact. Consequently, the opportunity for the character to create community with others also remains intact. It is this opportunity that Ovid seeks to emphasize and express in the *Metamorphoses*, and the most frequent vehicle through which he attempts to do so is stories involving speech loss.

In the previous chapter, I laid out two concepts foundational to the discussion of speech loss in Ovid and with which this chapter will deal. First, I identified speech loss as a frequent motif in Ovidian literature and discussed some of the major scholarly positions on it. Second, I attempted to frame my discussion of speech loss in Ovid by indicating the major cognitive associations with speech loss in the time period spanning from the beginning of the first century BCE to Ovid's death in 18 CE. The schematic model produced from that discussion showed that speech loss was associated with the nonhuman, emotionality/lack of reason, and the subsequent curtailment of community through the lack of reason.

In this chapter, I turn to the manner in which Ovid interacted with and innovated on this schematic model through his use of the motif of speech loss in the *Metamorphoses*. In that work, Ovid mentions speech loss in roughly 40 of the 250 stories (appendix A). In each of these episodes, Ovid routinely follows a schematic model and associates speech loss with the nonhuman, the emotional, and the curtailment of community. When a character is transformed from a human into a nonhuman (e.g., an animal, an inanimate object, a plant), like Kafka, Ovid focuses his attention on the character's inability to speak in his or her transformed state. Likewise, often when a character is transformed into a speechless animal, Ovid indicates that the character also experiences an increase in emotion. As a result of the transformed character's speech loss and heightened emotion, the character is also removed from community, as she or he is no longer able to communicate with it.[2]

Yet, as these characters are not entirely transformed and are in an ambiguous state, they need not be permanently cut off from community. In fact, Ovid uses this notion to emphasize the complete opposite. In the case of some characters, he provides a method by which they can communicate, state their identity, and reconnect with society: the written medium. Through writing, characters are able both to replace speech as a vehicle of communication and, possibly, to regain their human form altogether.

In order to explore Ovid's innovation in stories of speech loss in the *Metamorphoses*, this chapter is divided into two sections. First, I examine tales of speech loss in which Ovid exhibits the traditional features of the schematic model of speech loss: the nonhuman and the emotional. This section places Ovidian depictions of speech loss within the larger context of speech loss in antiquity. I have chosen five narratives that exemplify this aspect of the Ovidian depictions of speech loss: Lycaon, Callisto, Actæon, Echo, and Dryope. These five stories represent the narratives with the fullest depiction of speech loss and, subsequently, provide the best, most substantial handlings to analyze.

Second, I turn to the stories of speech loss in which Ovid innovated within the schematic model through the inclusion of the written medium as a communicative means of reintegration with society. The two tales discussed in this section are those of Io and Philomela, two verbally gifted characters who, after having their speech stripped from them, transfer their communicative skills to the written medium (in particular, poetry in the written medium). This section highlights Ovid's unique construction of the relationship between speech loss, identity, and community in the *Metamorphoses* and sets the stage for my discussion in chapter 3 of how Ovid used his own conception of speech loss and the written medium of poetry as a major motif in his exile literature.

## Speech Loss and the Traditional Schema

As I discussed in the previous chapter, the basic concepts associated with speech loss in Ovid's Rome were the nonhuman and the emotional/nonrational. Speech (i.e., articulate speech) was seen as a uniquely human characteristic, and any nonhuman entity, therefore, was barred from exhibiting it. Likewise, humans who were experiencing high levels of emotion tended to be described as temporarily bereft of the ability to speak. In the stories that follow, Ovid works within this traditional schema of speech loss, associating speechlessness with (1) characters who are transformed from their human state into a nonhuman state and (2) characters who are so overcome with emotion that they are transformed from their human state and, consequently, are speechless.

### Lycaon

The first story of transformation in the *Metamorphoses* is also the one in which Ovid introduces the theme of speech loss: the story of Lycaon. Although there are multiple extant versions of the myth of Lycaon, the major thrust of the story is that Lycaon committed hubristic sacrilege against Zeus and, consequently, was transformed into a wolf.[3] The Ovidian handling of the myth, however, seems to be the only one to focus explicitly on Lycaon's metamorphosis and not on his crime.[4] Perhaps as a result of this shift in focus, Ovid's narration is the only extant version of the myth that mentions Lycaon's loss of speech. As such, it seems likely that Ovid created this portion of the tale.

Ovid's focus on speech and speech loss can be seen throughout the passage. First, Lycaon is introduced as a clever man capable of speaking, and Ovid emphasizes this ability by allowing him to speak in *oratio recta* and to assume the role of narrator:

> Inridet primo pia vota Lycaon,
> mox ait "experiar, deus hic, discrimine aperto,
> an sit mortalis; nec erit dubitabile verum."
> (*Met.* 1.221–23)

[At first, Lycaon scoffed at the pious votives; soon, he says: "I shall try with a clear test whether this is a god or a mortal; and the truth will be undoubtable."]

Ovid, as he does elsewhere (e.g., Actæon, Philomela), shows the audience the character to be transformed has the ability to speak in order to emphasize the later loss of it.

Second, the actual transformation of Lycaon is focused on speech loss and its schematic associations with emotion, the nonhuman, and the loss of community:

> *territus* ipse *fugit* nactusque *silentia ruris*
> exululat frustraque *loqui conatur*: ab ipso
> colligit os rabiem solitaque cupidine caedis
> vertititur in pecudes et nunc quoque sanguine gaudet.
> (*Met.* 1.232–35)

[He himself, terrified, flees, and, having reached the silence of the countryside, howls and tries in vain to speak: his mouth gathers foam from itself and by the accustomed desire for slaughter he is turned to the flocks and now rejoices also in blood.]

From the beginning of the metamorphosis, Ovid shows the progression of Lycaon's transformation with a tricolon as it moves from (1) initial fear and flight to (2) howling and retreat to the countryside and finally to (3) the realization of transformation through the loss of speech. First, Ovid shows the heightened emotion traditionally associated with speech loss, as the self-assured character who had earlier chosen himself to pass judgment on Zeus is now reduced to fear and flight (*territus ipse fugit*). Then Ovid shows Lycaon's removal from society, as he forsakes the city and takes up the silent countryside, howling upon his arrival.[5] The phrase *silentia ruris* serves two purposes here: (1) to provide a stark contrast to the sound of Lycaon's howling and (2) to mark the silence of the animals that inhabit the countryside, who, being nonhuman, lack the ability to speak. Now Lycaon finds himself a part of the animal world, a fact that may be gleaned from an alternate meaning for *nanciscor*: not only does the term mean "to happen upon" or "to reach"—the traditional translation of its occurrence in Lycaon's transformation—but it can also mean "to receive by birth."[6] Here Lycaon is receiving animality as part of his nature, perhaps one that had always been a part of him.[7] Finally, after two lines of buildup, Ovid delivers the final third of his tricolon: Lycaon's realization that he cannot speak but can only howl (*frustraque loqui conatur*). Lycaon's ability to produce articulate speech (*loqui*) is replaced by a new sound that is emphasized by the repetition of *v* and *u* in the following lines, a repetition that imitates the sound of howling (*vertitur in pecudes et nunc quoque sanguine gaudet. / in villos abeunt vestes, in crura lacerti: / fit lupus et veteris servat vestigia formae: / canities eadem, eadem violentia vultus*, *Met*. 1.235–38).[8] Likewise, as Frederick Ahl has noted, the description of Lycaon's howling emphasizes his movement from a member of society to an exile through the inclusion of the word *exul* in the term *exululare*.[9] When he loses the ability to speak, Lycaon loses the ability to communicate with his society.

Therefore, Lycaon's transformation is one replete with connections to speech loss. Moreover, the traditional schematic associations apply, as Lycaon's speech loss goes hand in hand with heightened emotion, transformation into a nonhuman, and the loss of community. Furthermore, as the first story of metamorphosis in Ovid's work, it gains paradigmatic force and provides the model of metamorphosis for the tales to follow. By spending so much time on speech and speech loss in this story, therefore, Ovid sets it up as a major motif for the metamorphoses to come.

## Callisto

In book 2, Ovid returns to the family of Lycaon and tells the tale of the metamorphosis of his daughter, Callisto. Like the myth of Lycaon, there are several extant permutations of a central core concept: Callisto, the daughter of Lycaon, is raped by Jupiter, gives birth to a son, Arcas, and is transformed into a bear.[10] In Ovid's version, Juno, jealous of Callisto's affair with Jupiter, transforms the maiden into a bear as a form of punishment through isolation. As we saw in the case of the Lycaon narrative, this Ovidian version of Callisto's tale is unique among the other extant versions in that it focuses the narrative on the schematic associations of Callisto's speech loss, her loss of identity, and, consequently, her loss of community.[11] These three concepts can be seen sequentially in the passage of her transformation:

> "haud impune feres: adimam tibi namque figuram,
> qua tibi, quaque places nostro, inportuna, marito."
> dixit et adversam prensis a fronte capillis
> stravit humi pronam. tendebat bracchia supplex:
> bracchia coeperunt nigris horrescere villis
> curvarique manus et aduncos crescere in unguis
> officioque pedum fungi laudataque quondam
> ora Iovi lato fieri deformia rictu.
> neve preces animos et verba precantia flectant,
> posse loqui eripitur: vox iracunda minaxque
> plenaque terroris rauco de gutture fertur;
> mens antiqua tamen facta quoque mansit in ursa,
> adsiduoque suos gemitu testata dolores
> qualescumque manus ad caelum et sidera tollit
> ingratumque Iovem, nequeat cum dicere, sentit.
> a! quotiens, sola non ausa quiescere silva,
> ante domum quondamque suis erravit in agris!
> a! quotiens per saxa canum latratibus acta est
> venatrixque metu venantum territa fugit!
> saepe feris latuit visis, oblita quid esset,
> ursaque conspectos in montibus horruit ursos
> pertimuitque lupos, quamvis pater esset in illis.
>     (*Met.* 2.474–95)

["You shall hardly go unpunished: for I shall take away your beauty, in which you and my husband take pleasure, crude girl." She spoke and flung Callisto down by the hair until her face lay on the ground. Callisto, suppliant, kept holding out her arms: her arms began to grow shaggy with thick black hair, and her hands to curve and to grow into hooked claws and did the duty of her feet, and the mouth once praised by Jove became deformed by a broad muzzle. So that neither prayers nor prayerful words could change minds, the ability to speak was taken from her: a voice angry and threatening and full of terror is borne from her hoarse throat; yet still her original mind remained in the formed bear; she bears witness to her grief with constant groaning and raises whatever hands she has to the sky and stars; she thinks Jove ungrateful, although she is unable to speak. Ah! How many times she did not dare to relax alone in the forest, she wandered into the fields before her former home! Ah! How many times she, a huntress, was driven through the rocks by the barking of dogs, and, terrified by the fear of the prey, fled! Often she hid when wild animals appeared; she, a bear, yet forgetful of what she was, shuddered at other bears she saw on the mountains, and feared wolves terribly, although her father was among them.]

In the first section of the passage (2.474–81), Ovid, as he so often does, shows us the actual transformation of Callisto as it progresses through her body. It begins with her arms (*bracchia*), moving slowly to her hands (*manus*) and fingernails (*ungues*). The climax of the transformation, however, is the last aspect of Callisto that is transformed: her face and her speech. Our vantage point shifts from Callisto's extremities to her transformed face (*ora*), as Juno makes good on her promise to destroy the beauty that delights her husband (474–75). However, *ora* here is referring not simply to the face as a whole but to its more specific, semantic meaning of the part of the face that speaks.[12] Maurizio Bettini, in his recent study on communication and identity in antiquity, provides a detailed discussion of *os, oris*:[13]

> In Latin, os *has strong connotations: it evokes a capacity that chiefly distinguishes human beings from other animate creatures: language.* For Latin speakers, the connection between *os* and words such as *oro* or *orator* was probably immediately recognizable. But even ignoring etymological speculation, such common idioms as *in ore esse* ("to be much spoken of"), *uno ore* ("by general agreement") and *aperire ora* ("to speak") leave little doubt about the relationship between *os* and *oro*. Likewise the great number of passages in which *os* is used in the sense of "discourse, speech," "the sound of voice" or "pronunciation." Os *is first and foremost "speech."* (Bettini 2011, 135, emphasis added to first and last sentences)

Thus, in addition to destroying Callisto's beautiful appearance by changing her human mouth into a broad muzzle, Juno also robs her of her ability to speak articulately, as the broad muzzle of a bear is unable to form human words. The reading of *ora* as regarding speech as well as beauty helps to make sense of the subsequent lines. As she attempts to pray to the gods for help, she is unable to articulate *verba* and *preces*. Her articulate voice, her *vox*, is transformed from a human voice to one that is described as angry (*iracunda*) and threatening (*minaxque*), whose harshness is emphasized by the rare trisyllabic ending to an Ovidian hexameter line.[14] The fact that her voice is borne from her throat (*rauco de gutture fertur*) and not a *lingua* emphasizes the fact that she, transformed, is no longer able to produce articulate speech but is reduced to an inarticulate roar.[15] Still, though her speech is lost, Ovid takes care to emphasize that her essence remains intact (*mens antiqua tamen . . . mansit*).[16]

With her speech having been removed, Callisto's conception of herself, her identity, begins to waver, and the rest of the passage emphasizes this confusion. Resorting to an all too human act of supplication, she attempts to pray to the gods, creating a pathetic and somewhat humorous scene in which a bear raises its paws to the heavens for assistance. Although Callisto is unable to articulate her pain through prayer, she is still able to communicate in a fashion with the gods, for Jupiter is said to have felt (*sensit*) her message, despite her inability to speak (*nequeat cum dicere*). Anderson remarks that this is possible because "one of the sounds which human beings and animals share is that of groaning. Callisto voices her agony. As the adjectives in 483–84 suggest, in bears that same sound usually connotes anger, menace, and fearsomeness" (1997, *ad* 2.585–86). Although Callisto is unable to articulate the particulars of her pain as a bear, she is nonetheless able to communicate that she is suffering.

However, as there is no reply from Jupiter, Callisto assumes that her appeals have failed and that she is isolated and alone. Such isolation is emphasized by the final portion of this passage (2.488–95), as Callisto is trapped between two worlds, the animal and the human, never fully fitting into either. Not wholly animal, she cannot stay in the woods, so she attempts to return to her human abode (*domum*) and the civilized fields (*agris*).[17] The verb *quiescere*, which describes the alternative to returning to her previous home, emphasizes the silence of the nonspeaking animal realm, as *silentia ruris* had done in the case of Lycaon.

Likewise, Callisto's isolation is amplified by her inability to connect with any community of which she had previously been a part. First, although Callisto still considers herself to be a huntress (*venatrix*), fear has driven her away from the sound of dogs and hunters.[18] Such a flight belies Callisto's identity crisis, as she cannot understand why she is frightened by members of a community of which she is supposedly a part. The fear that envelops her now is that of animal nature, and *metu territa* should be read as a close synonym of *mutus metu*, the fear associated with nonhuman speechlessness.[19] Second, beyond connecting with her hunting community, she cannot even reconnect with her family, as she is terrified by wolves, a group in which, according to Ovid, her father was numbered. This inability to reconnect with her father stems from her inability to recognize herself, as Ovid points out that she is *oblita quid esset*. Not only does her identity crisis prohibit the realization that she is a bear and should not fear wolves, but it also keeps her from understanding that she herself has been transformed in the same manner in which her father had been. If she had realized this, although she may not have been able to locate her father in a pack of wolves, she might have found a connection with her family, for she has suffered the same fate as her father.

The transformation of Callisto, therefore, follows the same basic schema of speech loss as the metamorphosis of Lycaon did. Having become nonhuman, Callisto loses her ability to speak and, consequently, loses her community. In contrast with the Lycaon episode, Ovid focuses more on Callisto's psychological anguish: the identity crisis and inability to reconnect with any form of past community, neither with her friends nor with her family. However, the fact that she retains her basic ability to rationalize does allow for a glimmer of hope, as she is able to communicate somewhat with Jupiter, although she is unaware of this fact and unable to communicate in any way with humanity. Still, the opportunity provided by the persistence of the human mind is one that will be exploited by Ovid in other stories of metamorphosis.

*Actæon*

In book 3, Ovid continues to explore the motif of speech loss with the story of Actæon (3.138–252). As with the tales of Lycaon and Callisto, the myth of Actæon did not originate with Ovid but is well attested in the Greek tradition, and multiple versions have come down from antiquity.[20] In all these versions, however, the core of the myth remains essentially unchanged: the hunter Actæon stumbles upon the nude goddess Diana, is transformed by her into a stag as a form of punishment, and finally is killed by his own hunting dogs, which are unable to recognize their master in his transformed state. As with the other stories examined above, the Ovidian version deviates from the other permutations: whereas the previous stories of Actæon focused more on the *error* of Actæon and the harsh punishment of Diana,[21] Ovid shifts the focus more toward our schematic progression and Actæon's loss of speech, identity, and community.[22] Ovid's emphasis on these themes can be seen throughout the narrative as Actæon's progression from a member of human society with the ability to speak, to his transformation into a nonhuman being, to his realization of his predicament through the persistence of his mind, and to his crisis of identity and his ultimate removal from community.

At the beginning of the narrative, Ovid introduces Actæon to his audience as a member of the human community with a heightened ability of speech in order to draw a greater contrast with his ultimate fate. As he often does in tales of speech loss, Ovid has the character who will be transformed speak in *oratio recta*:

> lina madent, comites, ferrumque cruore ferarum,
> fortunaeque dies habuit satis; altera lucem
> cum croceis invecta rotis Aurora reducet,
> propositum repetemus opus: nunc Phoebus utraque
> distat idem meta finditque vaporibus arva.
> sistite opus praesens nodosaque tollite lina!
> (*Met.* 3.148–53)

[The nets, comrades, and the sword are wet with the gore of beasts, and the day has had enough of good fortune; when another dawn leads back the light, having driven on red wheels, we shall seek our proposed work: now Phoebus likewise stands equally on each side and cleaves the fields with his rays. Cease the present work and put up the knotted nets!]

Not only does the fact that Actæon speaks point to speech loss as a key concept in the story, but the content of his speech also matters. Actæon locates himself in a community of hunters, calling to his comrades (*comites*) as the recipients of his statements. Moreover, his words are extremely polished and ornate, leading Ovid's readers to believe that Actæon is actually a skilled speaker. His speech is bookended by the same word, *lina*, emphasizing not only Actæon's skill with language but also his sense of order. Likewise, he favors the epic floridity of description, choosing to describe the next day of hunting with an elaborate description of dawn and Apollo. In addition, Actæon is said to have spoken with a *placidum os*, an aspect that draws attention (1) to his serenity, which has drawn parallels to the ideal Virgilian prince who favors serenity over traditional notions of violence and arrogance, and (2) to his ability to speak with his *os* at the beginning of the narrative (see Bettini above).

Having introduced Actæon as a character who is part of an active community and with a gift for the spoken word, Ovid focuses on his loss of both in his transformation. The metamorphosis itself (3.194–98) is enclosed by explicit mentions of speech loss in such a manner that the concept is emphasized by its placement in the first and last positions of the narrative section. Before transforming him, Diana first mocks him, stating that he is free to tell (*narrare*) the world he saw her naked, if he is able to speak that fact. This raises the anticipation that

Actæon's speech will truly be lost in his transformation. Moreover, the use of the verb *narrare* to describe the act of telling brings with it the assumption of an audience to tell, a community of listeners. This community also is threatened by Actæon's impending speech loss, as he will not able to interact with community without his ability to speak. However, no mention of a transformed voice is made as in other tales. Instead, suspense is held until the transformation is complete and Actæon sees his reflection in the water:

> "*nunc tibi me posito visam velamine narres,*
> *si poteris narrare, licet!*" nec plura minata
> dat sparso capiti vivacis cornua cervi,
> dat spatium collo summasque cacuminat aures
> cum pedibusque manus, cum longis bracchia mutat
> cruribus et velat maculoso vellere corpus;
> *additus et pavor est*: fugit Autonoeius heros
> et se tam celerem cursu miratur in ipso.
> ut vero vultus et cornua vidit in unda,
> "*me miserum!*" dicturus erat: vox nulla secuta est!
> ingemuit: vox illa fuit, lacrimaeque per ora
> non sua fluxerunt; *mens tantum pristina mansit.*
> quid faciat? repetatne domum et regalia tecta
> an lateat silvis? *pudor hoc, timor inpedit illud.*
>     (Met. 3.192–205)

["Now it is allowed for you to tell that I was seen with my garment put aside, if you are able to tell!" And not threating more, she gives his head the horns of a long-lived stag, and gives space to his neck and pointed the tips of his ears and changes his hands to feet, his arms to long legs and covers his body with a spotted skin; fear was also added: the son of Autonoë, a hero, marvels that he is so fast in the course itself. Truly, when he saw his appearance and horns in the water, he was about to say, "Woe is me!" but no voice followed! He groaned: that was his voice, and tears flowed down a face not his own; yet, his mind remains as it had been. What could he do? Should he seek home and the regal roofs again, or should he hide in the woods? Shame keeps him from the former, fear from the latter.]

His attempt to speak is met with severe resistance, as he is unable to even utter a sound. Like Callisto, who had her articulate *vox* transformed into something incapable of producing articulate sounds, Actæon is unable to find his voice as well (*vox nulla secuta est*). All he can do is groan (*ingemuit*).[23] This sound takes the place of his human, articulate voice. In fact, throughout the remainder of the passage, all Actæon's attempts to communicate are described in terms of either complete failure or rudimentary and confusing noise:

> clamare libebat:
> "Actaeon ego sum: dominum cognoscite vestrum!"
> verba animo desunt; resonat latratibus aether.
> (*Met.* 3.229–31)

[He kept wanting to shout: "I am Actæon: recognize your master!" The words failed his mind; the air resounds with barking.]

> gemit ille sonumque,
> etsi non hominis, quem non tamen edere possit
> cervus
> (*Met.* 3.237–39)

[He groans a sound, even if not human, still not one a stag is able to produce.]

In the first instance, Actæon wants to speak and can even form the words in his head (*animo*), but he lacks the ability to articulate them. Therefore, instead of speaking, he fails to make a sound at all, and all that is audible is the barking of Actæon's dogs (*resonat latratibus aether*). In the second instance, Ovid describes the strangeness of the sound, as it is neither human nor animal.[24] Beyond the distinction of articulate *verba* and *voces*, Actæon's sound is so foreign that it can only be described as a *sonum*, a noise belonging neither to humanity nor to the animal realm;[25] the foreignness of the *sonum* not only shows the futility of Actæon's attempt at communication but also his isolation, as it is neither animal nor human.

It reflects the crisis of identity that can be directly attributed to Actæon's speech loss. As with other transformed characters, although he lost his speech when he was transformed, Actæon's mind has remained intact, trapped inside an animal's body with no manner of communication. As a result, he cannot return to his human community, nor can he live as a deer. This inner conflict is exemplified in Actæon's internal monologue at 3.204–5 (see passage above):[26] *pudor*, a uniquely human conception, constructed and maintained by community, keeps him from living with the animals (Kaster 2005, 28–65); *timor*, the traditional animal fear from our schematic model, with which Diana had imbued him at his transformation (*additus et pavor est*, 3.198), keeps him from civilization. Likewise, his conflicted nature is present in his attempt at supplication to Diana. As Callisto had done, Actæon also tries to contort his animal form into a stance of supplication and attempts to pray for mercy. Yet, as with Callisto, this is in vain, as his human attempts at communication with the gods are foiled by his new animal nature.

However, perhaps the most tragic result of Actæon's loss of speech is his death at the hands of his former community:

> at *comites* rapidum solitis hortatibus agmen
> ignari instigant oculisque Actaeona quaerunt
> et velut absentem certatim Actaeona clamant
> (ad nomen caput ille refert) et abesse queruntur
> nec capere oblatae segnem spectacula praedae.
>         (*Met.* 3.242–46)

[But his comrades, unaware, spur on the rapid group with their customary encouragements and look for Actæon with their eyes and call Actæon in turn as if he were absent (he lifts his head at the name) and complain that he is absent and that he, lazy, is missing the spectacle of the offered prey.]

The same community with which the story started is present at the end. Yet this time the transformed Actæon is no longer able to speak to his comrades (*comites*) at all. Although they still look for him and consider him part of their community, they cannot recognize him in his animal form and Actæon cannot reclaim his identity without his voice.

And so, as with the stories of Lycaon and Callisto, Ovid changes the traditional myth of Actæon to emphasize the role of speech loss in a character's identity crisis and loss of community. Because he could not speak, Actæon became trapped in an animal form and was thrown into a middle state between man and beast, but fully neither. As such, he was unable to create a solid identity. Moreover, because of his lack of speech, he felt the full force of the schematic associations of speech loss: he became unable to identify himself to his former hunting community and was cut off from them, eventually being murdered at their own hands.

## Dryope

In book 9, Ovid offers another story of transformation focused on the schematic progression of speech loss and the effects it has on identity and community. However, the manner in which these concepts are presented differs greatly from other stories of transformation we have seen. In this tale of metamorphosis, Ovid focuses on the fate of Dryope (*Met.* 9.324–93), who, according to the only two extant versions of the myth, was either transformed into a nymph associated with a spring or, as the Ovidian version describes, into a lotus tree.[27] Based on the extant versions—which indeed may not have been all the versions available to Ovid—it seems as if the metamorphosis of Dryope into a lotus tree originated with Ovid.[28] The emphasis on speech loss and community also is likely to have been an Ovidian invention, judging from the other stories of metamorphosis in which Ovid focuses on that issue.

Indeed, the Ovidian story of Dryope does focus on speech loss and community similar to the stories of Callisto, Lycaon, and Actæon. Ovid follows his typical pattern of allowing the character about to be transformed to speak in *oratio recta* so that the character's loss of the ability to speak will create all the more contrast between the present and the past version of the character.[29] Likewise, the transformation itself serves to highlight speech loss, as the progression of metamorphosis works its way up from Dryope's feet throughout her body and head, while leaving her face and mouth intact. By leaving her face temporarily intact, the story remains focused on her ability to speak throughout her speech.

The final act of metamorphosis, however, further emphasizes Ovid's focus on speech loss. As Dryope's mouth is overcome by the bark of her new, nonhuman form, her voice is cut off: *Desiderant simul ora loqui, simul esse* (*Met.* 9.392). Anderson, commenting on these lines, suggests that Ovid includes this concluding statement to satisfy his need for witticism.[30] Yet when read against the other stories of speech loss and transformation, this sentence reads more like a gnomic statement capping the end of a Pindaric stanza: this is the point, the climax of Dryope's transformation. The force of the *esse* refers not solely to Dryope's mouth but to her entire self: when her mouth stopped speaking articulately (*ora loqui*), *she herself*, her *human* identity, ceased to be. Henceforth, her human identity was lost to her family forever, being no longer able to communicate with them. Her original, human identity was thus replaced by a new, nonhuman one, as the subsequent emphasis on *recentes* and *mutates* implies.[31] The loss of speech, therefore, was not merely a witticism but the actual moment of identity crisis and dislocation.

Still, even though this story shares much in common with other tales of transformation in terms of an emphasis on speech loss and identity crisis, it also adds a new wrinkle. Whereas other characters examined thus far in this chapter have suffered transformation and speech loss alone, Dryope undergoes her metamorphosis in the presence of her community, her family. This major difference in detail has profound consequences for Dryope's continued participation in her community. As her community watches her transformation, Dryope's identity within that community is not severed: they know she is a lotus tree. With that knowledge, as Dryope hopes, they can keep the memory of her human identity alive after her transformation into a nonhuman form.[32] She asks that her son know his mother's transformed state and that he play under her branches:

> hunc tamen infantem maternis demite ramis,
> et date nutrici, nostraque sub arbore saepe
> lac facitote bibat, nostraque sub arbore ludat.
> cumque loqui poterit, matrem facitote salutet,
> et tristis dicat "latet hoc in stipite mater."
> (*Met.* 9.375–79)

[However, send this infant below his mother's branches, and give him to the nurse that she may make him drink milk often under my tree, play often under my tree. And whenever he is able to speak, see to it that he acknowledge his mother and, sad, say, "My mother lies hidden in this bark."]

Likewise, she asks her husband to continue to protect her, only now from the sharp knife and cattle:

> care vale coniunx, et tu, germana, paterque!
> qui, siqua est pietas, ab acutae vulnere falcis,
> a pecoris morsu frondes defendite nostras.
> (*Met.* 9.382–84)

[Farewell, dear spouse and you, sister, and father! You who, if there is any loyalty, defend my foliage from the wound of the sharp scythe, from the bite of the cow.]

To Dryope, her transformation is not death; it is merely a metamorphosis into a new form. For this reason she rejects her family's attempts to perform funerary rites and to place coins on her eyes.[33] Her request is not simply to prevent an unnecessary step of ritual, as Anderson suggests, but it is to explain explicitly to her family that she is not dead, just different.[34] All she wishes is that her human form be remembered and her nonhuman form continue to be included in the community. Moreover, her wish for remembrance is granted, as attested by her sister Iole's narrative of Dyrope's very transformation for Ovid's audience.

And so, as with the other stories of transformation, Ovid reinvents the myth of Dryope to include a focus on the schematic dimensions of speech loss: the nonhuman, the removal from community, and the subsequent identity confusion brought about by such a removal. Dryope ceases to be human only when she loses the ability to speak. Yet she does not suffer the same removal from community as Lycaon, Callisto, or Actæon because her community was present at the time of her metamorphosis. Instead, all she wants is for her community to consider her not deceased but transformed and to continue to involve her in communal life.

*Echo*

As with the other stories discussed above, in the tale of Echo Ovid again points to the schematic relationship between speech, identity, and community.[35] Echo, having deceived Juno, undergoes a transformation and is stripped of her power of speech, an act that isolates her and prohibits her from expressing her identity through language. As a result, she is unable to express fully her love for another individual, Narcissus, a limitation that leaves her isolated and shut off from human contact.[36] Her removal from the human community is ultimately expressed in her loss of bodily form. Unable to express her inner identity through speech, Echo loses her external being, literally evaporating into the ether and fading from the narrative focus. Throughout the narrative, Ovid uses the connected concepts of speech loss and identity to focus on Echo's liminal state between a social being and an isolated, metamorphasized one.

The metamorphosis of Echo itself presents us with a starting point for discussion, as Juno's threats toward and ultimate punishment of Echo provide a prime example of the instability of Echo's linguistic ability. The narrative had introduced Echo as a *vocalis nymphe*, a description not only looking forward to the close connection Echo will have with speech after her transformation but also seeking to identify pretransformation Echo as one with the ability to produce articulate speech. Shilpa Raval, whose penetrating analysis of the Echo narrative is greatly instructive for our discussion of speech loss, points out that although the use of *vocalis* to describe Echo reminds the audience of Echo's original talents as a speaker, since the term can be translated as "babbling" or "chatty," it often was used to designate "artistic abilities, particularly in Ovid and other Augustan and Imperial poets" (2003, 206).[37] Raval goes on to give examples of individuals who enchant with words, such as Orpheus in *Odes* 1.12 or Arion in *Fasti* 2.84–92, being described with the term *vocalis* (206–7), and concludes that Ovid's use of *vocalis nymphe* to describe Echo highlights Echo's original ability "to manipulate her voice in order to capture (and retain) Juno's attention" (207). In terms of our discussion, this is akin to Ovid's use of *oratio recta* in the tales of Lycaon, Actæon, and Dryope to indicate the original ability of the character to speak; yet, in Echo's case, this ability is highlighted further as a special ability to use language.

Having been prevented from exacting revenge on her adulterous husband and his lovers by Echo's verbal ability, Juno vows to rob Echo of this gift of speech that makes her *vocalis*:

> fecerat hoc Iuno quia cum deprendere posset
> sub Iove saepe suo nymphas in monte iacentes,
> illa deam longo prudens sermone tenebat
> dum fugerent nymphae. postquam hoc Saturnia sensit,
> "huius" ait "linguae, qua sum delusa, potestas
> parva tibi dabitur vocisque brevissimus usus."
> (*Met.* 3.362–67)

[Juno had done this because, although she was able to recognize that nymphs were often lying with Jove on his mountain, Echo, clever, kept delaying the goddess with a long conversation until the nymphs could flee. Afterward the daughter of Saturn realized this, she said, "A small power of this tongue, by which I have been deceived, and the most fleeting use of voice will be given to you."]

Juno's threats state the loss of Echo's existence as *vocalis* and the basic instability of Echo's new linguistic state: she has a small amount of control over her *lingua* and a fleeting ability to speak through a *vox*. The *lingua*, as was discussed in the previous chapter, is the body part that gives humans the ability to produce articulate speech, since it is with the tongue that humans are able to differentiate their utterances. *Vox* too carries a similar connotation and is linked with the communicative act of the individual who speaks. For humans, this entails the articulate communication unique to human speech. Therefore, Echo's loss of control over her *lingua* and *vox* is tantamount to her loss of the ability to speak in a human fashion and, consequently, her ability to communicate her identity to others in the form of expressing herself through speech. Still, her *vox* and *lingua* are not entirely curtailed, and Echo is left with the physical ability to use them, provided that another individual speak first. So, as a result of her transformation and the curtailment of her speech, Echo finds herself in an in-between state: although she retains the physical tools for human speech, she lacks the control over them that would allow her to express her feelings, her thoughts, and, in essence, her identity.

However, the most prominent method through which Ovid identifies Echo's liminal existence between the human and nonhuman realms is through the repetition of *vocare* and *sonare*, along with their derivatives.[38] *Vocare* and *sonare*, although both describing a type of sound, are on opposite ends of the spectrum of articulate speech. The sound represented by *vocare* and its derivatives is that of human, articulate speech. *Sonare*, on the other hand, indicates a basic sound, most often a noise emitted by inarticulate beings (e.g., moos, howls, or lows) or objects (e.g., the wind, instruments, or thunder). In the narrative, Ovid describes Echo with both of these terms, frequently alternating between the two, even within a single sentence or line. The effect is to show Echo's true wavering identity: although she can produce articulate speech (i.e., *vocare*), she cannot fully control it in order to communicate her identity; thus, the sound she produces is not entirely a human voice in the truest sense but is limited to a sound (*sonare*) somewhat beyond her control and incapable of communicating her identity.

Ovid indicates the essential nature of this *vocare*/*sonare* tension in Echo's identity at the beginning of the narrative, introducing her for the first time as an individual stuck between these two extremes of articulate speech:

adspicit hunc trepidos agitantem in retia cervos
vocalis nymphe, quae nec reticere loquenti
nec prior ipsa loqui didicit, resonabilis Echo.
   (*Met.* 3.356–58)

[She sees him [Narcissus] driving the frightened deer into the nets, the *vocalis* nymph, who neither knows how to remain quiet when one speaks nor knows herself how to speak first, the *resonabilis* Echo.]

Here the two concepts are indicated through adjective-noun pairs (*vocalis nymphe*, *resonabilis Echo*) arranged chiastically with two clauses controlled by the coordinating conjunctions *nec . . . nec*. The chiasmus creates a picture of the ambiguity in Echo's identity: on opposite ends are the two poles of articulate speech, *vocalis* and *resonabilis*; between the two is the uncertain ability of Echo, who can speak (*loquor*) but lacks the total control over her voice to allow her to initiate a conversation (*nec prior ipsa loqui*).

Likewise, when Ovid describes the "conversation" between Narcissus and Echo, he uses the same opposition of *vocare*/*sonare*:

forte puer comitum seductus ab agmine fido
dixerat: "ecquis adest?" et "adest" responderat Echo.
hic stupet, utque aciem partes dimittit in omnis,
voce "veni!" magna clamat: vocat illa vocantem.
respicit et rursus nullo veniente "quid" inquit
"me fugis?" et totidem, quot dixit, verba recepit.
perstat et alternae deceptus imagine vocis
"huc coeamus" ait, nullique libentius umquam
responsura sono "coeamus" rettulit Echo
et verbis favet ipsa suis egressaque silva
ibat, ut iniceret sperato bracchia collo;
ille fugit fugiensque "manus conplexibus aufer!
ante" ait "emoriar, quam sit tibi copia nostri";
rettulit illa nihil nisi "sit tibi copia nostri!"
 (*Met.* 3.379–92)

[By chance, the boy, led away from the familiar field of his companions had said: "Is anyone there?" and Echo had responded, "She is here." He is astonished, and as he seeks high ground in all parts, calls in a great voice, "Come!"; she calls to him, calling. He looks back and again, since no one is coming, says, "Why do you flee me?" and as many times as he spoke, he receives words in reply. He stands still and, deceived by the appearance of another voice, says, "Let's meet here," and Echo, never more ready to reply to one, brought back, "Let's meet" in a sound and herself burned at her words and, having left the woods, began to go forth so that she might wrap her arms around the hoped-for neck. He flees and, fleeing, says, "Take back your hands from your embrace! May I die before my bounty be for you!" She brought back nothing other than "May my bounty be for you!"]

Throughout this "conversation," Ovid makes clear the distinction between the linguistic abilities of Narcissus and those of Echo with his choice of verbs to describe each. Ovid uses verbs of human speech to portray Narcissus as a human fully capable of speech: *dicere, clamare, vocare, inquit, ait*. But whereas Narcissus's ability to speak is consistent throughout, Echo speech is referenced roughly half as often (four verbs compared to seven) and is anything but consistent. At the beginning of the conversation, Echo is described as able to respond (*respondere*) and to call out (*vocare*) to Narcissus. In fact, she is afforded the same active ability to form speech as Narcissus (*vocat illa vocantem*). Her speech sounds like a human voice and, as such, convinces Narcissus that he is speaking to another.

At the point, however, when the audience may be beginning to believe that it is a real conversation between two fully communicative beings, Ovid brings them back to reality. First, he reminds his audience that Echo's speech is not a true *vox* but an *imago vocis*, the mere appearance of a voice. Second, the verbs describing Echo's speech shift from the realm of articulate language (*respondere, vocare*) to that of the inarticulate. Twice Ovid refers to her speech as *rettulit sono*, a phrase that emphasizes the true nature of Echo's voice. Her speech is incapable of communicating her feelings and expressing her identity; thus it cannot be truly described by *vocare* but instead is relegated to the realm of sound unable to articulate identity (*sonare*). This disconnect between Echo's ability to produce speech and her inability to express herself through it is summed up in the clause *nullique libentius umquam / responsura sono "coeamus" rettulit Echo*. Ovid presents Echo as attempting both to fulfill the same verbal action she had mimicked earlier (*responsura ≈ responderat*, 380) and to express her own feelings in her own way (*libentius*), but she lacks the ability to do so and is, in fact, not free. In such a manner, Ovid portrays Echo as the same individual whom he introduced at the outset of the tale: trapped in an ambiguous state between *vocare* and *sonare*, the opposite poles of articulate speech.

After Echo is spurned by Narcissus, she undergoes a second metamorphosis: from an individual with a speech impairment to nothing but a sound. In this transformation, Ovid brings the tension between Echo's ability to speak and her inability to communicate to its natural conclusion, as he depicts Echo's disintegration from the realm of *vocare* to that of *sonare*:

> spreta latet silvis pudibundaque frondibus ora
> protegit et solis ex illo vivit in antris;
> sed tamen haeret amor crescitque dolore repulsae;
> extenuant vigiles corpus miserabile curae
> adducitque cutem macies et in aera sucus
> corporis omnis abit; vox tantum atque ossa supersunt:
> vox manet, ossa ferunt lapidis traxisse figuram.
> inde latet silvis nulloque in monte videtur,
> omnibus auditur: sonus est, qui vivit in illa.
>         (*Met.* 3.393–401)

[Spurned, she hides in the woods and shamed, she cloaks herself in the foliage; she lives apart from him in lonely caves. Yet still the love of the rejected one endures and grows on grief; vigilant cares waste away her miserable frame, and her body shrivels; all its moisture dries. Only voice and bones are left. At last, only voice; her bones are turned to stone. So she hides in the woods and is seen on no mountain but is heard by all: 'tis but a sound that lives on in her. (translation adapted from Melville 2009)]

As the physical manifestation of Echo disintegrates, her entire being exists only in her *vox*, her ability to speak articulately, albeit in a curtailed manner. However, as Ovid prepares for the end of her place in the narrative, her active participation in the story ceases and her ability to communicate is lost. Echo fades to the background and is described only with passive verbs; now her speech is called not a *vox* but a *sonus*, highlighting both the end of her narrative importance and her final loss of whatever vocal agency she had. Ovid at last releases the tension of Echo's linguistic identity; her metamorphosis is now complete. Totally bereft of her voice and personal agency, Echo now enters the isolation afflicting other transformed characters in the *Metamorphoses*.

In all these cases, Ovid works within the prevalent cognitive schema of speech loss and its salient features of the nonhuman and emotionality in order to emphasize the resulting loss of community and identity confusion. When the character is transformed, the voice is stripped away and, with it, a sense of communal identity. However, although they lose the ability to speak, the characters retain their humanity and are simply enveloped by the tree or animal *forma*. Furthermore, all except Daphne were transformed involuntarily, either by their own fault or by the whim of a deity. Yet, to reiterate the main point, all these instances involve speech loss. Furthermore, speech loss is a key symptom of transformation and loss of community. Therefore, to continue the analysis of this theme, we will now expand our investigation to explore Ovid's manipulation of the schematic associations of speech loss.

## Speech Loss and the Written Medium

Until this point, it has been shown that the schematic associations of speech loss, the nonhuman, and emotionality, as well as their subsequent effects on community and identity, are critical aspects of Ovid's depictions of metamorphosis. When a character loses the ability to speak, he or she does not regain it and, as a result, loses a uniquely human trait. However, these characters do not lose their minds, so to speak. The persistence of the characters' internal, rational sense of identity keeps each character somewhat human. Still, since their form is not that of a human, they exist fully in neither the realm of humanity nor of animality. Thus, they are left with no true community and are forced into isolation, a solitary, "wavering" existence as neither animal nor human. Still, in a few cases, most notably those of Io and Philomela, Ovid manipulates the schematic associations of speech loss and uses the same internal sense of identity that prevents characters from being fully animal to provide a way back to humanity: convinced of their human identity, these human characters strive to reconnect with their communities and to communicate their identities through writing. In essence, Ovid specifically points out that they are not fully animal and, consequently, they have not lost their speech. Instead, their speech has just been transformed, and they can still communicate through a written medium. To examine this path to restoration, let us first start with the story of Io (1.568–746).

## Io

The myth of Io is one of the most well attested in antiquity, appearing first in fragments of the *Aiginios* and another Hesiodic work (most likely the *Catalogue*), enjoying an increase in popularity in fifth-century Athens, and persisting through the Roman period.[39] The only extended accounts of the story, however, come from the Roman period in Calvus's lost *Io* and Ovid's handling in *Metamorphoses* 1. The basic narrative of the myth remained relatively constant throughout antiquity, although some minor variations can be identified.[40] At its core, the story runs as follows: Io, a daughter of Peiren and a priestess of Hera, was seduced by Zeus, who then transformed Io into a cow and swore to Hera that he had not touched her. Hera, rightfully distrustful of her husband's oath, charged Argos with the task of guarding Io, a task that he performed until he was killed by Hermes. Hera then forced Io to wander the world in her bovine form, continually tormented by a gadfly. Eventually, Io was allowed to return to her human form.

Although other differences between the various versions can be identified, a major one germane to the current discussion is the presentation of Io's ability to speak. Whereas in all the extant Greek versions either Io has the ability to speak in her human voice (e.g., her extended monologues in Aeschylus's *Prometheus Bound*) or the topic of speech is never mentioned, in Ovid explicit reference is made to the fact that Io can no longer speak, a fact continuously exploited for the sake of pathos. The introduction of speech loss to the myth, therefore, has been seen as an Ovidian innovation. Such an inclusion, however, need not be only for the sake of pathos but instead can be read as an extension of the Ovidian manipulation of the schema of speech loss discussed in this chapter. Before we consider Ovid's emphasis on Io's speech loss, a brief examination of a previous Ovidian handling of the myth on a smaller scale is useful. The Ovidian innovation of speech loss in the Io myth appeared first not in the *Metamorphoses* but in the earlier *Heroides*.

In *Heroides* 14, Ovid presents a letter written from Hypermestra to her husband, Lynceus. According to that myth, Danaus, Hypermestra's father, and his brother Aegyptus father respectively fifty daughters and fifty sons. These two brothers fight over the kingship of Egypt, and Aegyptus seeks to marry his sons to Danaus's daughters to prevent Danaus from marrying the daughters to another's sons and forming an alliance against him. Danaus eventually agrees to the marriages but arms his daughters with daggers and tells each of them to murder her respective husband on the wedding day. All the daughters follow through with the plan except Hypermestra, who is unable to kill her husband, Lynceus. When Danaus discovers Hypermestra's disobedience, he throws her in prison. It is at this point that the epistle of *Heroides* 14 is written.

In the poem, Hypermestra explains her side of the story to a supposedly dual audience, with both Lynceus and Danaus as prospective addressees. Included in the letter is a lengthy "digression" on the myth of Io, which ostensibly acts to show commonalities between Io and Hypermestra. In the description of Io, Hypermestra emphasizes the bovine heroine's inability to speak, devoting much effort to describing the frustration such speech loss brought about:

Scilicet ex illo Iunonia permanet ira,
    cum bos ex homine est, ex bove facta dea—
at satis est poenae teneram mugisse puellam
    nec modo formosam posse placere Iovi.
adstitit in ripa liquidi nova vacca parentis
    cornuaque in patriis non sua vidit aquis
conatoque queri mugitus edidit ore
    territaque est forma, territa voce sua.
        (*Her.* 14.85–92)

[Just like that one the Junonian anger persists, when she was made a cow from a human, goddess from a cow—but it is enough of a penalty that the tender girl should moo and, no longer beautiful, be able to please Jove. She stands, the new cow, on the shore of her liquid parent, and horns not her own she sees in her father's waters, and sends forth moos from a mouth trying to complain, terrified at her form, terrified at her voice.]

As we have already established, all prior, extant handlings of the Io myth remain mute on her speech loss, either allowing her to speak in a human voice or leaving Io's speech out of the myth entirely. Thus, Ovid's insertion of Io's speech loss in his version seems to be intentional and innovative, adding another layer of meaning to Hypermestra's allusion to the myth. I would argue that this emphasis on Io's speech loss be read in conjunction with the predominant view that Hypermestra included the myth in her letter so as to set Io up as an analogy to herself. For as James Reeson (2001, 283) puts it, Hypermestra offers "no empty retelling of the story." Laurel Fulkerson (2003, 136n44), following the basic argument set out by Howard Jacobson (1987, 134–35), provides a good listing of the close parallels between the stories of the two heroines: "Both women are confused and terrified at their new surroundings, Io because she is a heifer, Hypermestra because she is in prison. Each woman is described as *exul*, an exile, and each must come to terms with unfamiliar weapons—horns for Io and *tela* for Hypermestra. Finally, both women were said to be priestesses of Hera at Argos."[41]

Although scholarship is right to point out the clear similarities between the positions of each heroine, the similarity between their methods of communication with their fathers also deserves attention and explains Ovid's choice to describe Io as speechless.[42] Since their situations are so closely parallel, it is also appropriate to equate the methods in which the heroines communicate with the respective fathers: Io, because she is voiceless, does so through writing, and Hypermestra, since she too is voiceless in the sense that she is unable to speak face-to-face with her father, also turns to writing as a means of communication.

By equating herself with the speechless Io, Hypermestra suggests that she too is suffering the schematic associations of isolation and relegation in Io's speechlessness. Therefore, like Io she turns to writing as a means of mediating that isolation and communicating with her father. The Ovidian addition of speech loss to the Io myth, therefore, serves a poetic purpose for *Heroides* 14: a means to express Hypermestra's sense of isolation and to explain the reason for the letter's existence itself as a method of mediating communication without speech. Still, what of the Ovidian handling of the Io myth in the *Metamorphoses*, a version that also includes a heavy emphasis on Io's loss of speech in her bovine form?

In the account of the Io myth given in the *Metamorphoses*, Ovid again depicts the bovine Io as bereft of speech, and as he did in *Heroides* 14, Ovid uses the schematic associations of speech loss to emphasize her isolation from community. Thus, in many respects, the story of Io in the *Metamorphoses* resembles the other tales we have examined from Ovid's *magnum opus*: after being transformed, Io loses the ability to speak and is consequently removed from her community, both familial and human. In her transformed state, she exists in a liminal state between animal and human, Fränkel's state of "wavering identity." Yet this is where the similarities between Io's tale and the other tales of metamorphosis end. She does not remain isolated from her community, nor does she suffer an unfortunate death in her transformed state. Instead, she is the first character in the *Metamorphoses* to communicate with her community and to effect the change of her state from one of isolation and transformation to one of reintegration and community. The means through which Io is able to achieve her reintegration is significant, for it is the written medium that effectively mediates the communication gap brought on by speech loss. (As we will see in chapter 3, the ability of the written word to bridge such communication gaps will form a large portion of Ovid's poetics of exile.) After she communicates her identity to her family through her writing, she initiates the course of events that results in her transformation back into her human form and her reintegration into her lost community.

An analysis of the narrative needs to begin with Ovid's description of Io in terms of liminality, after she is transformed into a cow by Jupiter in an effort to hide her rape from Juno: Io exists in a state of ambiguity between man and beast. Although she is able to rationalize as a human, she lacks the human ability to vocalize it due to the transformed state of her physical body. This liminality is identified at the moment of her transformation.

> coniugis adventum praesenserat inque nitentem
> Inachidos *vultus mutaverat* ille *iuvencam*;
> (bos quoque *formosa* est). *speciem* Saturnia vaccae,
> quamquam invita, probat nec non, et cuius et unde
> quove sit armento, veri quasi nescia quaerit.
>     (*Met.* 1.610–14)

[[Jupiter] had already sensed the arrival of his spouse and had changed the *vultus* of the daughter of Inachus into a brilliant *iuvenca* (for a heifer is also shapely). The daughter of Saturn, although unwilling, approves of the beauty of the cow and, as if ignorant of the truth, inquires both who owned the cow, where it came from, and to what flock it belonged.]

In these lines, Ovid depicts the actual moment of transformation and describes to us what type of transformation occurred that resulted in Io's loss of ability to communicate her inner emotions and intentions. First, Ovid seems to recognize that the only aspect of Io that was changed was the outward appearance, as the only vocabulary used to describe Io is that of outward appearance: *vultus*, *species*, and *forma*. The traditional explanation of these lines, therefore, is that all these terms be taken as synonyms pointing to the outward change of Io.[43]

These three terms for "outward appearance," however, have underlying meanings that need to be unpacked, for Ovid is expressing the exact nature of Io's transformation through these terms. The aspect of Io's identity that was transformed by Jupiter, her *vultus*, was not merely her outward appearance but her human ability to communicate her identity through her appearance.

In his recent study of identity and communication in the ancient world, Bettini devotes an entire chapter to expressions of communicative appearance in Roman thought, a chapter that touches on two of the terms employed by Ovid here: *species* and *vultus*.[44] Bettini suggests that *species* referred to an individual's "capacity to be seen" and focused exclusively on the outward appearance of an individual (i.e., what one "looked like").[45] As such, this seems to confirm the traditional interpretation that when Juno marveled at Io's *species*, she was impressed by the beauty of Io's bovine form. Moreover, Bettini's discussion of *vultus* adds another dimension to what Ovid is describing. For Bettini, the *vultus* was "a vehicle for expressing personality traits and internal emotions" (2011, 139), and since both of these aspects were not the purview of animals, animals did not have a *vultus*.[46] Likewise, Anthony Corbeill, in his study of gestures in the Roman world, describes *vultus* as the facial expression that voicelessly expressed an individual's inner will.[47] As Corbeill hints at with the term "voicelessly," such a focus on expression of an individual's interiority naturally includes notions of communication and speech, the vehicles through which one can verbally describe the inner emotions expressed nonverbally by the *vultus*:[48]

> The *vultus* is the central focus of interpersonal communication. This part of the head becomes a *locus* of hints and signs, to the point of functioning as a true and proper "language" that people can use to decipher the feelings and intentions at work in another person's soul. (Bettini 2011, 141)

Against this cognitive background, much more is happening in the metamorphosis of Io than a superficial transformation. When Io's *vultus* is transformed, her ability to express her inner feelings to her human community is lost. Furthermore, the ability of other humans to "read" her *vultus* for keys to her identity is obstructed. Although her human ability to have internal emotions and intentions remains intact, her ability to express them through her *vultus* is inhibited by her new bovine outward appearance. Io, thus, is placed in an ambiguous state between human and beast.

Ovid continues his emphasis on that state with the term *iuvenca*, the actual descriptor of what Io had become. Typically translated as "heifer," *iuvenca* is actually an ambiguous word that carries the semantic meaning of "young" and can refer either to young cattle or to young humans. In fact, Ovid, in *Heroides* 5, uses the term to refer to Helen of Troy (*Graia . . . iuvenca*, 5.117–18, 124), and he was clearly aware of the term's ambiguous connotations.[49] Moreover, if we stress the ambiguity of the term, Ovid's subsequent parenthetical reference to a *bos* makes more sense, as it serves to clarify Io's ambiguous nature stated at the end of the preceding line (one may even imagine the break between the lines being lengthened in a recitation of the poem to emphasize the ambiguity).

Secondly, since Io's transformation left her in such an ambiguous state between human and beast, Ovid emphasizes her loss of the human ability to speak, a loss that results in her schematic and literal removal from both her human and her familial communities. Under the watchful eyes of Argus, Io wanders the countryside and attempts to complain about her situation:

luce sinit pasci; cum sol tellure sub alta est,
claudit et indigno circumdat vincula collo.
frondibus arboreis et amara pascitur herba.
proque toro terrae non semper gramen habenti
incubat infelix limosaque flumina potat.
illa etiam supplex Argo cum bracchia vellet
tendere, non habuit, quae bracchia tenderet Argo,
conatoque queri mugitus edidit ore
pertimuitque sonos propriaque exterrita voce est.
    (*Met.* 1.630–38)

[In the day, [Argus] allowed her to graze; when the sun dropped below the earth, he locked her up and bound her undeserving neck with a chain. She eats tree leaves and bitter grasses. Instead of a bed, she, unlucky, sleeps on the ground, which not always has grass, and drinks from muddy streams. When she wished even to extend her arms to Argus in supplication, though she had none, which she might extend to Argus, a moo poured forth from the mouth trying to complain, and she was afraid of the sounds and frightened by her own voice.]

When Io attempts to complain, all she is able to do is produce a moo (*mugatus edidit*), as her physical form has been transformed into that of a cow.[50] For as much as Io's *mugatus* can tell us about her loss of speech, the subsequent line tells us much more, particularly regarding the type of sound that was produced. In that line, Ovid describes Io's moos as both a *sonus* and a *vox*, commenting on her speech loss in much the same manner that he had with Echo.[51]

*Sonus*, as we have seen, was traditionally associated with noise or the inarticulate speech of animals, whereas *vox* indicated some form of the articulate speech of humans. Here Ovid describes the sequence of Io's realization of and fright at her loss of speech with a past participle (*exterrita*) and a perfect verb (*pertimuit*). The participle *exterrita*, due to its relative tense, indicates the first action: when Io attempted to speak, she was shocked and thoroughly terrified at what she had expected to be her own voice (*propria voce*).[52] Sometime between the participial action and that of the main verb, Io comes to the realization that her voice had been changed along with her physical form (Payne 2010, 126–28). Instead of being able to voice her complaints as earlier versions of the character had been able to do, Ovid's Io is voiceless. There will be no monologues of complaints as in Aeschylus (*PV* 589–886). After this realization, Io is gripped by an intense fear (*pertimuit*) that she is able to produce only the *sonos* of a cow.

Because of her loss of speech, Io falls into the same schematic trap as other metamorphosed characters and is isolated from both her human and her familial communities and is relegated to the animal realm. Ovid describes her transformed state in terms of comparisons with humanity. Io, whom Jupiter had extolled as worthy of his love and of bringing a young prince to her wedding bed (*o virgo Iove digna tuoque beatum / nescioquem factura toro*, 590–91), now is forced to submit her unworthy neck to animal chains (*indigno circumdat vincula collo*), to exchange her human resting place for the ground (*proque toro terrae non semper gramen habenti / incubat*), and to eat tree leaves and bitter grass (*frondibus arboreis et amara pascitur herba*).[53] This last line, although typically described as an allusion to Calvus's lost *Io*, also alludes to a line in Virgil's *Georgics* in which the life of a lonely, exiled bull is described:[54]

> nec mos bellantis una stabulare, sed alter
> uictus abit longeque ignotis exsulat oris,
> multa gemens ignominiam plagasque superbi
> uictoris, tum quos amisit inultus amores,
> et stabula aspectans regnis excessit auitis.
> ergo omni cura uiris exercet et inter
> dura iacet pernox instrato saxa cubili
> frondibus hirsutis et carice pastus acuta,
> et temptat sese atque irasci in cornua discit
> arboris obnixus trunco, uentosque lacessit
> ictibus, et sparsa ad pugnam proludit harena.
>     (Verg. *G.* 3.224–34)

[It is not the custom for the [cattle fighting over a heifer] to stable together, but the beaten one leaves and lives in exile on unknown shores, bemoaning often his disgrace and the blows of the proud victor, then the loves which he, unavenged, lost, and looking at the stables, he leaves his ancestral realms. Therefore, he trains his strength with care and lies all night on a naked bed among hard stones, having eaten rough leaves and sharp reeds, and he tests himself and learns to attack with his horns, having pressed them against the trunk of a tree, and beats the winds with blows, and practices for the fight on the spread-out sand.]

The Virgilian bull is exiled from his herd, lives alone, and sleeps on a grassless patch of earth just as Io. Io, then, is bereft of a place in both the human community and the animal realm. Her lack of acceptance in either realm thus recalls the similar situations of the transformed Actæon and Callisto, who both struggle to find a place where they belong.

Beyond her schematic isolation from humanity, Io is also removed from her familial community. Ovid draws attention to this removal in the following lines:

venit et ad ripas, *ubi ludere saepe solebat,*
Inachidas: rictus novaque ut conspexit in unda
cornua, pertimuit seque exsternata refugit.
*naides ignorant, ignorat et Inachus ipse,*
quae sit; at illa patrem sequitur sequiturque sorores
et patitur tangi seque admirantibus offert.
    (*Met.* 1.639–44)

[And she comes to the shores, where she often used to play, the ones of Inachus: when she saw her jaw and new horns in the water, she was frightened and, having seen herself, she fled back. The naiads were unaware, and unaware was Inachus himself, of who she was; but she followed her father and followed her sisters and suffered to be touched and offered herself to those admiring her.]

In her wanderings, Io returns to the shores of her father's river, the location of her community where she used to play as a young girl (*ubi ludere saepe solebat*). Now, however, she is no longer a girl—or a human. Ovid emphasizes the separation of the bovine Io from her memories of her childhood by delaying Io's recognition scene until this moment. Even though she has been in a bovine form for some time, this is the first time Io actually sees herself. The sight of her new (*nova*) form in the waters of her childhood creates a displacement of identity that causes Io to flee: she sees a foreign face reflected back in her father's waters and is again reminded of her changed form.[55] Andrew Feldherr provides another interpretive angle that moves Io's moment of revelation beyond the narrative, bringing the reader into the text as a participant: this moment not only is the moment of Io's recognition of reality but also *the reader's realization* of Io's perception of reality:

> This moment of self-recognition as cow, then, comes when she literally sees herself as others see her, and those others are her readers, and yet the very same device makes the reader himself a reflection of Io, and so gives access to her experience as perceiving subject. (2010, 20)

At this moment, then, both the reader and Io see both narrative perspectives: although Io is truly a human in bovine form and perceives herself as such, she and the reader now understand that she no longer has a place in her father's realm;[56] her reaction to this realization is nearly identical to her initial response to that her transformed speech (*pertimuitque sonos propriaque exterrita voce est*, 638 ≈ *pertimuit seque exsternata refugit*, 641).

In addition to Io's displacement from her communal location and her failure to recognize herself, members of her community are also unaware of her identity and presence. The chiastic line following Io's reflective episode highlights the lack of awareness in her community, a fact heightened by the anadiplosis of the verb *ignorare*. Neither the naiads nor Inachus himself recognizes her in her bovine form. Io, of course, still recognizes them, and in her mind, they are her sisters and father.[57] The disconnection between Io and her family is emphasized by the repetition in lines 632–33: whereas the community members are identified by their proper names in relation to a cow in the first line, in the second, seen through Io's eyes (*at illa*), these same members are her sisters (*sorores*) and father (*patrem*).

Yet, although Io is in the presence of her community and recognizes it as such, she still is not a part of it because she has no means of communicating her identity to the community:

> illa manus lambit patriisque dat oscula palmis
> nec retinet lacrimas, et, si modo verba sequantur,
> oret opem nomenque suum casusque loquatur.
> (*Met.* 1.646–48)

[She licks [Inachus's] hands and gives kisses to the fatherly palms, but she cannot hold back tears, and, if only words were able to follow, she would beg for help and say her name and misfortunes.]

She attempts to indicate her identity by performing a variety of loving, human-like gestures: she kisses the hand of one she herself recognizes as her *pater*, she allows herself to be embraced, and she weeps.[58] However, these gestures are interpreted as those of a cow, and the effect they produce is one of astonishment (*admirantibus*) but not recognition. Io is now in a position similar to that of Actæon in book 3: although she knows what she wants to say, she lacks the verbal ability to do so.

This is the point at which all of the other tales of speech loss we have examined end, as Ovid emphasizes speech loss's schematic associations with the nonhuman, emotionality, and the subsequent effects on community and identity: the character's speech loss has isolated him or her from community, enclosing him or her within a foreign body and prohibiting him or her from communicating identity. With Io, however, Ovid manipulates this schema and starts a different narrative pattern, one that—as we shall see in chapter 3—he continues into his exile literature. For, Io, although lacking both a *vultus* and a *vox* by which to communicate her identity, is not truly an animal, as she retains her *mens*. Therefore, Ovid does not make her speech completely lost, as much as he alters it, allowing her to find another manner of communication with humanity: the written word:[59]

> *littera pro verbis*, quam pes in pulvere *duxit*,
> corporis *indicium* mutati triste peregit.
> "*me miserum!*" exclamat pater Inachus inque gementis
> cornibus et nivea pendens cervice iuvencae
> "*me miserum!*" ingeminat; "tune es quaesita per omnes
> nata mihi terras? tu non inventa reperta
> luctus eras levior! retices nec mutua nostris
> dicta refers, alto tantum suspiria ducis
> pectore, quodque unum potes, ad mea verba remugis!
> at tibi ego ignarus thalamos taedasque parabam,
> spesque fuit generi mihi prima, secunda nepotum.
> de grege nunc tibi vir, nunc de grege natus habendus.
> nec finire licet tantos mihi morte dolores;
> sed nocet esse deum, praeclusaque ianua leti
> aeternum nostros luctus extendit in aevum."
>
>    (*Met.* 1.649–63)

[In place of words, her hoof traced letters in the dust, a sad token of her changed body. "Miserable me!" father Inachus cried and clasped the moaning heifer's horns and snow-white neck. "Miserable me!" he groaned: "Are you the child I sought through all the world? Oh, lighter grief 'twas it when you were unfound than found. You give no answer. Silent, but from your heart so deep a sigh! A moo—all you can say—is your reply! I, knowing naught, made ready for your marriage, hoped for a son-in-law and grandchildren. But now the herd must find your husband, find your child. For me death cannot end my woes. Sad bane to be a god! The gates of death are shut; my grief endures for evermore." (translation adapted from Melville)]

In an effort to communicate with her family, Io writes a symbol (*indicium*) of her identity in the sand, trading the spoken word for the written medium (*littera pro verbis*).[60] The term *indicium*, incidentally, also is used to describe the written indication Philomela creates to communicate with her sister, Procne (see discussion below). Hardie (2002) reads the following lines as a progression of realization for Inachus, as he first translates what Io had written on the ground into its Latin equivalent (*me miserum*), and then, when he realizes the identity of the *iuvenca*—again pointing out a double meaning—he exclaims in grief, "*me miserum!*"[61] Yet despite the grief expressed by Inachus, Io has successfully reconnected with her society and has communicated her identity through the written medium.

In fact, Ovid emphasizes the importance of writing—especially that of the poetic variety—to the successful communication of identity through his phrase *pes duxit*. The word *pes* is consistently used by Ovid and other poets as a reference to poetic composition because of its relation to the metrical feet. Furthermore, the word *ducere* harkens back to Ovid's principal goal in writing *Metamorphoses*: *deducere perpetuum carmen* from the creation of the world to the present day (1.4). The term *ducere* itself has an artistic meaning in the sense of fashioning and casting, especially read along with *pes*.[62] By using such poetic terminology, Ovid emphasizes the importance of the medium of writing to overcome the schematic associations of speech loss, while offering an expression of the importance of poetry: through her writing, Io is able to communicate with her father and reintegrate herself into her family; through his writing, Ovid is able to communicate his identity as a gifted poet.

Despite her success in communicating her identity, Io still cannot be fully reintegrated into her community because of her bovine form, a fact that Ovid continues to highlight. His use of the words *gementis* and *iuvencae* plays on the duplicity of Io's nature, as both words have double meanings that can refer to either the animal or the human world.[63] Ovid, however, refuses to clarify, leaving Io's identity in the same ambiguous state. Likewise, Inachus's list of plans he had for his daughter serve not only to clarify his bourgeois tendencies but also to emphasize the continued disconnect between Io's human and animal nature.[64]

After this meeting of daughter and father, Ovid separates them again. However, although Argos takes her father away (*patri diversa*), he is unable to break the newly reconstituted bond of community, for Ovid now describes Io as a *natam* separated from her father, not as an isolated cow. Io's act of communication starts a series of events that eventually leads to her total reintegration into her community. Jupiter is moved by the scene of reconciliation and suffering between daughter and father (*nec superum rector mala tanta Phoronidos ultra / ferre potest*) and sends Mercury to slay Argos and free Io.

Once free, Io is returned to her former shape. Her mouth is narrowed (*contrahitur rictus*), and she is at last able to speak again. In addition, Ovid uses the word *erigitur* to show how Io's posture changes from that of an animal to that of a human. However, she still fears to speak lest she moo in the manner of a young cow (*metuitque loqui, ne more iuvencae / mugiat*, 745–46).[65] Her loss of speech and brush with isolation have scared her. But in the end, she finally is able to return to her long-abandoned speech (*et timide verba intermissa retemptat*). Moreover, she takes up an important place in the religious world of her community as a priestess of Isis. Ovid's choice of the Isis cult for Io continues the link between cow and human but in a communal setting. The ambiguous status between animal and human that once had removed Io from society now involves her in the community as a link between the human and the gods.

Io's story could well have ended as the stories of Lycaon, Callisto, Echo and Actæon. She could have fallen further into isolation and possibly death, both of which are salient features of speech loss. However, after Io loses her ability to speak and suffers isolation from society, Ovid resuscitates her humanity by manipulating the schema and pointing out that since Io is not truly an animal, she has not suffered total speech loss as much as a speech alteration. Thus, Io is able to communicate through *writing*. Because of this, not only does she regain her ability to speak, but she is also reintegrated into community as a link between humanity and the divine (*nunc dea linigera colitur celeberrima turba*).

## *Philomela*

The story of Philomela, Procne, and Tereus is one of the oldest tales discussed in this chapter, as the earliest traces date to Hesiod and Sappho.[66] The most definitive form of the myth, however, is Sophocles's *Tereus*, a play based on the

Attic version of the myth and not the Homeric one. In the story, Tereus, the king of Thrace, marries the Athenian Procne and takes her back to his kingdom. Then, sometime later, Tereus rapes her sister Philomela and cuts out her tongue to prevent her from reporting his misdeed. Philomela, now unable to speak, sends Procne a message about her situation woven into a piece of cloth. Then the two sisters take revenge on Tereus by killing his son, Itys, and serving Itys to Tereus in a banquet. When Tereus discovers their deed, he, enraged, chases the sisters in an attempt to kill them. However, before he succeeds, all three are transformed into birds: Procne into a nightingale, Philomela into a swallow, and Tereus into a hawk or a hoopoe.[67]

The Ovidian version of the myth follows the Attic version in most regards, with the exception of the assignment of transformation to the characters.[68] The Roman authors in general changed the types of birds into which the characters were transformed, instead identifying the nightingale as Philomela and the swallow as Procne.[69] Ovid, however, purposefully leaves this aspect ambiguous, as we shall see. Beyond the handling of the transformation itself, the only major difference the Ovidian story has in comparison with the other Ovidian metamorphoses we have discussed is the fact that speech loss was already a key aspect to the myth and Ovid did not have to create it out of whole cloth. Yet Ovid does spend a great deal more time on speech loss—and on the senses in general—in his version than in the earlier versions and uses it to focus on the schematic associations of speech loss and the subsequent effects on community and identity that we have traced throughout the *Metamorphoses*.

Throughout the tale, Ovid makes use of speech loss's schematic associations and Philomela's ability to speak (or lack thereof) to identify her relationship with both her familial community and the human community at large. Before her rape at the hands of Tereus, Philomela is portrayed as a woman with the power to speak and the determination to use that power to spread news of Tereus's misdeed to the community at large. After her tongue is removed, however, she becomes physically isolated from community through her inability to produce articulate speech and her physical removal from society in the woods. Still, like Io, Philomela overcomes her loss of speech by weaving an *indicium* of her identity into a cloth and sending the cloth to her sister, thus effecting her reintegration into society.

At the beginning of the tale, Ovid places the setting of the story in the realm of human community and palace civilization as a foil to Philomela's movement from it to the animal realm, a shift that results in her entrance into a state of "wavering identity" between human and animal schematically associated with the isolation of speech loss. As the plot opens, the action takes place in a wholly urban, civilized setting: the palaces of Tereus and Pandion in Thrace and Athens, respectively. Tereus, at the request of Procne, sails from his palace to Pandion's and asks that Philomela return with him to Thrace. After Pandion's approval is gained, Philomela is transported from Athens to Thrace. However, upon arrival in Thrace, Philomela is taken not to the palace but to the wilderness:

> Barbarus et nusquam lumen detorquet ab illa,
> non aliter, quam cum pedibus praedator obuncis
> deposuit nido *leporem* Iovis ales in alto:
> nulla fuga est capto, spectat sua praemia raptor.
> Iamque iter effectum, iamque in sua litora fessis
> puppibus exierant, cum rex Pandione natam
> *in stabula alta trahit, silvis obscura vetustis,*
> atque ibi pallentem trepidamque et cuncta timentem
> et iam cum lacrimis, ubi sit germana, rogantem
> includit fassusque nefas et virginem et *unam*
> vi superat frustra clamato saepe parente,
> saepe sorore sua, magnis super omnia divis.
> illa tremit velut *agna pavens*, quae saucia cani
> ore excussa lupi nondum sibi tuta videtur,
> utque *columba* suo madefactis sanguine plumis
> horret adhuc avidosque timet, quibus haeserat, ungues.
>     (*Met.* 6.515–30)

[The barbarian [Tereus] never casts his eyes down away from her in a manner no different than that in which the predator looks at his prey, when the bird of Jove clutches a hare with its taloned feet in the bright heights: there is no escape for the captured one. Now the journey was complete, now they had gone out of the tired ships into their lands, when the king dragged the one born of Pandion into the high stables, hidden by the old woods, and there the girl, pallid and trembling and fearing all things and now with tears asking where her sister was, he locks up and, professing his unspeakable act, takes both the girl, alone, and her maidenhood by force, while parent's names are often called out, often her sister's, and above all the names of the great gods. She trembles like a frightened lamb, who, though wounded, has shaken off the mouth of the gray wolf, yet still doesn't consider herself safe, and as a dove, with her feathers soaked in her own blood, shudders and still fears the greedy claws in which she had been ensnared.]

This passage presents the violent shift in setting from civilization to wilderness and begins to show Philomela's movement from human to animal or, as Hardie has observed, emphasizes the dehumanization that comes from "Tereus' removal of Philomela from the world of palace civilization to the wild woods (521)" (2002, 262).[70] No longer is Philomela in her own land, but she is in the land of the Thracians (*sua* [i.e., Tereus] *litora*) and is dragged (*trahit*) as an animal would drag its prey (*cum pedibus praedator . . . ales in alto*) to the high stables (*stabula alta*). Such a location emphasizes both the sense of foreboding for Philomela and her impending dehumanization through allusions to the journey made by Aeneas on his way to the underworld in *Aeneid* 7 (*itur in antiquam silvam, stabula alta ferarum*, 7.179). Moreover, in addition to the relocation of Philomela to the animal realm, Ovid also points to the impending schematic consequences of her speech loss through his use of three similes, all of which portray Philomela as a frightened animal,[71] as she is likened to a hare (*leporem*), a frightened lamb (*agna pavens*), and a dove (*columba*).[72]

Beyond Ovid's emphasis on Philomela's entrance into the animal realm, in this passage there is a distinct focus on her isolation from her community that also works within the dominant schema of speech loss. First, the stable to which Philomela is taken is described as *silvis obscura vetustis*, isolated deep in the most ancient part of the woods, removed from society by its depth. Second, the phrase *et unam* emphasizes Philomela's isolation regardless of whether it is read as hendiadys or polysyndeton with *et virginem*. Likewise, in addition to the constant emphasis on her isolation, the community from which she is isolated is brought to the forefront. Philomela calls to her sister and her father for help, but there is no response. Moreover, the fact that Ovid identifies Procne and Pandion not by their proper names but by their relationship to Philomela (*soror, parens*) highlights the familial relationship as the focus of the passage. Furthermore, Philomela herself is mentioned not by name but only through her relationship to her family as *Pandione natam*, further stressing Ovid's focus on the familial bonds that are threatened by Tereus's abduction.

Against this background of Philomela's impending isolation from her familial and human communities and her movement into the animal realm, Ovid now focuses his attention on the aspect of Philomela's identity that must be removed in order for this transformation to occur: her speech. First, he allows his audience to see Philomela's voice in action, as she delivers a threatening speech to Tereus, in the wake of her rape, in which she promises to expose him with her voice in public, community fora. Second, after her speech, Ovid shifts the entire narratological focus from the rape, which had been the dominant focus of the first half of the narrative, to the removal of Philomela's tongue, the very instrument with which she was planning to articulate her revenge on Tereus.

After her rape, Philomela delivers a powerful speech to Tereus that is so effective that it strikes fear in Tereus and causes him to cut out the tongue that had spoken it. In terms of our analysis of speech loss, Philomela's speech accomplishes two things. First, it highlights the fact that she could speak—and speak well—and thus had an ability to lose her speech (see the use of direct speech in the Actæon episode and the focus on *vocalis* in the Echo narrative). Second, and more importantly, the content of the speech focuses on speech as a means of getting revenge on Tereus. Moreover, the ways in which Philomela promises to use her speech are all communal and public in nature. An example is the end of her speech in which she levies her threats against Tereus:

si tamen haec superi cernunt, si numina divum
sunt aliquid, si non perierunt omnia mecum,
quandocumque mihi poenas dabis! *ipsa pudore
proiecto tua facta loquar: si copia detur,
in populos veniam; si silvis clausa tenebor,
inplebo silvas et conscia saxa movebo*;
audiet haec aether et si deus ullus in illo est!
    (*Met.* 6.542–48)

[However, if the gods above perceive these actions of yours, if the powers of the gods are indeed something, if everything has not perished with me, at some point you will pay the price! I myself, with my modesty put aside, shall speak your deeds: if an opportunity is given, I shall come into the people; if I shall be held, enclosed in the woods, I shall fill the woods and I shall move the rocks as witnesses; this air shall hear and whatever god there is in it!]

Philomela's threats are based on one concept: her ability to tell the world of Tereus's misdeeds (*tua facta loquar*). As we have seen, *loqui* is a verb of communication that describes articulate speech. The two *si* clauses that follow Philomela's statement qualify the type of articulate speech that Philomela has in mind, but both require some sort of communal interaction. The first option Philomela mentions is that she could go into a crowd of people and deliver a speech on Tereus's deeds. Such a civic locus for her speech is made clear by the terms *copia* and *populos*, both of which carry connotations of delivering a speech in public fora. Doing so is clearly a communal act of communication with which Philomela can counter Tereus's attempt to isolate her in the wilderness.

The second option Philomela provides is that she will fill the woods with her complaints of Tereus's misdeeds and make the rocks her witnesses. This form of speech is a far cry from the delivery of oratory in the forum; yet it is just as communal. Instead of drawing on oratory, this option depends on poetry and the ability to communicate complaints through it. The verb *implere* in particular deserves attention, as it is used multiple times in the Ovidian corpus in descriptions of poetic complaints and poetic production.[73] Ovid himself uses the term in regard to his own poetry in *Tristia* 4.3.72–73 as a description of how he fills his poetry with stories of his wife (*exemplumque mihi coniugis esto bonae / materiamque tuis tristem virtutibus imple*). Here Philomela is the poet who will fill (*implebo*) the woods with her complaints.

In addition to the semantic meaning of *implere*, the entire depiction of Philomela in the woods evokes images of Orpheus, the master poet who was famed for moving nature (*movere*) with his songs.[74] Instead of performing her complaints in a civic setting, in this option Philomela would shift her attention and engage in the pastoral and elegiac complaints of shepherds,[75] speaking to the community of the creatures of the woods and perhaps to other victims of transformation.[76]

After setting such a background for Philomela's impending movement into isolation in the animal realm and drawing the audience's attention to her verbal abilities, Ovid shifts the focus of the narrative to her loss of speech and the completion of her transformation:

> Talibus ira feri postquam commota tyranni
> nec minor hac metus est, causa stimulatus utraque,
> quo fuit accinctus, vagina liberat ensem
> arreptamque coma fixis post terga lacertis
> vincla pati cogit; iugulum Philomela parabat
> spemque suae mortis viso conceperat ense:
> ille indignantem et nomen patris usque vocantem
> luctantemque loqui conprensam forcipe *linguam*
> abstulit ense fero. radix micat ultima linguae,
> ipsa iacet terraeque tremens inmurmurat atrae,
> utque salire solet mutilatae cauda colubrae,
> palpitat et moriens dominae vestigia quaerit.
>     (*Met.* 6.551–60)

[After the anger of the savage tyrant had been stirred by such words and not a small fear arose at this, having been goaded by each cause, Tereus freed the sword from its sheath by its side, and seizing her hair, gathered it together, to use as a tie, to tether her arms behind her back. Philomela, seeing the sword, and hoping only for death, offered up her throat. But he severed her tongue with his savage blade, holding it with pincers, as it struggled to speak in indignation, calling out her father's name repeatedly. Her tongue's root was left quivering, while the rest of it lay on the dark soil, vibrating and trembling, and, as though it were the tail of a mutilated snake moving, it writhed, as if, in dying, it were searching for some sign of her.]

In this scene, Philomela ceases to be the subject of Tereus's outrage, and the source of her verbal threats attracts Tereus's wrath (*Talibus ira feri postquam commota tyranni*). Thus, Ovid shows the audience the tongue of Philomela, the source of her articulate speech, brutally cut out by the root (*radix micat ultima linguae*). Amy Richlin comments on this narratological shift, adding, "Ovid has shifted the focus of dramatic attention in this tale forward off the rape and backwards off the metamorphosis, onto the scene of the cutting out of Philomela's tongue" (1992, 164).[77] Ovid takes this aspect of the story directly from Apollodorus's version (καὶ τὴν γλῶσσαν ἐξέτεμεν αὐτῆς); however, with typical Ovidian vividness, he adds a new pathos and horror to the story by making the tongue itself the subject of the narrative.[78]

By these shifts of emphasis to the tongue and its actions, Ovid is pointing out to his audience that the most central transformation that is occurring is not Philomela's change from virgin to victim or the climax of Tereus's metamorphosis from husband to adulterer, but Philomela's move from the speaking world to the nonspeaking world through the loss of her ability to produce articulate speech. In so doing, Ovid activates all the schematic associations with speech loss, and Philomela is placed completely in an ambiguous state: she is isolated from her familial and human communities in an animal realm without the ability to express her identity through articulate speech; she is neither fully animal nor fully human but in a state in between both.

For the next year, Philomela remains locked away from her community, and her identity is refashioned by Tereus.[79] Tereus informs her family that she died on the journey (6.565–66), and they go through the appropriate rituals of mourning. Procne, believing the new identity of Philomela as dead professed by Tereus, creates a cenotaph for her sister. However, as Hardie has noted in his discussion of illusions in Ovid, the identity created by Tereus for Philomela is merely a mirage, and Ovid hints at this by describing Procne's cenotaph as an *inane sepulcrum* and her offerings as those for *falsis manibus et fat[ibus] lugendae sororis* (6.568–70).[80]

At this point in the narrative, however, Procne is unaware of the false nature of Tereus's story, and Philomela's connection with her community and her identity has been broken. This is nowhere more evident than in Ovid's description of her alone in the stables after Procne's "funeral" for her:

> Signa deus bis sex acto lustraverat anno;
> quid faciat Philomela? fugam custodia claudit,
> structa rigent solido stabulorum moenia saxo,
> *os mutum* facti caret indice. grande doloris
> ingenium est, miserisque venit sollertia rebus.
>      (*Met.* 6.571–75)

[The god had brightened twice six signs with the year having been completed; what could Philomela do? A guard closed off flight, the walls of the stable, built with solid stone, stand firm, and her *os mutum* lacks a means of describing the deed. Her mind is heavy with grief, but cleverness comes in miserable affairs.]

In addition to indicating her physical isolation in the stables, Ovid also calls attention to her lack of speech with the phrase *os mutum*.[81] As we discussed in chapter 1, *mutus* was a term used to describe the type of speech loss schematically associated with animality and emotionality. Likewise, *os* was a term for the face that more precisely described the human ability to speak.[82] Bettini, as we saw above, describes *os* as a term the salient features of which serve to distinguish the human from the animal, articulate speech from inarticulate utterings. By describing Philomela as having an *os mutum*, Ovid encapsulates the entirety of her existence through the speech-loss schema: because of her speech loss, she is isolated in an animal realm. Her verbal identity (*os*) lacks the physical means (*indice*) with which Philomela could proclaim Tereus's deed and make good on her threats to proclaim his deeds (*tua facta loquar*, 6.545).

Still, as in the story of Io, Ovid does not close off all the schematic possibilities; Philomela also finds a means of communicating her identity to her lost community through the written medium, and the shift from Philomela's isolated existence to her attempts to reconnect begin immediately after the climax of *os mutum*. Making use of a bucolic dieresis, Ovid quickly shifts from what Philomela has lost to what she still has: *os mutum facti caret indice. grande doloris /*

*ingenium est, miserisque venit sollertia rebus.* Although her mouth is mute (*os mutum*), Philomela, like Io, has her *ingenium* intact. In ancient literary criticism, especially that regarding Callimachean poetics, *ingenium* referred to the raw poetic talent in a poet and was traditionally juxtaposed with *ars*, the actual polished skill of poetic composition.[83] In the context of the Philomela narrative, Ovid employs the term as a means of indicating Philomela's continued schematic connection with humanity and her ability to create a narrative of her identity to undo that of Tereus.

As she had threatened to do if she were enclosed in the woods (*si silvis clausa tenebor*, 546), Philomela, enclosed in the stables (*fugam custodia claudit*, 572), turns to poetry both to fill the woods (*inplebo silvas*, 547) surrounding the stables (*in stabula alta trahit, silvis obscura vetustis*, 521) with her complaints and to move the very stones of the stables that were indeed witness to her rape (*conscia saxa movebo*, 547 ≈ *structa rigent solido stabulorum moenia saxo*, 573). However, with no voice to sing her poetry, she turns to a written medium, weaving, to voice her identity:[84]

> stamina barbarica suspendit *callida* tela
> purpureasque notas filis *intexuit* albis,
> indicium sceleris; perfectaque tradidit uni,
> utque ferat dominae, *gestu rogat*; illa rogata
> pertulit ad Procnen nec scit, quid tradat in illis.
> evolvit vestes saevi matrona tyranni
> germanaeque suae *carmen miserabile* legit
> et (mirum potuisse) silet: dolor ora repressit,
> verbaque quaerenti satis indignantia linguae
> *defuerunt*, nec flere vacat, sed fasque nefasque
> confusura ruit poenaeque in imagine tota est.
> (*Met.* 6.576–86)

[She hangs the clever warp on the foreign web and interweaves purple markings with white thread, a symbol of [Tereus's] wickedness; she handed the completed weaving to her one servant so that she might bring it to her mistress; she asks with a gesture; the servant, having been asked, carried it through to Procne and knew not what she handed over in the weaving. The wife of the savage tyrant unrolled the cloth and read the miserable song of her sister and (amazing to have been able to do so) was silent: grief held back her voice, and words with enough scorn failed to come to her tongue seeking them, and there is no room for crying, but she rushed round, about to confuse right and wrong, and was entirely engrossed in the *imago* of vengeance.]

Weaving, such as the kind in which Philomela engages here, was frequently associated with the creation of poetry, especially in the Callimachean tradition with which Ovid frequently associated himself.[85] Ovid even describes his creation of the *Metamorphoses* as a product of his weaving, using the most common image from writing poetry in Latin (*deducere carmen*).[86] Thus, the image of Philomela as poet continues, as she actually weaves the story of her true identity to oppose Tereus's, a story that indeed is called a *miserabile carmen*. Ovid's description of Philomela's narrative with these words marks her poetry as the type of pastoral lament that her threats against Tereus had promised. The combination of *miserabile carmen* together with the verb *implere* creates an allusion to *Georgics* 4.511–15, in which Virgil describes the sad song of the nightingale, appropriately marked by the term *philomela*:

qualis populea maerens *philomela* sub umbra
amissos queritur fetus, quos durus arator
observans nido implumes detraxit; at illa
flet noctem ramoque sedens *miserabile carmen*
integrat et maestis late loca questibus *implet*.

[As the sorrowing nightingale seeks her lost children under the shade of the poplar, which the harsh plowman, noticing them, unfledged, has taken from the nest; but she cries through the night and, sitting on a branch, renews her miserable song and fills the whole place with sorrowful complaints.]

Furthermore, terms such as *callida* and *intexuit* continue the metaphor of weaving poetry, portraying Philomela as a poet. Her warp is described as *callida*, "clever," another term closely related to the Callimachean concept of elaborate, learned poetry resulting from τέχνην (fr. 67.3), typically translated into Latin as *ars*.[87] Likewise, the verb *intexuit* comes from the semantic field of weaving that derives from the metaphor of *textus*, the interlacement of both written and verbal strands of poetry, and further casts Philomela in the role of the poet.[88]

In addition to Ovid's image of Philomela as poet attempting to renegotiate the depiction of her identity, two other aspects germane to the discussion of speech loss in her woven creation are *barbarica* and *indicium*. When Philomela hangs a *barbarica tela* on her loom, it is generally read as a reference to Thrace. However, in light of Philomela's speech situation, it should also be read with an eye to our schema of speech loss. The foreignness of the web is not only because of its nationality but also because it represents a foreign method of communication for Philomela. Now she can communicate not with her accustomed speech but in a strange, new manner: weaving. *Barbarica* can also be read in its other sense of that which is foreign to one's cultural community, and thus Philomela is shown as excluded from her community because of her use of a *barbarica tela*.

The final word of interest in this passage is so mostly because of its allusion. Philomela weaves her *notas* to evidence of the wickedness done to her (*indicium sceleris*). This reminds the audience of what Io produced for her father and sisters while in her bovine form (*corporis indicium mutati triste peregit*). Ovid's thematic and literal repetition serves to link the stories of Io and Philomela: both undergo a transformation that excludes them from society and strips them of their ability to speak. Still, both are able to overcome their afflictions and to communicate their identities through the written medium.

When Philomela completes her artistic creation, she gives it to a servant and communicates to her what to do with it (*gestu rogat*).[89] This is significant. Philomela, from the moment she completes her tapestry, is able to communicate. Oddly enough, she is no longer alone in the secluded hut: an attendant appears, and the *uni* that fills the end of line 578 and designates the new, single servant (*indicium sceleris; perfectaque tradidit uni*) has replaced the *unam* that marked the isolated Philomela at the end of line 524 (*includit fassusque nefas et virginem et unam*). However, this narrative oddity of the appearance of the attendant ex nihilo should not be overlooked because it serves to push the story forward and to introduce the final important aspect of speech in the Philomela episode. The attendant represents the first instance of Ovid's unraveling of the schematic associations of speech loss and community loss, and humanity's return into Philomela's world.

When Procne receives the web from the sister whom she thought to be dead, she is overcome by grief. Ovid describes Procne's grief by creating a sympathetic mirror image of Philomela. The silence of Philomela is transferred to her sister, as Procne reads her Philomela's *carmen* in complete silence. Ovid remarks that it would have been amazing if she had been able to speak (*mirum potuisse*). Procne, like her sister, has undergone a metamorphosis by the loss of speech. Ovid furthers his point by adding the fact that grief restrained her mouth (although Frank Justus Miller's Loeb translation [1939] "Grief chokes her words" exemplifies best what is happening here). Anderson comments that just as Philomela had been stimulated to communication by her *dolor* (574), Procne, ironically, is stifled by it. It is also important that Ovid focuses on Procne's tongue and describes it as searching for words that were scornful enough (*verbaque quaerenti satis indignantia linguae*). Procne's indignation echoes Philomela's resentful tongue (555–56) and her inability to express her scorn. Even more telling and important is the fact that Ovid describes the tongues of both sisters in the same manner: both are depicted with the verb *quaerere*. In such a manner, Ovid is able to create a connection between the sisters, a connection that had been stripped from Philomela from the moment at which she had been isolated from society.

Feldherr, in his analysis of the Philomela narrative (2010, 199–239), draws a more particular connection between the two sisters, arguing that throughout the tale the sisters are inextricably bound to each other as they switch roles: Procne slowly loses her individuality and eventually becomes her sister, whereas Philomela slowly takes back her identity and becomes more herself. The point at which this slippage reaches a breaking point is when Procne reads the *miserabile carmen*:

> Procne's recognition of her sister throughout the written signs she receives begins two contradictory processes that anticipate precisely her later transformation into her sister. As the text becomes a song, a *carmen*, Procne perceives it as a song about herself, the *carmen suae fortunae*. At the same time that she sees herself in what she reads, though, we watch her from without and see her changed into Philomela precisely by losing the capacity to speak, by becoming an image herself (*poenaeque in imagine tota est*). . . . From the moment when she crafts her *carmen miserabile*, the person that Philomela represents is herself. (Feldherr 2010, 230)

Feldherr's analysis, in addition to identifying a point of slippage between the characters, also emphasizes this moment as key in the reintegration of Philomela into community. She has told the narrative of her identity, and Procne has recognized it, retying the bond between the two that had been broken by Tereus's narrative of Philomela's death. This moment is the beginning of the victory of Philomela's narrative of her identity over Tereus's.

Having successfully communicated with Procne, Philomela's isolation in the animal realm does not last for long. A mere fifteen lines later, Procne, adorned with the trappings of the bacchic festival, goes to the secluded hut, breaks into it, and finds her sister.[90] Her first action is key: Procne does not attempt to do anything but dress her sister as a fellow bacchante. Anderson (1997, *ad* 595–97) reads this scene as an indictment of Procne's humanity and that Procne, dressed as a bacchante, completes her transformation into the irrational mother who later murders her son and feeds him to his father. However, this is best read as a twofold transformation. While temporarily losing her rational mind (*mens*) as a bacchante, Procne becomes more like an animal. Therefore, it is easier for her to run from civilization and to free her sister. Indeed, her mental state is just as passionately irrational as Tereus's was when he first arrived with Philomela. Both Tereus and Procne are described as being violent to Philomela, dragging (*trahens*) her to their destination (521, 600). Philomela is, in turn, terrified and pallid in both instances (522, 602). Thus, Procne's crazed state is made clear. However, a transformation also occurs for Philomela. She is incorporated into the bacchic ritual by her sister. This marks a reintegration into society for Philomela. As a bacchante, she is brought back into the walls of the city and reconnected with civilization and her family.

Once in the palace, Philomela cannot look her sister in the eye due to her disgrace, and she tries to call on the gods (for the first time since her rape) by using her hand as her voice (*pro voce manus fuit*). However, the crazed Procne cares little for this and hatches a plan to kill Itys, her son, and feed him to Tereus. Procne looks at her son and damns the fact that he can make pretty little speeches (*blanditias*), while Philomela's tongue remains silent (*silet altera lingua*). At this point, she kills her son and, together with Philomela, cooks and feeds him to Tereus. Again, we see Philomela wishing that she were able to speak, as she flings Itys's head into Tereus's face (*nec tempore maluit ullo / posse loqui et meritis testavi gaudia dictis*). Philomela is still unable to speak words; however, she can now communicate sufficiently. Feldherr (2010, 230ff.) goes as far as to assert that, although still voiceless, the act of throwing Itys's head at Tereus marks Philomela's final act of reasserting her identity, as it exposes rather than conceals her crime.

Ovid, however, never tells his audience that Philomela recovers her human voice.[91] In fact, his omission is striking when compared with his focus on how Io regained her speech. In addition to regaining her community, Philomela also regains a voice that, although not human, is capable of articulate speech through her transformation into a bird. The type of bird Philomela becomes, however, is left ambiguous by Ovid, most likely to emphasize the reconstitution of community between the sisters. He states that one becomes a swallow on the roofs and that the other flies to the woods (*quarum petit altera silvis, altera tecta subit*). The reader is left to wonder whether Philomela or Procne goes into the wilderness. However, as mentioned at the beginning of this section, the entire Roman tradition of the myth asserts that Philomela was transformed into a nightingale and Procne into a swallow. This reading seems most likely for Ovid's tale as well, as the multiple descriptions of Philomela singing in the forest and his allusion to the passage from the *Georgics* about the nightingale (*philomela*) singing a *miserabile carmen* in the forest make most sense in that context.

The import of the identification of the bird into which Philomela was transformed comes from ancient theories on the relationships between animals and humans.[92] As mentioned in chapter 1, one of the key schematic distinctions made between animals and humans was linguistic ability: humans are able to speak; animals are not. However, the linguistic abilities of all animals are not equal. In fact, in ancient treatises on the relationship between man and beast, the animal whose linguistic ability is closest to that of humans is the bird.[93] Aristotle, though not believing birds to have the rational ability (νοῦς) of humans,[94] still hints at the fact that they may have a higher linguistic ability than other animals.[95] Likewise, Plutarch, in both his *De esu carnium* (994E) and his *De sollertia animalium* (972F-73E), attributes to birds the ability to speak in an articulate manner to one another, as they have developed through self-instruction (αὐτομάθειαν) the ability to communicate (Newmyer 110–99, 1999). Humans, however, lack the ability to understand bird communication and, therefore, take it for mere inarticulate gibberish. Finally, in his chapter on birds (*NH* 10.43), Pliny the Elder devotes an entire section to the nightingale, attributing to the species sounds unique to each nightingale,[96] the ability to choose what to sing and how to sing it,[97] and a means of instruction and communication between nightingales.[98]

In all these instances, the bird is set apart from the rest of the animal kingdom in regard to the species' ability to produce articulate speech. Moreover, Pliny the Elder extends this ability to nightingales in particular, describing their utterances as a type of *vox*, a term for articulate speech. What this means for the Philomela narrative is that, when she is transformed into a nightingale, she regains a type of speech for herself. Although different from her human voice, the voice of the nightingale was considered articulate, and, thus, Philomela is able to speak in an articulate fashion again. Now she is reunited with her community in an avian form and can continue to sing her songs with the articulate speech of the nightingale.

Thus, the story of Philomela, like that of Io, highlights the schematic associations of speech loss and its effect on community and identity. As speech loss is associated with the nonhuman, emotionality, and the subsequent destruction of community and identity, both characters lose their ability to speak at the hands of a lustful rapist and are isolated in the wilderness, far from their familial and human communities. However, both find their voices again through the written medium. As such, Philomela and Io separate themselves from other transformed and speechless characters such as Lycaon, Callisto, Echo, Dryope, and Actæon.

An analysis of the topic of speech loss in the *Metamorphoses* shows that the schematic connotations laid out in chapter 1 are amply in evidence in Ovid's description of transformations within the *Metamorphoses*. In the stories discussed in this chapter, Ovid engages with the connections between speech loss, the nonhuman, and emotionality and embellishes his unique take on metamorphosis. When characters are transformed, they become isolated from the human community, and that isolation takes the form of speech loss. Without speech, a character is trapped in a state of "wavering identity" between the nonhuman and the human. Although most characters perish or remain trapped for the duration of the narrative in this state, some, such as Philomela and Io, are able to escape their ambiguous states by communicating their true identities through the written medium. In chapter 3, I will further trace Ovid's manipulation of the schematic associations of speech loss, identity, and communication, analyzing its presence throughout Ovid's exile literature, as he depicts his existence in exile in much the same fashion and attempts to use his poetry as a written medium to reconnect with his lost community and effect his return to it.

*chapter 3*

## Speech Loss in the Exile Literature

Haec, utcumque potui, longo iam situ obsoleto et hebetato animo composui. Quae si aut parum respondere ingenio tuo aut parum mederi dolori uidebuntur, cogita quam non possit is alienae uacare consolationi quem sua mala occupatum tenent, et quam non facile latina ei homini uerba succurrant quem barbarorum inconditus et barbaris quoque humanioribus grauis fremitus circumsonat.[1]

—Seneca the Younger, *De Consolatione ad Polybium* 18.9

Si qua videbuntur chartis tibi, lector, in istis
Sive obscura nimis sive latina parum,
Non meus est error: nocuit librarius illis,
Dum properat versus adnumerare tibi.[2]

—Martial 2.8.1–4

In the previous chapter, I examined Ovid's use of the schema of speech loss and its salient associations of animality, emotionality, and community in the tales of transformation in the *Metamorphoses*. In nearly 20 percent of all the stories in Ovid's magnum opus, characters who undergo metamorphosis are rendered speechless. When these characters lose their ability to speak, they subsequently are stripped of the ability to indicate their identity through words, and for characters transformed into animals, trees, or inanimate objects, any ancillary means of communication (e.g., gestures, facial expression) become problematic. As a result, these speechless characters are cut off from their communities, and for all save Io and Philomela, this isolated state is permanent.

In 8 CE, Ovid found himself in a situation similar to those of his characters. As a result of the famous *carmen et error* mentioned at *Tristia* 2.207, Ovid, the fifty-year-old poet laureate of Rome at the height of his popularity, was relegated by Emperor Augustus from the center of the Roman world, the city of Rome itself, to the periphery of Roman rule in Tomis (modern-day Constanța in Romania). As Ovid describes it, almost overnight his identity was transformed from the poet whose voice had been so prominent in Rome in the form of his numerous successful works to an exile bereft of his society and stripped of his ability to interact with his poetic circles. Throughout his literature from exile, Ovid focuses his attention on the physical and psychological consequences of his banishment and the negative effects such consequences have on his poetic ability. In what has become known as Ovid's "pose of decline," Ovid professes that his physical isolation in exile has prohibited him from having the peace of mind, the inspiration, and the technique necessary to write successful poetry. The key aspect in which Ovid grounds all these complaints is the speech loss that he suffers due to his separation from the Latin-speaking world.[3] Hinds (2011a, 60) sums this up succinctly: "For Ovid, the exile's alienation on the margins of civilization is manifested, strikingly, in a sense of alienation from his native tongue; and, under pressure from the broader anxieties which pervade Ovid's exile poetry, this comes to define a wholesale crisis of linguistic capacity and intelligibility."

Although in antiquity the topic of exile was not a frequent one,[4] the focus Ovid placed on speech loss in his description of exile found a place in subsequent authors, ranging from antiquity to today, who discussed exile or related topics.[5] Two of the most prominent examples of allusions to Ovidian, exilic speech loss from the Roman world are the two excerpts at the beginning of this chapter, from Seneca the Younger and Martial.[6]

Seneca, writing his *de Consolatione ad Polybium* from actual exile on Corsica, recalls an Ovidian emphasis on speech loss in exile at *Tristia* 3.14.27–30, 43–50 and applies such linguistic slippage to his own exilic persona:

quod quicumque leget—si quis leget—, aestimet ante,
*compositum* quo sit tempore quoque loco.
aequus erit scriptis, quorum cognoverit esse
*exilium tempus barbariamque locum*

. . .

saepe aliquod quaero verbum nomenque locumque,
nec quisquam est a quo certior esse queam.
dicere saepe aliquid conanti—turpe fateri!—
verba mihi desunt dedidicique loqui.
Threïcio Scythicoque fere *circumsonor* ore,
et videor Geticis scribere posse modis.
crede mihi, timeo ne Sintia *mixta Latinis*
inque meis scriptis Pontica *verba* legas.

And again Seneca, *De Consolatione ad Polybium* 18.9:

> Haec, utcumque potui, longo iam situ obsoleto et hebetato animo *composui*. Quae si aut parum respondere ingenio tuo aut parum mederi dolori uidebuntur, cogita quam non possit is alienae uacare consolationi quem sua mala occupatum tenent, *et quam non facile latina ei homini uerba succurrant quem barbarorum inconditus et barbaris quoque humanioribus grauis fremitus circumsonat.*

Seneca blames his loss of the ability to speak fluent and acceptable Latin on his exilic location in the same manner in which Ovid had done in *Tristia* 3.14 (Degl'Innocenti Pierini 1990, 112–22; Fantham 2007, 190–91). Yet, the equation between the two situations should not be pushed too far. For as Hinds has noted, Seneca was not in a remote part of the Roman world but in Corsica, an island just 250 miles from Rome: "Seneca, remember, is in Corsica. Even allowing for the fact that then, as for much of its history, this was an island more resistant than most to the Mediterranean mainstream, the reference to barbarism sounds like overkill" (2011b, 62). Therefore, instead of presenting a relatively accurate portrayal of his exile, it is more likely that Seneca is responding to the Ovidian invention of the linguistic sufferings of exile. Ovid's self-depiction as speechless had become a topos unto itself within the literary context of exile.[7]

Martial, though not in exile as Ovid and Seneca, acknowledges an Ovidian source in his discussion of his hampered Latin, alluding to Ovid's claim to have lost the ability to produce proficient Latin at *Tristia* 3.1.17–18:

> siqua videbuntur casu non dicta Latine,
> in qua scribebat, barbara terra fuit.

And again Martial 2.8.1–4:

> *Si qua videbuntur* chartis tibi, lector, in istis
> Sive obscura nimis sive *latina* parum,
> Non *meus est error*: nocuit librarius illis,
> Dum properat versus adnumerare tibi.

Whereas Ovid blames his loss of speech on his physical isolation from Latin speakers, Martial blames his copyist and transfers the topos from exilic poetry to "mundane poetry."[8] For Martial, the Ovidian allusion indicates not necessarily his own loss of speech in exile but rather his avoidance of the heightened diction of higher forms of poetry than his epigram.[9] Moreover, Martial's second couplet contains a second allusion to Ovid, to the *carmen et error* of *Tristia* 2, an allusion read as a "footnote" to the *Tristia* allusion in the first couplet (Hinds 2007, 131): whereas Ovid's Latin was indeed compromised due to his exilic situation, Martial's, as he was safe in Rome, was not.

What the Senecan and Martialian allusions to Ovid's exile literature point to is the fact that, despite the relative paucity of references to Ovid's physical exile, the Ovidian poetics of exile were picked up by subsequent authors of both poetry and prose. In particular, these authors identified Ovid's focus on his loss of speech as one of the seminal aspects of his exile. In this chapter, I will examine this exilic emphasis on speech loss in Ovid's exile literature by treating it as an extension of the manipulation of the schema of speech loss that was shown in chapter 2 to be prominent in the *Metamorphoses*. My analysis is divided into three parts: First, I discuss the narrative sequence that Ovid describes in *Tristia* 1 and, in particular, 1.3, analyzing the manners in which Ovid follows the standard schematic progression and portrays his transformation from vocal member of the Roman community to an isolated exile suffering from speech loss. Like his characters in the *Metamorphoses*, as Ovid undergoes his transformation, he loses the ability to speak. Second, I then turn to Ovid's description of his resulting speech loss and examine it through the comparisons Ovid makes between his speech loss and that of characters from the *Metamorphoses*, most notably Philomela; I note that the same schematic associations of animality and emotionality are activated in the removal of Ovid from community. Third, after having examined Ovid's narrative of transformation into a speechless exile and his subsequent existence in silent isolation, I conclude this chapter with an analysis of how Ovid manipulates the schema of speech loss and attempts to reintegrate with his lost Roman community in the same manner that his characters in the *Metamorphoses* did: the written medium. Ovid set up his *Tristia* and *Ex Ponto* as letters written from an absent poet to his friends and family back home and chose to do so because the epistolary genre was seen as one through which an individual could negotiate separation and communicate with others as if he or she were *speaking* with them in person. Thus, Ovid's use of the epistolary genre should be seen as an effort to overcome the schematic consequences of his loss of speech through the written word. Moreover, the content of his letters, written to members (*sodales*) of his poetic circles, are focused on communicating his identity and reclaiming his position within the social, spoken world of Roman poets.

## Ovid Transformed: Becoming Voiceless in *Tristia* 1

In *Tristia* 1, the first book of the *Tristia* and of the exile literature as a whole, Ovid describes the exile's journey both the progression into physical exile and the metamorphosis from loquacious *vates* to speechless *exul*.[10] The book's focus on such movement both physical and emotional has led it to be named a "Journey into Exile" by multiple scholars.[11] The book, in accordance with Augustan poetic tradition, describes the exile's transformational journey not in a chronological sequence but in a more "artful and symmetrical" style. Harry Evans (1983, 46) has identified the organization of the book as one that emphasized the theme of the journey through a chiastic series of frames (figure 2):[12]

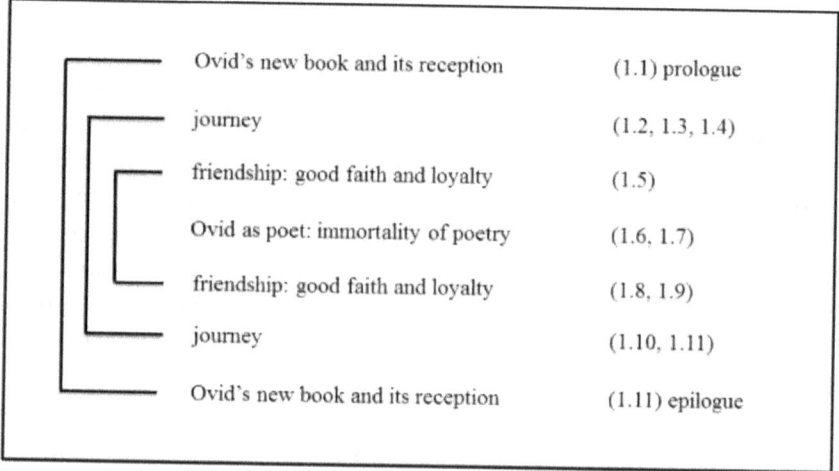

FIGURE 2. Organization of *Tristia 1* from Evans 1983.

*Tristia* 1.1 and 1.11 bookend the collection as a prologue and an epilogue focused on the exile's *libellus*; the group of 1.2, 1.3, 1.4 and the pair of 1.10 and 1.11 form the second level of the structure and describe the journey itself; the third level is created by *Tristia* 1.5 and the pair *Tristia* 1.8 and 1.9, which deal with the theme of friendship; finally, the innermost level of the book is the pair *Tristia* 1.6 and 1.7, both of which discuss the immortality of the exile's poetry.

The strength of Evans's arrangement is that it allows the poems narrating the journey to surround the other more topical and epistolographic poems that the exile says were written along the journey (*Tr.* 1.11.1–2: *littera quaecumque est toto tibi lecta libello, / est mihi sollicito tempore facta viae*; "Whatever letters have been read by you in the whole *libellus*, have been made by me, vexed, at the time of the storm"). Such an arrangement creates the visual appearance that these topical and epistolographic poems were indeed composed *in* the course of the journey and *during* the described storms.[13]

More recently, Eleonora Tola (2008) has reanalyzed the order of the poems in *Tristia* 1 from a narratological perspective (figure 3). She too notes that the story of the exile's journey is "far from the narration of a chronological event" (55). Whereas Evans saw the organization of *Tristia* 1 as an exercise in ring composition, Tola, taking her starting point from the work of Anne Videau-Delibes (1991), sees the organization as a means through which Ovid can portray the discontinuity in his life brought on by exile; as his new life is confused and disjointed, thus is his narrative of it.[14]

In this section we will focus on the series of poems narrating the exile's transformational journey (*Tr.* 1.2–1.4). For in addition to describing the exile's physical movement from Rome to Tomis, these poems also describe how the exile is transformed from *vates* to *exul*. Moreover, the manner in which Ovid chooses to describe the exile's transformation follows the same schema of metamorphosis and speech loss that was identified and explored in chapters 1 and 2. As described in *Tristia* 1.3, when the day of the exile's relegation arrives, he is removed from his community of family and friends and forced to leave for Tomis. At the same moment that this removal occurs, the exile also loses his ability to speak. Henceforth, like the characters of the *Metamorphoses*, whenever the exile attempts to communicate on his journey in *Tristia* 1.2 and 1.4, these attempts are thwarted, and he finds himself unable to control the same linguistic and poetic *ars* that had marked his identity in the Roman community as *vates* and *lusor tenerorum amorum*. Consequently, as Io and Philomela before him, the exile turns to the written medium to communicate his identity and to tell his narrative of change in exile.

### *Tristia* 1.3: The Metamorphosis of the Exile

As we have just established, Ovid arranged the poems of *Tristia* 1 not in a chronological order but in an artistic, chiastic one aimed at emphasizing the book's major themes of journey, friendship, and poetic immortality. However, if the

| Sea journey | Sea journey and mention of terrestrial places | Other motifs |
|---|---|---|
| Tr. 1.2 | | Tr. 1.1 |
| Tr. 1.4 | Tr. 1.10 | Tr. 1.3 |
| Tr. 1.11 | | Tr. 1.5, 6, 7, 8, 9 |

FIGURE 3. Organization of *Tristia* 1 from Tola 2008.

poems were to be arranged chronologically, the book would necessarily begin with *Tristia* 1.3, which describes the point of the exile's departure from Rome, followed by 1.2, 1.4 and 1.10, which portray the exile's stormy nautical journey to Samothrace, where he paused before continuing to Tomis. As the chronological starting point of the exile's journey, *Tristia* 1.3 has extreme importance to our understanding of the whole of the exile literature because, in the words of Claassen, "*Tristia* 1.3 depicts graphically, but selectively, the break between 'present' and 'past'" (1999, 174). It portrays "graphically" the very moment of the exile's metamorphosis from his past state as *vates* to his present one as *exul*.

The poem is set up as the exile's flashback to his last night in Rome in which he recalls in his mind's eye (*imago*) his final, emotional moments with his friends and family:[15]

cum subit illius tristissima noctis imago,
    qua mihi supremum tempus in urbe fuit,
cum repeto noctem, qua tot mihi cara reliqui,
    labitur ex oculis nunc quoque gutta meis
        (*Tr.* 1.3.1–4)

[Whenever comes to mind the image, most grievous, of that well-known night, on which was my final time in the city, when I think back to the night on which I left so many things dear to me, there falls even now from these eyes of mine a tear.]

The exile's flashback falls neatly into four temporal frames divided by references to the time of day:[16] after the prologue, given above, there is (1) the evening before his departure (ll. 5–26), (2) the following nighttime hours (ll. 27–46), (3) the early morning hours of the following day (ll. 47–70), and (4) the break of dawn on the exile's day of relegation (ll. 71–100).

Scholarship on *Tristia* 1.3 has historically focused on the ways in which Ovid depicts the last moments of the exile in Rome with special regard to the generic coloring of those depictions. Some scholars closely align the poem with the tragic genre due to the highly dramatic nature of the poem.[17] Hermann Froesch (1976) compares the description of the exile's departure from Rome to Euripides's portrayal of the flight of Hippolytos, banned by Theseus, and the reaction of the exile's friends and wife to that of the Euripidean chorus.[18] Georg Luck focuses on the tragic roles played by each character in the poem and provides the most succinct example of this scholarly trend, describing the poem thus:

Die Elegie... ist einem Drama vergleichbar mit Ovid als Protagonisten; seine Frau spielt die zweite Rolle; Freunde und Gesinde bilden den tragischen Chor, der mit seinen Klagerufen das Geschehen begleitet. (Luck 1977, 36)[19]

Likewise, the poem's elegiac affinities have also been noted. Hubert Poteat (1912, 25ff.) has observed that similarities in literary devices linked *Tristia* 1.3 to Ovid's earlier elegiac corpus, particularly the use of pointed anaphora in consecutive clauses. Helmut Rahn (1958, 110ff., esp. 112–13) reads the theme of departure in the poem as within a larger elegiac topos of "Darstellungen des Abschieds." Sara Mack (1988) connects the role of the exile's wife with the traditional depictions of loyal elegiac mistresses in elegy (e.g., the depiction of Delia mourning the departure of Tibullus in Tib. 1.3).[20]

Moreover, scholars have also commented on the similarities between the poem and epic. Stephen Harrison (2002, 90ff.) sees the analogies between the descriptions of the voyage in *Tristia* 1.2–1.4 as an explicit comparison to the voyages of Odysseus and Aeneas in the *Odyssey* and the *Aeneid*. Samuel Huskey (2002, 88–99) too has commented on the close relationship between the description of the exile's departure in *Tristia* 1.3 and that of Aeneas's departure from Troy at the end of *Aeneid* 2 with particular attention paid to the concept of exile and the loss of the wife.

Such "blending" of different genres into one narrative is typical of Ovid's work in general (e.g., the *Metamorphoses*) and speaks to the difficulties inherent in creating the black-and-white pictures of genre and form that characterized the scholarship of the mid-twentieth century. By bringing elements of drama and epic into the elegiac medium, Ovid is able to create a more holistic narrative that allows him more freedom to emphasize or downplay certain generic elements. However, this discussion of *Tristia* 1.3 will focus not on its generic affinities but on the ways in which it describes the metamorphosis of the exile as one involving the loss of speech and community. Throughout the poem, Ovid employs multiple allusions to characters from the *Metamorphoses* who undergo transformations and, subsequently, lose their ability to speak, such as Dryope, Actæon, Callisto, and Philomela. These allusions are scattered throughout the poem and help to depict a progressive deterioration in the exile's ability to speak and connect with his loved ones. Therefore, our analysis will proceed through *Tristia* 1.3 in narrative order and will break the poem into its four narrative "acts." In each of these acts, we will discuss the descriptions of the exile's metamorphosis and how the portrayal of the exile in each act builds on itself, leading to the climax of the poem: the exile's loss of speech and subsequent removal from community along schematic lines.

### ACT 1: THE EVENING BEFORE EXILE (LL. 5–26)

> iam prope lux aderat, qua me discedere Caesar
> finibus extremae iusserat Ausoniae.
> nec spatium nec mens fuerat satis apta parandi:
> torpuerant longa pectora nostra mora.
> non mihi seruorum, comitis non cura legendi,
> non aptae profugo vestis opisue fuit.
> non aliter stupui, quam qui Iouis ignibus ictus
> *vivit et est vitae nescius ipse suae.*
> ut tamen hanc animi nubem dolor ipse remouit,
> et tandem sensus conualuere mei,
> *alloquor* extremum maestos *abiturus amicos,*
> qui modo de multis unus et alter erat.
> *uxor* amans flentem flens acrius ipsa tenebat,
> imbre per indignas usque cadente genas.
> *nata* procul Libycis aberat diversa sub oris,
> nec poterat fati certior esse mei.
> *quocumque aspiceres, luctus gemitusque sonabant,*
> *formaque non taciti funeris intus erat.*
> *femina virque meo*, pueri quoque funere maerent,
> inque domo lacrimas angulus omnis habet.
> si licet exemplis in parvis grandibus uti,
> haec facies Troiae, cum caperetur, erat.

The first narrative section—or dramatic act—of *Tristia* 1.3 begins after a short four-line prologue that details the exile's reaction when he calls to mind the events described in the poem. This portion of the exile narrative (or *Abschiedsbericht*) describes the "reaction of Ovid, his family and friends, to the sentence of exile"; these reactions are presented in a type of "outward looking" progression, proceeding sequentially from a focus on Ovid, to his friends and family, to the extended household, and finally to the level of the city as a whole (Dickinson 1973, 164). Our analysis will focus on the manner in which this narrative section sets the thematic foundation of the whole poem as a foundation grounded in the schematic concepts of speech loss, community, and identity. First, in this section Ovid depicts the exile as a speaking individual whose vocal abilities are juxtaposed with the lack of articulate speech surrounding him. Second, as he is able to communicate, the exile is shown as a member of a community that is all around him. Yet the third point made in this section is the fleeting nature of the exile's communicative ability and communal identity, for his very ability to speak and his experience in his community highlight the beginnings of a slippage in his communication and a breakdown in identity that foreshadow the exilic speech loss and isolation that will face him at the end of the poem.

The section's—and indeed the entire poem's—emphasis on speech is brought to the audience's attention not at the beginning of the section but toward the middle with the use of the term *alloquor* to describe the exile (l. 15). The exile's first act of the dramatic narrative is to speak to the friends who had come to grieve his impending departure. As first noted by Sebastian Posch (1983, 132), the verb *adloqui* is the first verb in the section that is placed in the present tense, a fact that gives it added significance in the poem as the poem's first real narrative "act." Posch goes on to interpret the tense of *adloqui* as an indication of Ovid's psychological engagement (*seelisches Engagement*) in the poem, and this may be true, despite the difficulty of reaching the feelings of "Ovid" through the actions of the exile. It is not difficult, however, to conclude that the use of a verb of speech as the first present, narrative act in the poem sets up the theme of speech as central to the poem's meaning.

The emphasis on the exile's verbal ability is again highlighted a few lines later in the juxtaposition between the exile's articulate speech and the inarticulate wailings of the others in his house. After the exile is described as speaking with his friends (*alloquor . . . amicos*, 15), the tenor of the scene shifts to one of gloom and sadness as the exile's wife weeps quite bitterly (17), and every corner of the house is engulfed in tears (*inque . . . habet*, 24). The sounds that the mourning of these individuals makes is summed up in the couplet:

quocumque aspiceres, luctus gemitusque sonabant,
    formaque non taciti funeris intus erat.
      (*Tr.* 1.3.21–22)

[Wherever you might have looked, griefs and groans were sounding, and the situation inside took the form of an unquiet funeral.]

As was shown in preceding chapter's discussion of the Echo narrative from the *Metamorphoses*, the verb *sonare* refers to inarticulate sounds and is frequently juxtaposed with verbs of articulate speech (*vocare, loqui*) in Ovid's poetry. Here the juxtaposition is with the exile's speech to his friends and serves two purposes. First, and obviously, the verb helps set the background of the emotion and pain felt by those present on the last night of the exile's time in Rome, a background imbued with a high frequency of emotional words typical in descriptions of funerals (*luctus, gemitus, funeris, funere maerent, lacrimas*). Second, and more important for our purposes, the juxtaposition serves to highlight the fact that the exile starts the poem with the ability to speak articulately, and he is largely set off from all others in this section as the only individual capable of speaking, despite his impending exile.

In addition to the exile's ability to communicate, this section of *Tristia* 1.3 also highlights his membership in a community. As already mentioned, one of the main points of this section is the effect of the news of the exile's *relegatio* on his family and friends. Throughout the section, the audience sees the community of the exile surrounding him, particularly in lines 15–24. The exile's friends (*maestos . . . amicos*), wife (*uxor*), household staff and—possibly—clients (*femina virque . . . pueri*) are all present in the scene and interact with the exile, as he speaks to his friends and weeps with his wife. The only member of the exile's family not present is his daughter, but even she is mentioned here (19–20). In short, this opening scene depicts the exile, an individual with the ability to speak articulately, immersed in and interacting with his community.

Yet the exile's linguistic ability and his communal identity are not as secure as their overt depiction in this section may make them out to be, for one can see, even this early in the poem, the linguistic slippage and the destabilization of identity that will come to mark the exile by the poem's end. First, let us return to the line with which I began this section: *alloquor extremum maestos abiturus amicos*. Earlier, these lines were read as evidence for the importance of speech to *Tristia* 1.3 and for the exile's ability to produce such speech. These two aspects still remain vital; however, there is more to the picture. As noted by Luck, although the exile speaks to his friends, there is no reply to him (1977, 38).[21] Such one-way communication foreshadows the eventual inefficacy of the exile's voice: he may speak, but such speaking is not successful in procuring communication in return. The exile is, in a sense, speaking in isolation within what Huguette Fugier (1976) calls a "zone de silence."[22] This motif, which I will discuss more fully in the final portion of this chapter, is emblematic of Ovid's exile literature as a whole: attempts at communication by the exile, albeit it in epistolary form, to which there is never an actual reply. The only replies mentioned are those that the exile himself states he received.[23] In terms of *Tristia* 1.3, however, the lack of response to the exile's speech serves to undermine his linguistic ability and to foreshadow his loss of speech at the end of the poem.

In addition to the destabilization of the exile's linguistic ability, this section of the poem also foreshadows his eventual metamorphosis, his entrance into a state of wavering identity, and his removal from community. This process can most clearly be seen in the exile's description of his "stupefication" at the hands of Augustus. In lines 11–16, the exile relates how he was struck dumb like those struck by the thunderbolt of Jove and was covered in a cloud of grief. In addition to being a direct reference to Augustus's edict against the exile through the traditional connection between Augustus and Jupiter, these lines also depict the beginning of the exile's journey into a state of wavering identity (Fantham 2013, 132ff.). Doblhofer presents the clearest articulation of this transition:

> This ego-splitting is a process and a condition which already greatly attracted the poet of the "Metamorphoses," in the stories of which the process is rooted, and H. Frankel opened our eyes to this fact in his famous book on Ovid; Ovid only now painfully experiences it for himself. Even this painful predicament of the loss of his own poetic and human identity is a leitmotif of complaint poetry; for the similarly exiled Ovid it went so far that he sought, already in the first poem from exile (*Tristia* 1.1.117–22), to understand his banishment as a metamorphosis and to classify his range of experiences in this way. Here in the "Farewell to Rome," the idea of splitting of the ego into a "living" one and a "dead" one [i.e., 1.3.11–16] returns at the end of the poem in the description of the last departure from his house by the exiled poet: (v. 89) *egredior, sive illud erat sine funere ferri.* (1987, 91–92)

Doblhofer's focus on the splitting of the exile's persona and the exile's subsequent entrance into Fränkel's "wavering identity" is hinted at in line 12: *vivit et est vitae nesius ipse suae*. After being relegated, the exile is stunned and has an out-of-body experience, not sure of his own identity but still in existence. Moreover, as Tola (2008, 59–60) notes, in *Tristia* 1.3, the exile makes constant reference to his dismemberment (see the *exemplum* of Mettus at 1.3.73–74), describing his body in its constituent parts strewn through the entirety of the narrative (*oculis*, 4, 60; *membra*, 64, 73, 94; *pectora*, 8, 66, 78; *ore*, 44; *ora*, 90; *manus*, 78, 88; *genas*, 18; *pes*, 56; *umeris*, 79). Such a split in identity is remarkably similar to the experiences of characters in the *Metamorphoses* who undergo psychological trauma and, unsure of their identity, are rendered speechless.[24] Although each of these characters regains their speech, each is also eventually transformed into a nonhuman entity and, subsequently, loses the ability to speak for a second time.

Like these characters, the exile too regains his speech, and his eventual transformation is foreshadowed by the use of *abiturus* to describe him. When he recovers from his momentary "Ich-Spaltung," he immediately regains the ability to speak and communicates with his friends (*alloquor extremum maestos abiturus amicos*). The term *abiturus* is traditionally translated as a reference to the exile's impending physical departure to Tomis; however, the term has at least two other meanings that have a great bearing on this poem. First, *abiturus* is often used to refer to dying in the same fashion as modern English describes death as a "passing away."[25] This aspect of *abiturus* meshes well with the overarching motif of "exile as death" throughout the exile literature. When the exile physically leaves his home, he undergoes a type of social death. As mentioned in Doblhofer's quote, *Tristia* 1.3 itself ends with a scene of the exile being borne out of his house like a corpse in a funeral. Second, and more germane to the idea of metamorphosis, the term *abiturus* is used multiple times in the *Metamorphoses* to describe a character's transformation.[26] As such, the use of the term to describe the exile (1) places him in the same position as characters from the *Metamorphoses* who, having undergone an identity crisis, are transformed into a nonhuman entity and (2) foreshadows his eventual speech loss, transformation, and loss of the schematic association of communal identity.

The underlying associations of the term *abiturus* and the exile's lack of communicative connection with his friends thus undermine the seemingly positive picture of the exile in this first section and foreshadow his ultimate linguistic and communal downfall. Although the exile is surrounded by his community and has the ability to speak with that community, Ovid identifies underlying complications that foreshadow the exile's eventual metamorphosis.

### ACT 2: THE DEAD OF NIGHT (LL. 26–46)

iamque quiescebant voces hominumque canumque
    Lunaque nocturnos alta regebat equos.
hanc ego suspiciens et ad hanc Capitolia cernens,
    quae nostro frustra iuncta fuere Lari,
"numina vicinis habitantia sedibus," inquam,
    "iamque oculis numquam templa videnda meis,
dique relinquendi, quos urbs habet alta Quirini,
    este salutati tempus in omne mihi.
et quamquam sero clipeum post vulnera sumo,
    attamen hanc odiis exonerate fugam,
caelestique viro, quis me deceperit error,
    dicite, pro culpa ne scelus esse putet.
ut quod vos scitis, poenae quoque sentiat auctor:
    placato possum non miser esse deo."

> hac prece adoravi superos ego, pluribus uxor,
> singultu medios impediente sonos.
> illa etiam ante Lares passis adstrata capillis
> contigit extinctos ore tremente focos,
> multaque in aversos effudit verba Penates
> pro deplorato non valitura viro.

After the loud wailings and groans of the first "act" of *Tristia* 1.3, the scene shifts to a new location and tenor in the second. The second "act" no longer takes place inside the exile's noisy house but unfolds outside it, as the exile looks over the quiet city of Rome and makes his last plea to the gods for pardon from his relegation. Yet although the scene of the narrative action has shifted, Ovid continues to foreshadow the exile's eventual loss of speech and the schematic associations of identity and community for him. First, the exile's prayer, his attempt at verbal communication with the gods, fails to receive a reply from them; moreover, the content and description of the prayer point to the beginning of his linguistic slippage. Likewise, the linguistic slippage of the exile can also be seen in the description of his wife's prayer. Second, in addition to his loss of speech, the exile's impending loss of communal identity is foreshadowed through the consistent allusions to the *Aeneid* and the comparisons drawn between the exile and Aeneas: whereas Aeneas, although forced to leave his native Troy, was allowed to preserve his communal identity through the transport of his friends, family, and household gods, the exile is stripped of his place in society through his inability to bring any of these objects with him.

Turning first to Ovid's foreshadowing of the exile's loss of speech, let us begin with the exile's prayer. Three aspects of the prayer call the audience's attention to the exile's eventual loss of speech: (1) the very presence of the prayer, (2) an allusion made by Ovid in the exile's prayer to the story of Actæon from the *Metamorphoses*, and (3) the description of the prayer as a *sonus* at its conclusion.

Although it is indeed a prevalent topos in Latin literature for those in trouble to turn to the gods for assistance, one of the narrative situations in which this topos is employed within the Ovidian corpus is the tale of speech loss. Throughout the *Metamorphoses*, transformed characters are routinely depicted as appealing to the gods for rescue from their situations.[27] However, because of their compromised verbal abilities, their prayers are unsuccessful and they either remain transformed or undergo a transformation. Examining the stories analyzed in chapter 2, the tales of Actæon, Callisto, and Io all feature the failed attempts at communication for each character. Because they have been transformed into animals and are unable to speak in a human voice, all fail to communicate through prayer and all remain in their animal forms. A similar situation can be identified in the Philomela narrative, in which Ovid employs failed prayer to emphasize her isolation from community and civilization as well as her impending isolation through speech loss.[28]

Against this background, the exile's prayer to the gods for help and Ovid's remark that the prayers of the exile and his wife were ineffective (*non valitura*) place the exile in the position of these transformed characters. Moreover, the exile includes an allusion to Io's successful prayer through his statement that he hopes the gods will speak to Augustus and help him feel (*sentiat*) that the exile angered him not through willful wickedness but through innocent error:

> caelestique uiro, quis me deceperit error,
>    dicite, pro culpa ne scelus esse putet.
> ut quod vos scitis, poenae quoque *sentiat* auctor:
>    (*Tr.* 1.3.37–39)

> [And tell to that heavenly man what error deceived me lest he think wickedness be the same as fault; so that which you know, the author of this penalty may also feel:]

Whereas the focus of the exile is here clearly on his desire that Augustus not misconstrue fault for wickedness,[29] Ovid's allusion to a prayer of a verbally compromised individual that was actually successful highlights the importance of speech loss and sets up a juxtaposition with the exile's metamorphosis and eventual loss of speech.

In addition to Ovid's use of the topos of prayer from the *Metamorphoses*, he also creates a specific allusion within the exile's prayer that further equates the exile with a character who underwent metamorphosis and speech loss, the first of four such allusions in *Tristia* 1.3 (for the other allusions, see discussion of 1.3.47–68 below). In the prayer, the exile makes mention of the *error* that led to his relegation. He prays that the gods on the Quirinal tell Augustus (*caelestique viro*, 37) that the fault he ascribed to the exile was only an *error* and not a *scelus*. This vocabulary creates an allusion to the Actæon story *Metamorphoses* 3, an allusion that Ovid develops more fully in *Tristia* 2.[30] In the Actæon narrative, one of the key concepts that Ovid presents to his audience is that of blame: was Actæon's punishment by Diana deserved and due to a *scelus*, or was it an unfortunate consequence of his *error*?[31] The particular terms used in the *Metamorphoses* to illustrate the concept are the same terms used in the *Tristia*:

at bene si quaeras, Fortunae crimen in illo,
non *scelus* invenies; quod enim *scelus error*
habebat?
    (*Met.* 3.141–42)

[But if you inquire, you will find a crime of Fortune in the act, not wickedness; for what kind of wickedness does a mistake have?]

caelestique viro, quis me deceperit *error*,
    dicite, pro culpa ne *scelus* esse putet.
      (*Tr.* 1.3.37–38)

[And tell to that heavenly man what error deceived me lest he think wickedness be the same as fault.]

Through such an allusion, Ovid places the exile in a position identical to that of Actæon and foreshadows what will become of the exile. Both have angered a god through an innocent mistake, and both will be punished with metamorphosis, speech loss, and communal (in Actæon's case, literal) death.

The final portion of this section that foreshadows the exile's speech loss is the mention of *sonus* in the couplet immediately following the his prayer:

hac prece adoravi superos ego, pluribus uxor,
    singultu medios impediente sonos.
      (*Tr.* 1.3.41–42)

[With this prayer I begged the gods, with many my wife begged, all the while sobs were choking our half-spoken words. (translation adapted from Green 1994)]

This simple couplet, though easy to translate, leaves ambiguous the subjects of the actions in the second line because of the ablative absolute. Nonetheless, translators have typically written the exile's wife as the subject who produces the half-spoken words:

Luck 1977: Schluchzen unterbrach *sie* mitten in Sprechen.
Renato Mazzanti 1991: Con questi preghiera supplicai i celesti con molte
    più alter la sposa, fra I singhiozzi che *le* troncavano a mezzo le parole.
A. D. Melville 1992: I made that prayer to gods above; my wife made more,
    but *her* sobs cut short the words she said.

Peter Green 1994: Such my prayer to the powers above; *my wife's* were countless, sobs choked each half-spoken word.

A. S. Kline 2003: I spoke to the gods in prayer like this, my wife more so, sobs choking *her* half-heard cries.

At the same time, however, other scholars have noticed the emphasis placed on the connection and harmony between the exile and his wife in this portion of 1.3.[32] Therefore, I suggest that the ablative absolute typically ascribed to the wife alone be restored to its ambiguous nature and allowed to describe both the wife and the exile.[33] Doing so makes for better poetic organization. First, the ablative absolute portion of the couplet is made to reply to the whole of the first line and not to half of it, an organization that adds balance to the couplet and is further amplified by the synthetic word order. Second, it allows the subsequent couplet (*illa etiam ante Lares passis adstrata capillis / contigit extinctos ore tremente focos*, 43–44) to focus exclusively on the wife, an act that creates a parallelism between the exile's first appearance in the section and reflection on the Lares (*hanc ego suspiciens et ad hanc Capitolia cernens, / quae nostro frustra iuncta fuere Lari*, 29–30) and the wife's appearance and prostration before the Lares. Finally, such an organization creates a picture of harmony and shared action consistent with the rest of the poem (e.g., *uxor amans flentem flens acrius ipsa tenebat*, 1.3.17).

This reorganization is apropos to our discussion of speech loss because if the ablative absolute refers to both the exile and his wife, then the words spoken by the exile are described as *soni*, a term emphasizing their inarticulate nature and their ineffectiveness to produce human communication. Such a concept of ineffective communication is furthered four lines later, as the speech the wife produces is described as *verba non valitura* (45–46). Both of these instances again bring to the audience's attention a type of linguistic slippage that foreshadows the exile's ultimate metamorphosis marked by his loss of speech. Now, instead of being set apart from the other *soni* in the house as an individual capable of articulate speech, as he was described in the first section of the poem, the exile is portrayed as an individual whose voice is so affected by his situation that he can produce only *sonos*. His linguistic slippage has begun.

In addition to the references made to the exile's impending loss of speech, this section also continues the theme of communal identity from the opening "act." In the first "act," the exile is depicted as part of a community, but although his interaction with his community has marked him as a member of it on the surface, the lack of response from them foreshadows his ultimate removal from community. In this section, the exile's removal from community is again alluded to, though more overtly and forcefully, through repeated allusions to the *Aeneid* and comparisons drawn between Aeneas and the exile.

The major lines of comparison drawn between the two revolve around community: although both men are forced to leave their native city, only Aeneas is successful in retaining his communal identity. In the *Aeneid*, he famously leaves Troy with his family, domestic staff, and household gods:

> dixerat ille, et iam per moenia clarior ignis
> auditur, propiusque aestus incendia volvunt.
> "ergo age, care pater, cervici imponere nostrae;
> ipse subibo umeris nec me labor iste gravabit;
> quo res cumque cadent, unum et commune periclum,
> una salus ambobus erit. mihi parvus Iulus
> sit comes, et longe servet vestigia coniunx.
> vos, famuli, quae dicam animis advertite vestris.
> est urbe egressis tumulus templumque vetustum
> desertae Cereris, iuxtaque antiqua cupressus
> religione patrum multos servata per annos;
> hanc ex diverso sedem veniemus in unam.
> tu, genitor, cape sacra manu patriosque penatis;
> me bello e tanto digressum et caede recenti
> attrectare nefas, donec me flumine vivo
> abluero."
> (*Aen.* 2.705–20)

[He had spoken, and now a clearer fire is heard through the city, and the blaze rolls its heat nearer. "Come then, dear father, clasp my neck: I myself will carry you on my shoulders and that task will not be burdensome to me. Whatever may happen, the same and shared risk, the same salvation will be for both of us. Let little Julus be our companion, and let my wife follow our footsteps at a distance. You servants, heed with your whole hearts the things that I'm saying. At the entrance to the city there's a mound, an ancient temple of forsaken Ceres, and nearby an ancient cypress, protected through the years by the reverence of our fathers: we shall come to that one place by diverse paths. You, father, take in your hand the sacred objects and our country's Penates; until I will have washed in running water, it is a sin for me, coming from such fighting and recent slaughter, to touch them."]

> feror exsul in altum
> cum sociis natoque penatibus et magnis dis.
>     (*Aen.* 3.11–12)

[I am borne, an exile, onto the deep with my comrades, my son, the Penates and the great gods.]

Like Aeneas, the exile is surrounded by his wife, child, household staff, and gods, but he is forced to leave them behind:

> "numina vicinis habitantia sedibus," inquam,
>     "iamque oculis numquam templa videnda meis,
> dique relinquendi, quos urbs habet alta Quirini,
>     este salutati tempus in omne mihi."
>         (*Tr.* 1.3.31–34)

[I said: "Powers living in these seats nearby, and temples never to be seen again by my eyes, gods to be relinquished, who possess this high city of Quirinus, be propitious to me for all time."]

> multaque in aversos effudit verba Penates
>     pro deplorato non ualitura viro.
>         (*Tr.* 1.3.45–46)

[Many words she poured to averse Penates, words of no avail for her bemoaned husband.]

Huskey, in his article chronicling the consistent allusions to the *Aeneid* throughout *Tristia* 1.3, encapsulates the ramification of such Ovidian allusions perfectly:

> Aeneas leaves Troy as it is dying, but by bringing his friends, family, and household gods with him, *he preserves a vital kernel of his city*. Ovid [i.e., the exile], however, says farewell forever to the gods, temples, and the city itself. Unlike Aeneas, Ovid [i.e., the exile] does not have to preserve any remnants of his civilization, since Rome, its buildings, and its gods will remain intact without him. Indeed, *he does not bring any part of his civilization with him to Tomis.* (2002, 96; emphasis added)

Therefore, the foreshadowing of the exile's loss of speech and removal of communal identity that began with oblique references to his lack of communication with his friends and his momentary identity crisis in the first section is now extended into the second in more overt terms. The failure of the exile's prayer is highlighted to emphasize the beginning of his linguistic slippage; the references to the Actæon myth draw a stark equation between the exile as Actæon and individuals who undergo metamorphic speech loss at the hands of a vengeful deity; and the allusions to the *Aeneid* provide a clear juxtaposition between Aeneas, who maintains his communal identity, and the exile, who does not. This general movement toward more overt indications of the exile's linguistic slippage and loss of communal identity continues in the follow section, in which Ovid draws even closer parallels between the exile and characters from the *Metamorphoses* who suffer metamorphic speech loss.

### ACT 3: BEFORE THE DAWN OF EXILE (LL. 47–76)

iamque morae spatium nox praecipitata negabat,
    versaque ab axe suo Parrhasis Arctos erat.
*quid facerem*? blando patriae retinebar amore,
    ultima sed iussae nox erat illa fugae.
*a! quotiens* aliquo dixi properante "quid urges?
    vel quo festinas ire, vel unde, vide."
*a! quotiens* certam me sum mentitus habere
    horam, propositae quae foret apta viae.
ter limen tetigi, ter sum revocatus, et ipse
    indulgens animo pes mihi tardus erat.
saepe 'vale' dicto rursus sum multa locutus,
    et quasi discedens oscula summa dedi.
saepe eadem mandata dedi meque ipse fefelli,
    respiciens oculis pignora cara meis.
denique "quid propero? Scythia est, quo mittimur," inquam,
    "Roma relinquenda est, utraque iusta mora.
uxor in aeternum vivo mihi viva negatur,
    et domus et fidae dulcia membra domus,
quosque ego dilexi fraterno more sodales,
    o mihi Thesea pectora iuncta fide!
dum licet, amplectar: numquam fortasse licebit
    amplius; in lucro est quae datur hora mihi."
nec mora sermonis verba inperfecta relinquo,
    complectens animo proxima quaeque meo.
dum loquor et flemus, caelo nitidissimus alto,
    stella grauis nobis, Lucifer ortus erat.

> dividor haud aliter, quam si mea membra relinquam,
>   et pars abrumpi corpore visa suo est.
> sic doluit Mettus tum cum in contraria versos
>   ultores habuit proditionis equos.

The third "act" of *Tristia* 1.3 continues the themes of the earlier two sections: the exile's loss of speech and his removal from his community. Throughout the narrative section, Ovid makes multiple allusions to various characters from the *Metamorphoses* and compares them to the exile in order to foreshadow his impending metamorphic speech loss. In terms of speech loss and its schematic association with loss of community, three characters in particular are highlighted: Callisto, Philomela, and Dryope. As we saw in chapter 2, all three of these characters share the unfortunate distinction of having suffered metamorphic speech loss. For Callisto and Dryope, speech loss occurred simultaneously with their physical metamorphosis into a bear or a poplar tree, respectively. Philomela underwent a more symbolic, but no less brutal, metamorphic speech loss resulting from the excision of her tongue from her mouth.

Let us first turn our attention to the presence of the Callisto myth in the narrative. The myth is alluded to twice in the first eight lines of the narrative, with both instances serving to create a mythic background that foreshadows the exile's metamorphic speech loss:

> iamque morae spatium nox praecipitata negabat,
>   versaque ab axe suo *Parrhasis Arctos* erat.
> *quid facerem*? blando patriae retinebar amore,
>   ultima sed iussae nox erat illa fugae.
> *a! quotiens* aliquo dixi properante "quid urges?
>   vel quo festinas ire, vel unde, vide."
> *a! quotiens* certam me sum mentitus habere
>   horam, propositae quae foret apta viae.
>        (*Tr.* 1.3.47–54)

[And now the falling night began to deny time for delay, and the Arcadian bear had been turned bout her axis. What could I have done? I kept being held back by the sweet love of country, but the night was the last before my ordered exile. Ah! How often I spoke as someone hurried by: "Why do you hasten? Consider whither and whence you are hurrying to go." Ah! How often I lied that I had a set time that was appropriate for the intended journey.]

The first allusion to the Callisto myth establishes the background for the entire section. The "Parrhasian bear" that introduces the new temporal setting of the "act" is the constellation into which Callisto was metamorphosed by Jupiter after she had been transformed into a bear by the jealous Juno.[34] The constellation, which is most visible throughout the night, signals the arrival of the exile's day of relegation, a day on which he, like Callisto, would undergo metamorphic speech loss.[35]

The second allusion builds on the first and makes a direct link between the effects that metamorphic speech loss had on Callisto's human and communal identity and the effects it will have on the situation of the exile. As first mentioned in passing by Posch (1983, 151n359), the anaphoric *a! quotiens* is a direct allusion to the Callisto story from the *Metamorphoses*:

*a! quotiens*, sola non ausa quiescere silva,
ante domum quondamque suis erravit in agris!
*a! quotiens* per saxa canum latratibus acta est
venatrixque metu venantum territa fugit!
    (*Met.* 2.489–92)

[Ah! How many times she did not dare to relax alone in the forest, she wandered into the fields before her former home! Ah! How many times she, a huntress, was driven through the rocks by the barking of dogs, and, terrified by the fear of the prey, fled!]

Callisto, having been recently transformed into a bear and rendered speechless and, subsequently, unable to communicate her identity through a verbal means, is described as an individual with a "wavering identity": not entirely fit for either the human or the animal community. She stands before her house debating where she should go, in which community she belonged.

In *Tristia* 1.3, the exile faces the same situation. Having just stood outside his house and reflected on the city and identity that he was about to lose, he poses a question of direction similar to Callisto's: whither or whence is everyone hurrying to go? The exile himself is frozen in uncertainty between the desire to stay out of love for Rome and the necessity of leaving because of Augustus's order.[36] He too stands on the precipice of metamorphosis and "wavering identity," and the allusion to the Callisto tale serves to provide an allusive analogue to emphasize that situation (Posch 1983, 151n359).

Within the same eight lines in which Ovid makes allusions to the Callisto myth, there is an allusion to another Ovidian tale of metamorphic speech loss:

the Philomela narrative. The couplet between the reference to Ursa Major and the anaphoric *a! quotiens* begins with a deliberative subjunctive reminiscent of the beginning of a hexameter line from the Philomela narrative in the *Metamorphoses*:

> Signa deus bis sex acto lustraverat anno;
> *quid faciat Philomela?* fugam custodia claudit,
> structa rigent solido stabulorum moenia saxo,
> os mutum facti caret indice. grande doloris
> ingenium est, miserisque venit sollertia rebus:
> (*Met.* 6.571–75)

[The god had brightened twice six signs with the year having been completed; what could Philomela do? A guard closed off flight, the walls the stable, built with solid stone, stand firm, and her *os mutum* lacks a means of describing the deed. Her mind is heavy with grief, but cleverness comes in miserable affairs.]

In these lines, Philomela finds herself trapped in the forest stable with no way out.[37] Moreover, because of her speech loss, she has no way of communicating her identity. She is, in essence, stuck between the animal and the human, the nonspeaking and the speaking worlds.

In the context of *Tristia* 1.3, the deliberative subjunctive *quid facerem* looks back to this episode and uses the allusion to add depth to the exilic situation framed by references to the Callisto narrative. As just shown, the Callisto narrative provides an analogue to the exilic situation based on the concept of wavering identity and loss of community. The Philomela narrative also speaks to both of these points but superimposes on them the added dimension of speech loss.

A few lines after the allusions to Philomela and Callisto, we find another allusion to a transformed character from the *Metamorphoses*: Dryope. Elizabeth Forbis (1997, 252–54) has already identified the close relationship between the description of the exile's metamorphosis and that of Dryope, noting the similarities in situation and transformation: both the exile and Dryope are surrounded by their families at the time of the metamorphoses, both situations are ones of grief and sadness, and both characters suddenly lose the ability to speak because of their transformation. However, whereas Forbis is correct in identifying the similarities between the general situations, she omits the specific connections between the two narratives that cluster around the moment of the exile's transformation, for the moment of the exile's transformation occurs midspeech:

denique "quid propero? Scythia est, quo mittimur," inquam,
    "Roma relinquenda est, utraque iusta mora.
uxor in aeternum vivo mihi viva negatur,
    et domus et fidae dulcia membra domus,
quosque ego dilexi fraterno more sodales,
    o mihi Thesea pectora iuncta fide!
*dum licet, amplectar*: numquam fortasse licebit
    amplius; in lucro est quae datur hora mihi."
*nec mora sermonis verba inperfecta relinquo,*
    *complectens animo proxima quaeque meo.*
*dum loquor et flemus, caelo nitidissimus alto,*
    *stella grauis nobis, Lucifer ortus erat.*
dividor haud aliter, quam si mea membra relinquam,
    et pars abrumpi corpore visa suo est.
    (*Tr.* 1.3.62–72)

[Finally, I say. "Why should I hurry? It is Scythia to which I am sent and Rome must be left behind. Both are good reasons for delaying. My wife, living, is denied me, living, forever, and my house and the sweet members of my loyal house, associates whom I cherish as a brother would, O hearts joined to me with Thesean loyalty! While it is allowed, I shall embrace you: perhaps it will never be allowed again; whatever time that remains is a profit for me." Without delay, I leave the unfinished words of my conversation, embracing those closest to my heart. While I speak and we weep, the brightest Lucifer, a star grievous to me, had arisen high in the sky. I am torn hardly otherwise than if I leave my limbs, and part seems to be broken from its body.]

Leading up to his sudden transformation, the exile places a heightened emphasis on embracing those around him (*amplectar, complectens*) while he is still allowed to do so (*dum licet*). As he does this, he breaks off midspeech and never speaks again for the remainder of the poem. This moment marks the end of the exile's ability to speak: as his words go unfinished, the day of his relegation dawns (*Lucifer ortus erat*),[38] distinguishing his spoken past from his now-silent present (69–72).

Such a description of transformation shares verbal allusions to the moments in which Dryope was transformed:

spectatrix aderam fati crudelis, opemque
non poteram tibi ferre, soror, quantumque valebam,

crescentem truncum ramosque *amplexa* morabar,
et, fateor, volui sub eodem cortice condi.
    (*Met.* 9.359–62)

[I was present, a spectator to cruel fate, and I was unable to bring help to you, sister; how much I kept saying farewell, and kept delaying, embracing the rising trunk and limbs, and, I confess, I wished to be covered under the same bark.]

nil nisi iam faciem, quod non foret arbor, habebat
cara soror: lacrimae misero de corpore factis
inrorant foliis, ac, *dum licet, oraque praestant
vocis iter*, tales effundit in aera questus:
    (*Met.* 9.367–70)

[There is nothing but your face that was not already tree, dear sister: tears rain on the fashioned leaves down from your poor body, and while it was allowed and your mouth left a path for your voice, it poured out such laments into the air:]

In addition to the general situation of mourning and sudden speech loss identified by Forbis (1997), the description of the embrace of Dryope and her sister (*amplexa*) and Dryope's attempts to speak to her family while she was allowed to do so (*dum licet*) point to the specific linking of these passages with the portrayal of the exile's transformation. The force of this allusion is to repeat the concepts of speech loss, community loss, and wavering identity brought by the allusions to the Philomela and Callisto episodes, but what this allusion also provides is a descriptive angle for the exile's transformation: like Dryope, the exile's transformation is sudden and immediately removes him from the embraces of his community. As soon as the dawn of the day of his relegation occurs, his speech stops short, and he is removed from the closeness of those he loves.

Until this point of the poem, Ovid had been a part of a community, surrounded by his family and friends. However, when his words stop in midspeech, he loses his voice, and, consequently, he is schematically isolated from his community. Ovid emphasizes this removal from community in the next seven lines. Luck has rightly noticed their separation, writing that "der Akt des Zerreißens ist durch drei verschiendene Verben ausgedrückt: *dividior, membra relinquam*, [und] *abrumpi*" (1977, 44).[39] Ovid is literally torn from his society as Mettus (75–76) was torn apart by his horses (cf. Tola 2008, 59–60).

The "dismembered," separated Ovid is henceforth surprisingly (perhaps not) absent from the poem. In fact, the focus shifts to the grieving of his lost community. Then, Ovid writes, the cries and groans of *his* people arose (*tum vero exoritur clamor gemitusque meorum*, 77). This lament is furthered by the following line (*et feriunt maestae pectora nuda manus*) and truly begins to take on the shape of a funeral lament. Indeed, Ovid's wife clings to his body and begs him to take her with him, her speech creating a nice parallel to Ovid's earlier prayer. However, Ovid's character makes no reply to his wife's impassioned plea; perhaps he, transformed, is no longer able to do so verbally. Instead, Ovid leaves (*egredior*), bedraggled and as one fit for a funeral.

Therefore, the entirety of *Tristia* 1.3 centers on a crucial issue: the exile's loss of speech and subsequent schematic separation from community. Ovid brings these aspects to the forefront through his use of this schema of speech loss and his consistent allusions to characters from the *Metamorphoses* who undergo a similar transformation to that of the exile. As the poem progresses, the exile slowly moves from a position of speech to one of speech loss and, consequently, from one of communal membership to one of social death. Allusions to Callisto, Philomela, Dryope, and Actæon are deployed throughout *Tristia* 1.3 to emphasize particular aspects of the exile's impending loss of speech and community. Moreover, the use of *Tristia* 1.3, the first narrative poem in all the exile literature, to describe the transformation of the exile sets the tone for the remainder of the exile literature: having lost his ability to speak and his connection to community, the exile must spend the rest of the *Tristia* and the *Epistulae ex Ponto* attempting to find his voice again and to reconnect with his community.

### Tristia 1.2 and 1.4: Voicelessness on the Journey to Tomis

Surrounding the narrative of the exile's transformation in *Tristia* 1.3 is a pair of poems depicting his hard travels from Rome to Tomis, *Tristia* 1.2 and 1.4. These poems tell of the perils of a journey by sea to a foreign land in a fashion typical of both elegy and epic.[40] In the artistic ordering of the *Tristia* 1 already mentioned, 1.2 and 1.4 have typically been read together as a doublet surrounding the narrative of change in 1.3. In addition to the place of the organization of the doublet in describing the nature of his exile, these poems also present the first instance of the exile's new position as a speechless *exul*. As he travels from Rome to Tomis, on multiple occasions the exile attempts to speak and to communicate with the gods, only to have his attempts thwarted by the waves of the sea.

In *Tristia* 1.2, the exile opens with the observation that when one god opposes a man, often another brings him aid, and the exile hopes that this too will be the case for him if he prays. However, his attempts at prayers do not reach the ears of the intended divine addressees:

> *Verba* miser frustra *non proficientia* perdo.
>    ipsa graves spargunt ora loquentis aquae,
> terribilisque Notus iactat mea dicta, precesque
>    ad quos mittuntur, non sinit ire deos.
> ergo idem venti, ne causa laedar in una,
>    velaque nescio quo votaque nostra ferunt.
>       (*Tr.* 1.2.13–18)

[A wretch, I'm wasting idle words in vain. My mouth that speaks is drenched by heavy waves, and fearful Notus hurls my words away, and won't let my prayers reach the gods. So the same winds drive my sails and prayers who knows where, so I'm doubly punished. (trans. Kline 2003)]

> scilicet occidimus, nec spes est ulla salutis,
>    *dumque loquor*, vultus obruit unda meos.
> opprimet hanc animam fluctus, frustraque precanti
>    ore necaturas accipiemus aquas.
>       (*Tr.* 1.2.33–36)

[Surely we're done for, there's no hope of safety, while I speak the waves drench my face. The breakers will crush this life of mine, with lips praying in vain, I'll swallow the fatal waters. (trans. Kline 2003)]

Each time that the exile attempts to pray for assistance, his prayers are literally drowned out by the waves of his exile. His words amount to nothing (*verba non proficientia*), a phrase that is reminiscent of the failed prayer of the exile's wife in *Tristia* 1.3 (*verba non valitura*, 1.3.45–46). Moreover, the harsh realities of the exile's loss of speech and his seemingly impending death alone on the sea are contrasted with a death on land in which the dying individual is able to speak his last wishes to his family:

> est aliquid, fatove suo ferrove cadentem
>    in solida moriens ponere corpus humo,
> et mandare suis aliqua et sperare sepulcrum
>    et non aequoreis piscibus esse cibum.
>       (*Tr.* 1.2.53–56)

[Surely we're done for, there's no hope of safety, while I speak the waves drench my face. The breakers will crush this life of mine, with lips praying in vain, I'll swallow the fatal waters. (trans. Kline 2003)]

The newly exiled poet can now see the full ramifications of his exilic state. Instead of being surrounded by family and friends on his deathbed, able to speak his wishes to his community (*mandare suis*), he will die alone in isolation and unable to speak.[41]

The same imagery recurs in *Tristia* 1.4, as the exile again describes his peril on the sea, albeit in a less explicit manner:[42]

> *dum loquor* et timeo pariter cupioque repelli,
>   increpuit quantis viribus unda latus!
>     (*Tr.* 1.4.23–24)

[While I speak and equally fear and desire to be sent back, with what force a wave crushed the side of the boat!]

Here the exile shudders at the power of the waves crashing against his ship—and probably covering him with water—while he attempts to speak. Although this lone reference to speech in the poem does not explicitly detail the new speechless nature of the exile, it does create an allusion to *Tristia* 1.2 with the repetition of *dum loquor* (*Tr.* 1.4.23 ≈ *Tr.* 1.2.34). Whenever the exile tries to speak, something prevents him—in these poems it is the waves and the winds—from doing so. Moreover, the phrase *dum loquor* also points back to an important moment in the poem that *Tristia* 1.2 and 1.4 surround. In *Tristia* 1.3, the point of the exile's transformation is marked with the same phrase:

> *dum loquor et flemus*, caelo nitidissimus alto,
>   stella grauis nobis, Lucifer ortus erat.
> dividor haud aliter, quam si mea membra relinquam,
>   et pars abrumpi corpore visa suo est.
>     (*Tr.* 1.3.69–72)

[While I speak and we weep, the brightest Lucifer, a star grievous to me, had arisen high in the sky. I am torn hardly otherwise than if I leave my limbs, and part seems to be broken from its body.]

Therefore, by repeating the same phrase that indicated the moment the exile entered into a speechless state, Ovid points to the exile's continued state of speechlessness. Now, whenever the exile attempts to speak, there will always be a hindrance to prevent him from communicating successfully.

Furthermore, the picture of the exile painted in these storm poems sets a foundation for his portrayal throughout the exile literature that is built on the same schema of speech loss from the *Metamorphoses*. Now isolated in Tomis, the exile continuously attempts to communicate with his lost community, only to find some hindrance in his path. He no longer has a physical voice with which to identify himself. Therefore, the exile that we see after these opening poems of the *Tristia* is one struggling to overcome his speechlessness. Ovid draws attention to the exile's struggle, as he did in *Tristia* 1.3, by alluding to characters in the *Metamorphoses* who had undergone transformation and speech loss. It is to these allusions that we now turn our attention.

## Performing Voicelessness: Description of Speech Loss in the Exile Literature

Having described the exile's metamorphosis from a speaking member of community to a speechless exile in the opening three narrative poems of the *Tristia*, Ovid continues this description throughout the remainder of the exile literature, painting a picture of an exile bereft of the ability to communicate verbally. A number of scholarly treatments of the exile's speechlessness have pointed to his multiple complaints regarding his voiceless state, while others have indicated the similarities between the exile's voicelessness and that of characters from the *Metamorphoses*. In particular, Forbis and Stevens have most clearly laid out these parallels. Forbis identifies parallels between the exile's story and those of Actæon and the Swan and the Raven, the effect of which is to proclaim the exile's innocence and the unintentionality of his *error* against Augustus (1997, 249–52, 262–63); likewise, she also points to the fact that the description of the exile's transformation resembles that of Dryope and that the manner in which he attempts to navigate his voicelessness is similar to those taken up by Philomela and Io (252–62). Stevens (2009), on the other hand, focuses his attention more on the complaints of the exile and less on the allusions to the *Metamorphoses*.[43] Therefore, he discusses the exile's complaints of loneliness, lack of poetic inspiration, and inability to communicate with the Getans and the Sarmatians.[44]

Although these studies do well to point out the similarities between the exile's condition and those of characters in the *Metamorphoses*, they lack an in-depth discussion of why Ovid chose to depict the exile in such a manner and, more importantly, why he chose these particular characters as analogues for

## Speech Loss in the Exile Literature

the exile. In this section, therefore, I will build from the foundations set by Forbis and Stevens, seeking to explore the force of such self-allusive parallels and to situate them within the schematic associations of speech loss, isolation from community, and writing as reintegration that was identified in the previous chapter. In particular, I will take up the parallels drawn with the story of Philomela because, as an example of the full scope of the pattern in the *Metamorphoses*, it provides the hopeful ideal to which the exile aspires in the *Tristia* and the *Epistulae ex Ponto*.

I will begin the analysis with a discussion of the use of the Philomela myth in descriptions of speechlessness in the exile literature. As explained in the previous chapter, the story of Philomela was one that not only provided a full depiction of the movement from speech loss to the successful act of "writing oneself back into community" but also was pregnant with metaphors of the act of writing poetry. The description of Philomela's weaving as a *miserabile carmen* and the use of terms like *callidus*, *intexere*, and *tela* both call to mind the act of weaving poetry together and describe Philomela as a sort of poet character in the mold of Ariadne or Orpheus. Because of her state as poet character and victim of voicelessness, Philomela was a logical choice as an analogue to the exile and provided various angles for Ovid to explore the exile's situation. In this section, I focus on two methods in which Ovid uses the Philomela myth: (1) to make explicit statements about the exile's poetry through the repetition of similar vocabulary, and (2) to make explicit statements about *Ovid's situation* through the use of allusion and intertextuality.

To begin our discussion of the use of vocabulary from the Philomela myth to describe the exile's condition, we start with two passages from the *Metamorphoses*:

in *populos* veniam; si silvis *clausa* tenebor,
inplebo silvas et conscia saxa movebo;
*audiet* haec aether et si deus ullus in illo est!
    (*Met.* 6.546–48)

[I shall come into the people; if I shall be held, enclosed in the woods, I shall fill the woods and I shall move the rocks as witnesses; this air shall hear and whatever god there is in it!]

stamina barbarica suspendit callida *tela*
purpureasque notas filis intexuit albis,

*indicium* sceleris; perfectaque tradidit uni,
utque ferat dominae, *gestu* rogat; illa rogata
pertulit ad Procnen nec scit, quid tradat in illis.
      (*Met*. 6.576–80)

[She hung the clever warp on the foreign web and interwove purple markings with white thread, a symbol of [Tereus's] wickedness; she handed the completed weaving to her one servant so that she might bring it to her mistress; she asks with a gesture; the servant, having been asked, carried it through to Procne and knew not what she handed over in the weaving.]

In the first passage, Philomela threatens Tereus, claiming that she will expose his misdeed regardless of where he puts her. Philomela is supremely confident that her message will get through, that she will be successful in telling her story; though she herself may be contained in the woods (*clausa tenebor*), her voice will nevertheless overcome her physical location.

Let us compare Philomela's sentiments—along with the terminology used to profess them—with two excerpts from the exile literature in which the exile threatens an enemy and explains his condition to a friend:

quod Scythicis habitem longe summotus in oris,
    siccaque sint oculis proxima signa meis,
nostra per inmensas ibunt praeconia *gentes*,
    quodque querar notum qua patet orbis erit.
ibit ad occasum quicquid dicemus ob ortu,
    testis et Hesperiae vocis Eous erit.
trans ego tellurem, trans altas *audiar* undas,
    et gemitus vox est magna futura mei;
nec tua te sontem tantummodo saecula norint,
    perpetuae crimen posteritatis eris.
      (*Tr*. 4.9.17–26)

[Although I live, driven far off, on Scythian shores, and the dry signs are closest to my eyes, my heralds will go throughout many peoples, and my complaint will be known throughout the world. That which I shall say will go from east to west, and the eastern wind will be witness of a western voice. Across the land, across the deep seas I shall be heard, and great will be the future voice of my groan; moreover, not only your age will know you as a criminal, but you will be a crime to generations everlasting.]

*Clausa* tamen misi Scythica tibi *tela* pharetra:
   hoste, precor, fiant illa *cruenta* tuo.
Hos habet haec calamos, hos haec habet ora libellos,
   haec viget in nostris, Maxime, Musa locis!
      (*Pont.* 3.8.19–22)

[Yet, I have sent you weapons enclosed in a Scythian quiver: I pray that they be stained with the blood of your enemy. This shore holds these pens; this shore holds these booklets; in these places, O Maximus, this is the Muse that flourishes.]

In the first excerpt, the exile threatens his enemy in much the same manner as Philomela threatens Tereus: although he is isolated from his community, his voice will continue to travel and to tell of his enemies' misdeeds. Just as Philomela says she will go *in populos*, the exile affirms that his heralds will go *per inmensas gentes*.[45] Likewise, the two passages share in the use of *audire*, as both Philomela and the exile will be *heard* by all, despite the loss of their respective voices. Even though it would be pushing the comparison between these passages too far to call their relationship an explicit allusion, both profess the same schematic associations of speech loss and speak to the fact that the voiceless exile is experiencing a situation close to that of Philomela.

The second exilic excerpt, however, does seem to point to a closer relationship to the Philomela tale through the use of the terms *clausa*, *tela*, and *cruenta*. The exile opens this passage with a description of the poetry he has sent the addressee, Paullus Fabius Maximus.[46] The term *tela* serves double duty as both *tela,-ae* (warp) and *telum,-i* (weapons/spears). In one sense, Ovid has sent Maximus actual arrows from Scythia, as such arrows were a Greek literary topos, and elsewhere in the exile literature they were both the major threat to the exile's safety and the only worthwhile gift the Scythian could produce (Claassen 1999, 298n54).[47] In another sense, as Nagle observes, the *tela* represent the poetic material at hand for the exile, as the constant fighting and threats of attack furnished "material for poetry, since one recurring theme in the exilic poetry is the unpleasant nature of the place and its people" (1980, 59).[48]

In addition to these meanings furnished by the *telum*, the meaning of *tela*, *telae* also seems to be present beneath the literal surface. The function of *tela* as an object that the exile has sent to his lost community evokes the *tela* on which Philomela weaves her story to be sent to her lost sister, Procne. Moreover, this potential allusion is strengthened by the presence of two other strong terms from the Philomela tale: *clausa* and *cruenta*. As can be seen in the first excerpt above from the *Metamorphoses*, *clausa* is the manner in which Philomela describes her captured and isolated state. Likewise, since the exile is fond of conflating himself with his poetry (e.g., *I* [*as poetry*] will be heard, *audiar* above), it is not too much of a stretch to consider the *enclosed* material of the exile's letter to be the exile himself, placing him in the same enclosed state as that which Philomela described herself. Also, the exile confesses the wish that through poetry he may be able to stain Maximus's enemies with blood. This confluence of gore and the act of sending calls to mind the climactic moment of the Philomela tale: when Philomela throws the head of Tereus's son, Itys, in his father's face:

> prosiluit Ityosque caput Philomela *cruentum*
> misit in ora patris nec tempore maluit ullo
> posse loqui et meritis testari gaudia dictis.
> (*Met*. 6.658–60)

[Philomela leapt forth and sent the bloodied head of Itys into the face of his father, and at no other time would she have preferred to have been able to speak and to attest to her joy with deserved words.]

For Philomela, the *tela*, which she worked while *clausa*, delivers the bloostained (*cruentum*) head of her enemy's son. Likewise, the confluence of these three terms seems to underlie the meaning of the exile's letter to Maximus: as Philomela, he will travel through his enclosed poetry (*clausa tela*) and will bring about the bloody end (*cruenta*) for Maximus's enemies. Aside from setting forth the purpose of the exile's poem, it also serves to draw a direct relationship between the exile and Philomela: both are isolated and bereft of voice, but they still maintain the ability to write their way back into their community and to create devastating effects for their enemies through the continued efficacy of their writing.

The connections between the exile's condition and Philomela's situation, however, are not limited to a few isolated excerpts; many more systemic examples can be identified throughout the exile literature. Two similarities, in particular, are of import here: (1) the description of communicative attempts through gesture, and (2) the manner in which the content of "writing" is portrayed. To begin with the description of communication, we turn first to the method employed by Philomela in the *Metamorphoses*: the gesture.

As can be seen from the first excerpt provided above (*Met*. 6.576–80), when Philomela loses her ability to speak, she turns not only to writing but also to gesture, asking her servant to come and take her weaving to Procne (*gestu rogat*).

The act of gesture is also a prominent manner in which the exile's condition is described in both the *Tristia* and *Ex Ponto*.[49] Having lost his vocal ability, the exile turns to gesture in an attempt to communicate with the Getans and the Sarmatians around him:

> Exercent illi sociae commercia linguae:
>     per *gestum* res est significanda mihi.
> Barbarus hic ego sum, qui non intellegor ulli,
>     et rident stolidi verba Latina Getae;
> meque palam de me tuto mala saepe loquuntur,
>     forsitan obiciunt exiliumque mihi.
> utque fit, in me aliquid ficti, dicentibus illis
>     abnuerim quotiens annuerimque, putant.
>         (*Tr.* 5.10.35–42)

[They conduct conversations in a common tongue, but affairs must be dealt with by me through gesture. Here I am a barbarian, who is not intelligible to anyone; moreover, the foolish Getes mock my Latin words and in my very presence often deride me, perhaps upbraiding me for my exile. As usual, they think something is wrong with me whenever they speak to me and I only nod yes or no in response.]

The exile's attempts at communication are portrayed with the same term, *gestus*, as those of Philomela. However, whereas Philomela's gestures were understood by the servant, and Philomela could conceivably understand if the servant had spoken anything in reply, the exile does not enjoy such success. Since he does not speak the languages of the Getes, the exile is mocked openly and is unable to understand or defend himself from such ridicule. Moreover, his gestures are unsuccessful in communicating any meaning to the Getes other than a mental disability or extreme social awkwardness. In such a regard, the exile's condition resembles Philomela's in the use of gestures to communicate, but it is ultimately much worse and much more isolating. Unable to understand or to be understood, the exile feels a more potent version of schematic speech loss, lives in complete social isolation, and is limited to writing to Latin-speaking friends as his only means of social interaction.

Yet in other places, even writing is likened to an ineffective gesture such as the ones performed by the exile in the above excerpt. Consider, for example, the exile's complaints to Cornelius Severus:[50]

> Da veniam fasso, studiis quoque frena remisi
>     ducitur et digitis littera rara meis.
> Inpetus ille sacer qui vatum pectora nutrit,
>     qui prius in nobis esse solebat, abest.
> Vix venit ad partes, vix sumptae Musa tabellae
>     inponit pigras paene coacta manus,
> parvaque, ne dicam scribendi nulla voluptas
>     est mihi nec numeris nectere verba iuuat,
> siue quod hinc fructus adeo non cepimus ullos,
>     principium nostri res sit ut ista mali,
> *siue quod in tenebris numerosos ponere gestus*
>     *quodque legas nulli scribere carmen idem est*:
>         (*Pont.* 4.2.23–34)

[Forgive my saying, but I have dropped the reins of study, and rare is the letter that is led from my fingers. That sacred impulse that nourishes the breasts of poets, that used to be present in me before all, is absent. Scarcely does the Muse play her part, scarcely does she place her hesitant hand on my tablets, when I take them up—and she almost has to be forced to do even that; for me there is little to no joy to speak of in writing, and it does not please to interlace words in meter, whether it is the fact that thus far I have not gained any profit from it that makes this affair the genesis of my misfortune, or the fact that to write a poem that you can read to no one is akin to making numerous gestures in the dark.]

Here the exile states that he has begun to give up on the act of writing because no one is able to understand the poems that he is writing. The extent to which we should believe such a statement is debatable, especially since the statement was made in the very writing that the exile is promising to give up. However, the sense of isolation that began with speech loss in *Tristia* 1 has filtered through to the use of gesture and writing in *Tristia* 5, and finally to the loss of both in the final book of *Epistulae*. The gradual deterioration of the exile is apparent and, although the descriptions of his exile are grounded in the vocabulary and ideas of the Philomela tale, the effects of his isolation are much more devastating.[51]

In addition to the use of gesture to describe the exile's attempts at communication, the exile literature also shares another similarity with the Philomela tale: the description of the content of the character's "writing." In the *Metamorphoses*, Philomela is portrayed as weaving on her loom an *indicium sceleris*, the proof or evidence of the wicked act of Tereus. The term *indicium* is used throughout the exile literature as a means of describing the content of the exile's poetry.⁵² Consider two examples from the *Tristia* and the *Epistulae ex Ponto*:

> Dividimur caelo quaeque est procul urbe Quirini
>     aspicit hirsutos comminus ursa Getas.
> Per tantum terrae, tot aquas vix credere possum
>     indicium studii transiluisse mei.
>         (*Ponto*. 1.5.73–76)

[We're divided by the heavens, and the Bear, far from Quirinus's city, sees the wild Getae near. I can scarcely believe a judgment on my work could leap across so much land and sea. (trans. Kline 2003)]

> Adde quod, ut rerum sola es tutela mearum,
>     ad te non parvi venit honoris onus,
> quod numquam vox est de te mea muta tuique
>     indiciis debes esse superba viri.
>         (*Tr.* 5.14.15–18)

[Add that you're the sole custodian of my estate, a burden to you that comes with no little honour: that my voice is never silent about you, and you should be proud of your husband's testimony. (trans. Kline 2003)]

In the first excerpt, the exile, writing to Cotta Maximus, marvels at the fact that the content of his poetry can travel so great a distance and that he is able to communicate in some form with his friend. As in the Philomela narrative, *indicium* refers to the content of the poetry, a poetic content that is able to traverse long distances and to connect the exile to a lost community. In the second excerpt, the *indicium* again describes the content of the exile's poetry, but the content is now the exile's wife, and the force of the *indicium* is not only to connect the exile to his wife but also to communicate something about the his wife to a larger audience. Such an expanded effect that the written communication of the exile has on multiple audiences will be discussed further later in this chapter and in chapter 4, but for the present discussion, the important aspect to note is the use of the same vocabulary from the Philomela myth to describe the poetic writing of the exile, a writing aimed at mediating the social divide created by his relegation to Tomis.

To recap: thus far, we have seen a variety of similarities and allusions between the Philomela tale of the *Metamorphoses* and the story of the exile in the *Tristia* and the *Epistulae ex Ponto*. Both characters fit into the schematic associations of speech loss, are described as isolated and voiceless, and turn to gesture and writing to create an *indicium* of their situation. The only difference between the two narratives is that the exile's, though grounded in the vocabulary and situation of the Philomela tale, is taken further, and his attempts at communication are described as ineffective, rendering him completely isolated. Therefore, thus far the allusions that the exilic description makes to the story of Philomela have been relegated to the narrative level: the character in both texts undergoes a similar situation, and the knowledge of both narratives serves to deepen the understanding of both through a shared background.[53]

However, one of the main aspects of the intertextuality between Ovid's exilic oeuvre and the Philomela narrative of the *Metamorphoses* is the commentary that it provides not on the exile but on Ovid himself. We can perhaps catch a glimpse of the authorial Ovid through an exploration of a distinct chain of allusions linking his exile literature to the Philomela of the *Metamorphoses*, and the Philomela of the *Metamorphoses* to an intertext between Virgil's *Aeneid* and Ennius's *Annales*. Through this allusive chain, we can begin to see the extent to which the Philomela story truly encapsulates the exilic experience both for Ovid's exilic persona and, perhaps, for Ovid himself.

We begin our analysis of this chain of allusions with a seemingly straightforward reference to the Philomela narrative in a list of comparisons between the exile's situation and the situations of other literary characters:

> Nescio qua natale solum dulcedine cunctos
>     ducit et inmemores non sinit esse sui.
> Quid melius Roma? Scythico quid frigore peius?
>     Huc tamen ex ista barbarus urbe fugit.
> Cum bene sit clausae cauea *Pandione natae*,
>     nititur in siluas illa redire suas.
> Adsuetos tauri saltus, adsueta leones—
>     nec feritas illos inpedit—antra petunt.
>         (*Pont.* 1.3.35–42)

[By some sweetness one's native land leads back everyone and does not allow them to forget it. What is better than Rome? What is worse than the Scythian cold? Yet hither a barbarian flees from that city. Although it fares well for the daughter of Pandion, locked up in a cage, she strives to return to her forests. Bulls seek their accustomed glades, lions their accustomed caves—and their fierceness does not prevent them.]

*Epistulae ex Ponto* 1.3, written to a Rufinius, thanks the addressee for his kindness and his attempts to hearten the exile. The section in which the above excerpt is located attempts to prove to Rufinius that, although his attempts at assisting the exile are appreciated and even momentarily successful (*Cum bene firmarunt animum praecepta iacentem / sumptaque sunt nobis pectoris arma tui, / rursus amor patriae ratione ualentior omni / quod tua fecerunt scripta retexit opus*, 1.3.25–30), such attempts ultimately fail because the desire for one's native land (*natale solum*) always will turn the exile's mind back to the despair of his situation. The allusion to the Philomela story provides an example of such a yearning on multiple levels. First, the most literal reading is that the *nata Pandione* refers to an actual nightingale that has been relegated to a cage and desires to fly freely in her native forests.[54] Second, the very use of the phrase *nata Pandione* suggests an allusion to the Philomela narrative, as Philomela was traditionally the daughter of King Pandion of Athens. Indeed, the comparison of the exile and Philomela, as we have seen, is an extremely apt one, as both were trapped in isolation in Thrace and both attempted to negotiate a speech loss through the written medium. Yet the allusion should be pushed further as one that points back to a specific point in Ovid's Philomela narrative, for the only point in the version from the *Metamorphoses* at which the ablative of origin *Pandione* is present is at the very moment of Philomela's arrival in Thrace, a point at which the phrase *Pandione nata(m/e)* is placed in exactly the same metrical position as its exilic counterpart:

Iamque iter effectum, iamque in sua litora fessis
puppibus exierant, cum rex *Pandione natam*
in stabula alta trahit, silvis obscura vetustis,
atque ibi pallentem trepidamque et cuncta timentem
et iam cum lacrimis, ubi sit germana, rogantem
includit fassusque nefas et virginem et unam
vi superat frustra clamato saepe parente,
saepe sorore sua, magnis super omnia divis.
    (*Met.* 6.519–26)

[Now the journey was complete, now they had gone out of the tired ships into their lands, when the king dragged the one born of Pandion into the high stables, hidden by the old woods, and there the girl, pallid and trembling and fearing all things and now with tears asking where her sister was, he locks up and, professing his unspeakable act, takes both the girl, alone, and her maidenhood by force, while parents' names are often called out, often her sister's, and above all the names of the great gods.]

Therefore, it seems clear that this exact passage from the *Metamorphoses* is meant to be read with and against the exile's list of examples from *Epistulae ex Ponto* 1.3 and that, as we have seen, the Philomela narrative is an appropriate analogue to the exile's experience that provides an added dimension of meaning. However, perhaps Ovid is alluding to something beyond narrative similarity here, as this passage from the *Metamorphoses* is itself an allusion to another passage from the *Aeneid*, which in turn took its cue from a scene in Ennius's *Annales*. Here are the Ennian and Virgilian passages:

> Incedunt arbusta per *alta*, securibus caedunt,
> Percellunt magnas quercus, exciditur *ilex*,
> *Fraxinus* frangitur atque abies consternitur alta,
> Pinus proceras pervortunt: omne sonabat
> Arbustum fremitu siluai frondosai.
>     (Ennius, *Ann.* 175–79 Sk = Macrob. *Sat.* 6.2.27)

[They pass among the high groves, and hew with axes; they strike down great oaks; the ilex is chopped; the ash is shattered and the high fir laid low; they overturn lofty pines: the whole grove echoes with the leafy forest's din. (trans. Hinds 1998)]

> itur in *antiquam silvam*, stabula *alta* ferarum;
> procumbunt piceae, sonat icta securibus *ilex*
> *fraxineaeque* trabes cuneis et fissile robur
> scinditur, advolvunt ingentis montibus ornos.
>     (Verg. *Aen.* 6.179–82)

[The journey goes into an ancient forest, the high stables of beasts; the pitch pines fall forth, the ilex, struck by axes, resounds; ashen beams and split oak are cut by wedges; they roll from the mountains on huge lances.]

In the Ennian passage, a group of men engage in tree felling. In the Virgilian excerpt, Aeneas and his Trojans go out from Cumae to find and gather wood for the funeral pyre of Misenus, an act they must complete to continue on their journey to the underworld and, ultimately, to Italy. These two passages have been shown to be closely related through Virgilian allusion based on the term *silva*. Throughout Latin poetry, the term *silva* is often used metaphorically to represent ὕλη, "raw" or "poetic" material unworked by the art of poetry.[55] With regard to these two passages, *silva* provides Virgil with an intertextual linchpin.

Hinds provides the clearest description of the intertextual relationship between the two texts based on *silva*:

> It is precisely as *antiqua silva*, in this sense [i.e., as "raw" material], that the Ennian passage is laid under contribution by Vergil here in *Aen.* 6.179–82. *Itur in antiquam silvam*: on this interpretation the allusion includes its self-annotation; the epic project of the poet is seen to move in step with the epic project of the hero. As Aeneas finds his *silva*, so too does Vergil: the *tour de force* of allusion to poetic material from the *Aeneid*'s archaic predecessor, the *Annales*, is figured as a harvest of mighty timber from an old-growth forest—in a landscape (that of *Aeneid* 6) charged with associations of awe and venerability. (1998, 12–13)

In other words, Virgil uses this allusion to Ennius as a means by which he can show his poetic skill and, perhaps, his poetic superiority to Ennius through his ability to intervene in Ennius's poetic space. Even if we want to stop short of calling this poetic *aemulatio*, it still stands that Virgil has shown us an example of his poetic power.[56]

Turning now to Ovid, it is to this poetic intertext between Virgil and Ennius and to Virgil's expression of poetic power that Ovid is pointing in his Philomela narrative. Compare that passage to the Virgilian one, both reproduced here:

> *itur* in *antiquam silvam, stabula alta* ferarum;
> procumbunt piceae, sonat icta securibus ilex
> fraxineaeque trabes cuneis et fissile robur
> scinditur, advolvunt ingentis montibus ornos.
>     (Verg. *Aen.* 6.179–82)

[The journey goes into an ancient forest, the high stables of beasts; the pitch pines fall forth, the ilex, struck by axes, resounds; ashen beams and split oak are cut by wedges; they roll from the mountains on huge lances.]

> Iamque *iter* effectum, iamque in sua litora fessis
> puppibus exierant, cum rex Pandione natam
> in *stabula alta* trahit, *silvis* obscura *vetustis*
>     (*Met.* 6.519–21)

[Now the journey was complete, now they had gone out of the tired ships into their lands, when the king dragged the one born of Pandion into the high stables, hidden by the old woods.]

Throughout the opening of the Philomela narrative, Ovid makes an explicit allusion to the Virgilian passage, placing the eventual rape of Philomela in a location similar to that in which Virgil's tree felling took place.[57] However, this allusion seems to be misplaced or frustrated because of the lack of narrative commonalities, and one is tempted to consider this an example of Richard Thomas's "apparent reference."[58] Yet although there is no tree felling occurring in the Philomela episode, a type of rape does occur in the Virgilian episode, as Aeneas and his men are "raping" a natural area by felling trees. Moreover, issues of civilization and barbarity have been identified as key concepts undergirding both the Philomela narrative and Virgil's poetry as a whole.[59] Therefore, such a similarity in thematic conflict can partially explain Ovid's decision to allude to this Virgilian passage, but not completely. Latin literature—and Virgil's corpus—is littered with examples of the issue of civilization versus barbarity, so why did Ovid choose this particular one?

Perhaps the answer lies not on the narrative level but on the level of intertext. As we discussed in chapter 2 and throughout this chapter, the character of Philomela is a close analogue to that of the poet. She weaves her tale as a poet would and professes the ability of her telling powers as a poet would. Therefore, as a poet character she provides a compelling comparison to Virgil because, as Virgil's acts of allusion portray him as a powerful poet, Philomela's rape and loss of speech emphasize the very powerlessness of her poetry.

To take this one step further, let us consider when the Philomela narrative in the *Metamorphoses* was composed. It is now generally accepted that portions of the *Metamorphoses* were composed by Ovid in exile, but it is still unclear which ones (Hinds 1987, 10ff., 137n23; Wickkiser 1999). Yet if the Philomela episode is one that was composed in exile (which is likely given the themes of isolation and speech loss that, as we have seen, are prevalent in the exile literature as a whole), the character of Philomela could be seen as an analogue to Ovid himself: forcefully taken to Thrace by an overzealous ruler who, in Ovid's eyes, abused him and relegated him to a life of voicelessness and isolation.

If we can make that step, it is appealing to read the intertext between Virgil and Ovid as a commentary by Ovid on the effect of exile on his poetry. By drawing explicit attention to a passage in which allusion emphasizes Virgil's poetic power, Ovid can compare the effect that his exile at the hands of Augustus had on his own poetic power. This allusive chain is then activated again in the passage from *Epistulae ex Ponto* 1.3 with which we began our discussion of allusion:

Nescio qua natale solum dulcedine cunctos
    ducit et inmemores non sinit esse sui.

Quid melius Roma? Scythico quid frigore peius?
 Huc tamen ex ista barbarus urbe fugit.
Cum bene sit clausae cauea *Pandione natae*,
 nititur in silvas illa redire suas.
Adsuetos tauri saltus, adsueta leones—
 nec feritas illos inpedit—antra petunt.
 (*Pont.* 1.3.35–42)

[By some sweetness one's native land leads back everyone and does not allow them to forget it. What is better than Rome? What is worse than the Scythian cold? Yet hither a barbarian flees from that city. Although it fares well for the daughter of Pandion, locked up in a cage, she strives to return to her forests. Bulls seek their accustomed glades, lions their accustomed caves—and their fierceness does not prevent them.]

The exile alludes to the Philomela episode not merely to draw a narrative link between his situation and that of Philomela but also to draw an intertextual link between the effect of exile on his poetry and that of it on Ovid's. Like Ovid, the exile's poetic ability has been compromised, and two terms serve to make this clear: *silvas* and *cavea*. The term *silvas* needs no further elucidation, as it is an allusive link to both Ovid and Virgil and refers to its metaphorical meaning as "raw" poetic material. *Cavea*, although carrying a basic meaning of "cage," also can refer to the performance space of a theater.[60] Moreover, throughout the exile literature, the exile makes consistent reference to his performance in Getic and Sarmatian contexts, many times expressing his displeasure.[61] If *cavea* is read as referring to the theater instead of a cage, combined with the metaphoric meaning of *silvas*, the line can be interpreted to express the dissatisfaction of the exile with his relegation to a foreign stage. Although he longs to return to his native poetic fields (*suas silvas*), he must be content performing on a foreign stage (*cavea*).

Therefore, as I hope to have shown, after losing his speech and falling into the same schematic traps of death, emotion, and loss of community as characters in the *Metamorphoses* had done, the exile exists in a state of speechlessness and isolation. Again, Ovid uses characters such as Philomela to act as analogs to the exile and colors the exile's situation with the same brush he used to portray transformed characters in the *Metamorphoses*. Yet although Ovid uses much the same vocabulary to draw attention to this relationship, his poetic method goes far beyond the reuse of terminology but rather is a dynamic web of allusions and intertexts. Still, all these methods are employed to a single end: the characterization of the exile as existing in a schematic state similar to that in which transformed characters are trapped. Isolated and speechless, he constantly searches for methods of having his voice heard, of breaking out of the schematic trap of speech loss. In the end, he comes to the same conclusion as Io and Philomela: the written medium. Thus, it is to the exile's use of writing to mediate his social and linguistic isolation that I will now turn.

## Littera pro Verba:
## The Written Medium as Mediating Device

At the beginning of *Epistulae ex Ponto* 2.6, the exile explicitly describes the relationship between his exilic situation and the act of writing:

> Carmine Graecinum, qui praesens voce solebat,
>     tristis ab Euxinis Naso salutat aquis.
> *Exulis haec vox est*: praebet mihi littera linguam
>     et, si non liceat scribere, *mutus* ero.
>         (*Pont.* 2.6.1–4)

[With a song and from the Euxine sea, sad Naso greets Graecinus, who was accustomed to be present in voice. This is the voice of the exile: letters offer a tongue to me, and if it were not allowed to write, I would be mute.]

In these lines, the exile calls to mind many of the speechless situations in the *Metamorphoses*. As in the Echo narrative, in which Ovid emphasizes the distinction between articulate (*vocare*) and inarticulate (*sonare*) sounds, the exile describes an Echo-like voice. Because of his isolation, the exile does not have a true *vox*, over which he has total control. Instead, he must rely on a surrogate *vox* dependent on the written word. The written word can provide the exile with a *lingua*, the physical seat of articulate speech, the very appendage that was taken from Philomela to render her voiceless. Yet without writing, the exile would be relegated to a state of *mutus*, a term that we have seen has strong schematic associations with the nonhuman and noncommunal.

As such, the exile calls attention to the intention behind the adoption of the written word: in a similar situation to transformed characters from the *Metamorphoses*, the exile is attempting to write his way out of schematic voicelessness, following the pattern set forth by Philomela and Io. The close correspondence between the exile and these characters is made even more explicit in *Epistulae ex Ponto* 1.7:

> *Littera pro verbis* tibi, Messaline, salutem
>   quam legis a saevis attulit usque Getis.
> *Indicat auctorem locus*? An nisi nomine lecto
>   haec me Nasonem scribere verba latet?
>     (*Pont.* 1.7.1–4)

[A letter for words, Messallinus, has borne you the greetings, which you read, all the way from the savage Getes. Does the place identify the author? Or, unless the name has been read, does the fact that I, Naso, write these words escape you?]

At the opening of this letter to Messallinus, the exile describes his writing as *littera pro verbis* and wonders whether the addressee would recognize who had sent the letter if the name were not included. The phrase *littera pro verbis* is telling, however, as it alludes to the type of writing used by Io to identify herself to her family:[62]

> illa manus lambit patriisque dat oscula palmis
> nec retinet lacrimas et, si modo verba sequantur,
> oret opem nomenque suum casusque loquatur;
> *littera pro verbis*, quam pes in pulvere duxit,
> corporis indicium mutati triste peregit.
>     (*Met.* 1.646–50)

[She licks [Inachus's] hands and gives kisses to the fatherly palms, but she cannot hold back tears, and if only words were able to follow, she would beg for help and say her name and misfortunes. In place of words, her hoof traced letters in the dust, a sad token of her changed body.]

Like Io, who uses her writing as an attempt to describe the *triste indicium* of her misfortune, the exile writes his letters in an attempt to describe the misfortunes of his exile. Moreover, his line of questioning regarding his name and his ultimate statement of the name Naso correlates to the traditional interpretation that the *indicium* traced by Io is, in fact, her name.[63]

What these two excerpts from the *Epistulae ex Ponto* highlight is the emphasis placed on writing throughout the exile literature. In fact, scholars have long commented on the act of writing in the exile literature. Nagle associated Ovid's interest in writing with the concepts of *utilitas* and *gloria*, that the exile was writing (1) "as a means to an end, to influence others and thus obtain a transfer or recall from exile," (2) "for its immediate effect, as an ends in itself," and (3) as a means of garnering further poetic reputation (1980, 71–72). Gareth Williams reads Ovid's writing as a means through which the exile could represent the slippage of his poetic *ingenium*, as the "weight of his *mala* crushes his *ingenium*, depriving it of creative vitality [and creating] the lack of polish and correction in his verse" (1994, 50). Juliette Cherbuliez (2005), taking a different angle, associates the emphasis on writing as a means of emphasizing the metaphor of writing as a critique of authority.[64]

These discussions, and all those studies like them, however, focus on the larger questions of why Ovid the creator-poet decided to focus on the theme of writing. Our discussion instead focuses on *how the act of writing* fits into the schematic pattern of speech loss, community loss, and mediating writing, and not on the larger poetics of the topos of writing in the exile literature. In essence, in this section we are examining what the exile does on the narrative level, and not what Ovid's use of writing may reveal about his larger literary or political aims. That broader, more overarching level will be discussed in chapter 4, as well as the issue of why Ovid the creator-poet manipulated the schematic associations of speech loss from the *Metamorphoses* to describe the exilic condition.

On the narrative level of the exile, one particular aspect of the act of writing in the exile literature concerns us here: the writing of epistles.[65] Having been stripped of speech and isolated from community, the exile follows the lead of characters such as Philomela and Io and attempts to use epistolography as his means of reconnecting with his lost community. Therefore, each one of the poems in both *Tristia* and *Epistulae ex Ponto* is set up as a poetic epistle to friends and family of the exile in Rome. Moreover, as noted by Evans (1983, 171–74), the progression of epistolary form from the *Tristia* to the *Epistulae ex Ponto* dramatizes the increasing immediacy of the exile's condition: the poems move from a collection of *privata carmina* for unspecified addressees in *Tristia* 1–4 to *publica carmina* (*Tr.* 5.1.23) for unspecified addressees in *Tristia* 5 to finally a collection of public letters for specific and named addressees (*Pont.* 1.17–18: *et epistula cui sit / non occultato nomine missa docet*) in *Epistulae ex Ponto* 1–3.[66]

*Letters as Conversation: Ancient Epistolographic Theory*

As can be thus observed from the construction of this portion of the exilic corpus, epistolography is fundamental to understanding the characterization of the exile and his writing. This section, therefore, will focus on the use of epistolography to describe the exile's writing aims to mediate his speech loss and allow him to communicate with his lost community, completing the exilic schematic version of the pattern that Ovid developed in the *Metamorphoses*. First, we will consider how the epistolary form is the ideal *modus loquendi* for an individual suffering from physical speech loss by discussing how the epistle was seen as a surrogate for speech, an actual *littera pro verbis* in ancient epistolographic theory. Then we will explore how the use of the epistolographic form is used to describe the plight of the exile and identify the exact nature of this communication with friends and family. Finally, we will conclude our conversation about epistolography with a discussion of the audience of the letters to determine whether the exile, like Philomela and Io, was successful in his attempts to reconnect.

In his use of the epistolary form in the exile literature, Ovid depicts the exile's attempts at writing within the theoretical boundaries of epistolographic convention and uses that theory to emphasize the relationship between the exile's letters and his speech loss. In particular, Ovid calls attention to two aspects of epistolographic theory: (1) the letter as one half of a conversation spoken at distance, and (2) the letter as a symbol of the physical presence of the author. Both of these theoretical aspects serve to connect the exile both verbally and physically with his lost community: through letters he not only can communicate his identity to his community but also gains a surrogate voice.

Turning to the letter as conversation first, ancient epistolary theory defined a letter as a half of a dialogue and a medium through which an individual could have a conversation with an absent friend as though she or he were present.[67] Examples from the letters of Cicero and Seneca the Younger bear this out, as well as those from the, albeit much later, epistolary handbook of Pseudo-Libanius:

Epistularum genera multa esse non ignoras sed unum illud certissimum, cuius causa inventa res ipsa est, ut *certiores faceremus absentis* si quid esset quod eos scire aut nostra aut ipsorum interesset. (Cic. *Fam.* 2.4.1)

[You are not ignorant that there are many types of letters, but also one in particular, for which reason the whole business was invented, namely, that we might make those absent more certain, if anything happened that was important for them or for ourselves to know.]

tamen adlevor cum *loquor* tecum *absens*, multo etiam magis cum tuas litteras lego. (Cic. *Att.*, 12.39.2)

[Yet, I am lightened when I, though absent, speak with you, much more than even when I read your letters.]

Minus tibi accuratas a me epistulas mitti querereris. Quis enim accurate *loquitur* nisi qui vult putide loqui? Qualis *sermo* meus esset si una desideremus aut ambularemus, inlaboratus et facilis, tales esse epistulas meas volo, quae nihil habent accersitum nec fictum. (Sen. *Ep.* 75.1)

[You complain that letters sent to you by me are rather carelessly written. Indeed, who talks carefully unless he also desires to talk pedantically? I prefer that my letters, which have nothing strained or artificial about them, should be just like what my conversation would be if you and I were sitting together or walking together, spontaneous and relaxed.]

Φιλική. Γνησίων εὐπορήσας γραμματηφόρων ἐσπούδασα τὴν σὴν ἀγχίνοιαν *προσειπεῖν*. ὅσιον γὰρ ὑπάρχει τοὺς γνησίους φίλους παρόντας μὲν τιμᾶν, *ἀπόντας δὲ προσερεῖν*. (Pseudo-Libanius, *Epistolary Characters* 2.58)

[The friendly type: As I have noble letter carriers at hand, I hasten to address your shrewdness. For it is a holy thing to be ready to honor noble friends who are present, and to speak with those who are not.]

In all three of these examples, the letter form is described as a means of communicating with another person; for Cicero it is a way to make those absent understand what is going on in their absence (*certiores faceremus absentis*). Yet beyond a simple communicative device, the letter is described as an actual, *spoken* conversation (*cum loquor tecum absens*). For Seneca, a letter is a *sermo* in which he should speak (*loquitur*) as if he were conversing with someone in person. Pseudo-Libanius, in his handbook of epistolary forms, combines the Ciceronian and the Senecan concepts and asserts that an ἐπιστολη is a manner of verbally speaking to absent ones (προσειπεῖν; ἀπόντας δὲ προσερεῖν).

In addition to being considered as a surrogate for speech, the epistolary form could also be conceived of as a symbol for selfhood, a parchment-like personification of ones very identity.[68] In this sense, sending an addressee a letter was akin to sending a piece of yourself to that person, with the remnants of your touch, smell, and handwriting creating the illusion that you yourself are present. Consider these examples:

Quod frequenter mihi scribis, gratias ago. Nam quo uno modo potes, te mihi ostendis. Numquam epistulam tuam accipio, ut non protinus una simus. Si imagines nobis amicorum absentium iucundae sunt, quae memoriam renovant et desiderium falso atque inani solacio levant, quanto iucundiores sunt litterae, *quae vera amici absentis vestigia, veras notas adferunt*? (Sen. *Ep.* 40.1)

[I thank you for writing to me so often, for you are revealing your real self to me in the only way you can. I never receive a letter from you without being in your company forthwith. If the pictures of our absent friends are pleasing to us, though they only refresh the memory and lighten our longing by a solace that is unreal and unsubstantial, how much more pleasant is a letter, which brings us real traces, real evidences, of an absent friend?]

*complexus* igitur *sum* cogitatione *te absentem*, epistulam vero osculatus etiam ipse mihi gratulatus sum. (Cic. *Fam.* 3.11.2)

[Therefore, I embraced you, absent, in my mind, and truly also rejoiced in the letter.]

Seneca, writing to Lucilius, describes the letter that he received as containing traces of an absent friend (*amici absentis vestigia*). For him, the letter was a personification of the sender because it contained physical traces of the sender within it. The conception of letter-as-self is made even clearer in the Ciceronian passage, as Cicero equates the letter he received (*epistulam*) with the actual person who sent it (*te absentem*). Both of these examples are indicative of the way in which the physical letter was conceived of in antiquity.

The concept of letter-as-self is also of utmost importance to the exile throughout the *Tristia*. In the opening poems of both book 1 and book 3, the exile describes how he, as a poet, can return to Rome in the form of his *libellus* and how its metrical foot can go where his human foot cannot.

vade, liber, verbisque meis loca grata saluta:
   contingam certe quo licet illa pede.
      (*Tr.* 1.1.15–16)

[Go, book, greet places accepting of my words: those places where it is certainly permitted for me to touch with my foot]

Aspicis exsangui chartam pallere colore?
   Aspicis alternos intremuisse pedes?
      (*Tr.* 3.1.55–56)

[Do you see the paper pale with bloodless color? Do you see that its alternating feet have been trembling?]

Altera templa peto, vicino iuncta theatro:
  haec quoque erant pedibus non adeunda meis.
    (Tr. 3.1.69–70)

[I seek other temples, near the theater district: these also ought not to have been traversed by my feet.]

Likewise, in a letter to Ovid's stepdaughter, the exile employs the same concept of letter-as-self, but in this instance Perilla actually responds to the letter's arrival as if the exile were there in person and even engages in *sermonibus* with the letter:

Vade salutatum, subito perarata, Perillam,
  littera, *sermonis* fida ministra mei.
Aut illam invenies dulci cum matre sedentem,
  aut inter libros Pieridasque suas.
Quicquid aget, *cum te scierit venisse*, relinquet,
  nec mora, quid venias quidve, *requiret*, agam.
    (Tr. 3.7.1–6)

[Go quickly, scribbled letter, loyal servant of my conversations, to greet Perilla. Either you will find her sitting with her sweet mother or among books and her muses. Whatever she is doing, when she knows you have come, she will stop and, without delay, will inquire why you came and how I am doing.]

In addition to the theoretical aspects of epistolography linking the exile's writing with the recovery of a surrogate voice and a metaphorical means through which he could mediate his isolation from community, the audience to which the exile's writings were sent can also speak to such an attempt to reconnect with community. In the *Tristia* and the *Epistulae ex Ponto*, there are four major groups of identified addressees: (1) members of the exile's poetic community; (2) members of his family; (3) generic friends and enemies; and (4) Augustus. All these groups have one common denominator: their connection to the exile's poetry. Whereas the members of the exile's community and generic friends and enemies have clear associations with his poetry either through membership in a poetic circle or as topoi in literary letters,[69] the relationship between the two remaining groups, the exile's family and Augustus himself, and poetry are less clear-cut.

To take the relationship between Augustus and poetry first: in the exile's literary epistle to the *princeps*, *Tristia* 2, one of the overarching themes is Augustus's poor understanding of poetry and particularly Ovid's *Ars Amatoria*.[70] As Fulkerson has observed: "Ovid makes fun of the emperor's naïve but dogmatic insistence that literature serve as a model for real life, that fiction matters. We may, in fact, find Ovid's Augustus comically reminiscent of his Phyllis in their mutual inability to distinguish between truth and fiction" (2005, 149–50). Therefore, on the most basic level of reasons for the composition of *Tristia* 2, poetry and poetic composition play a major role.

Likewise, the presence of the exile's family can be read as having an even more direct relationship with poetry. The two family members with whom the exile communicates are his stepdaughter Perilla (*Tr.* 3.7) and his wife (*Tr.* 1.6, 3.3, 4.3, 5.2, 5.5, 5.11, 5.14; *Pont.* 1.4, 3.1). Perilla, in addition to being a member of the exile's family, is also a poetess, and the content of *Tristia* 3.7 focuses entirely on the concept of poetic fame: although old age will soon come, poetic talent and inspiration are immortal (*Tr.* 3.7.33–54).[71] The poetic nature of this letter to Perilla, therefore, is quite clear. The connection between the exile's wife and poetry is somewhat less so. Recently, analyses of the exile's wife have followed the same lines as scholarship on the exile literature more broadly, shifting from a more historical (Helzle 1989) to a more literary (Hinds 1998; Petersen 2005; Reeber 2014) angle. Instead of associating the exile's wife with one of Ovid's actual, historical wives, recent scholarship has increasingly identified the wife as an amalgam of elegiac personae: the fickle *puella*, the elegiac *domina*, and the *matrona* (Petersen 2005). Moreover, Joy Reeber (2014) has gone so far as to equate the wife with a metaphorical representation of a physical and literary corpus in the same way Maria Wyke (2002) has described Cynthia in Propertius.[72] As such, the group of addressees known as the exile's family may more accurately be subsumed under the group of members of his poetic community: Perilla is literally a *sodalis* in that community, and the wife is a metaphor for the exile's poetic contribution to that community.

Therefore, all the writings that make up the *Tristia* and the *Ex Ponto* are rooted in poetry in some fashion. Such a concerted emphasis on a poetic community consequently leads to the question of why and how the exile was attempting to use his writing to reconnect with that community. Whereas Philomela and Io use their writing to mediate the distance between themselves and their families, the exile chooses instead to reconnect with his poetic community. Due to his consistent self-identification as a poet, it is not surprising that the exile chose to focus on his poetic community over his familial, but our understanding of the exact nature of his reconnection with the poetic community and its relationship to our pattern of "speech loss–community loss–reconnection through writing" leaves much to be desired.

However, Sean Alexander Gurd's recent discussion of poetic communities may provide us with a means of exploring the relationship between the exile and his communication with his poetic community. In his analysis, Gurd (2012, 127) argues that the act of literary revision was a form of social performance in the late republic and the early principate. For Cicero, the act of revision—and even the discussion of that act—was a means by which a literary republic could be created: the texts, products of multiple hands, embody the concerns not only of their original authors but also those of entire communities of revision. Moreover, the process of revision substantiated and sustained the community, for "once the [revised product] has been achieved, there is no life in [the act of revision] any more; community consists not in having debated but in actually debating" (49). Gurd then traces the various reactions to this idea of communal revision in the subsequent works of Horace and Pliny, arguing that

> Horace's *Epistles* crossbreed the conventions of the letter with those of satire, and his *Satires* play with intimate confession in a way that is cognate to, if not dependent on, the familiar epistle; Pliny's *Epistles* themselves combine self-presentation in staged moments of epistolary familiarity with the artful design of the Hellenistic poetry book. (2012, 127)

In other words, both Horace and Pliny respond to Cicero's scheme in different manners: Horace took Cicero's emphasis on egalitarian revision and turned it into an imbalanced relationship between poet and reviser in which the poet always fell short of the reviser's expectations and dwelt on his failures in composition; Pliny, on the other hand, continued Cicero's insistence on a community of revision but did not extend that community into the political realm as an opposing scheme to autocracy, instead choosing to create a literary community that exists alongside the political.

Regardless of the angles taken by these three authors, the common denominator of revision as a means of community building has strong resonances in Ovid's exile literature. For throughout the *Tristia* and the *Epistulae ex Ponto*, the exile makes constant references to his participation in revision both past and present. Therefore, against the background of Gurd's concept of "communities of revision," the exile's repeated letters to his poetic community and his emphasis on the process of revising poetry can be read as an attempt to use his writing to reconnect himself with a poetic community and, more specifically, a community of poetic revision.

A clear instance of the exile's attempts to reestablish a presence in a community of revision can be seen at the end of *Tristia* 1.7, a poem written to an unnamed poet or member of a poetic community (*sodalis*, 10) in which the exile apologizes for the "unfinished" state of his *Metamorphoses*:

> ablatum mediis opus est incudibus illud,
>  defuit et coeptis ultima lima meis.
> et veniam pro laude peto, laudatus abunde,
>  non fastiditus si tibi, lector, ero.
> hos quoque sex versus, in prima fronte libelli
>  si praeponendos esse putabis, habe:
> "orba parente suo quicumque volumina tangis,
>  his saltem vestra detur in urbe locus.
> quoque magis faveas, non haec sunt edita ab ipso,
>  sed quasi de domini funere rapta sui.
> quicquid in his igitur vitii rude carmen habebit,
>  emendaturus, si licuisset, eram."
>          (*Tr.* 1.7.29–40)

[That work was borne off while still on the anvil, and the final polish was lacking for my undertakings. I seek forgiveness in place of praise, and I will be praised abundantly if you do not scorn me, reader. These six verses affix on the front of that little book if you think they are worthy: "You who touch these volumes, bereft of their begetter, at least let a place in your city be given to these, a greater favor, since they were not edited by the begetter himself but were snatched away just as from his funeral. Therefore, whatever fault this rough work may have, I'd have amended it, if I'd been allowed."]

In these lines, the exile writes to a *sodalis*, a member of poetic community—most likely of his lost community—and provides a revision for his earlier *Metamorphoses* along with the reasons why such revision is necessary. Yet it is not the quality of the work that concerns the exile here but the yearning for participation in a poetic community.

This distinction is made earlier in the poem, when the exile bestows on his work a sort of canonical status, describing how he has tried to destroy the text on his way to death in exile; however, the texts were not totally destroyed because other copies already existed:

> haec ego discedens, sicut bene multa meorum,
>     ipse mea posui maestus in igne manu.
> utque cremasse suum fertur sub stipite natum
>     Thestias et melior matre fuisse soror,
> sic ego non meritos mecum peritura libellos
>     imposui rapidis viscera nostra rogis:
> vel quod eram Musas, ut crimina nostra, perosus,
>     vel quod adhuc crescens et rude carmen erat.
> quae quoniam non sunt penitus sublata, sed extant
>     (pluribus exemplis scripta fuisse reor)
>         (*Tr.* 1.7.13–24)

[Leaving, mournful, I threw it on the fire, myself, along with so many other things of mine. As Althaea, they say, burning the brand, burned her son, and proved a better sister than a mother, so I threw the innocent books, that had to die with me, my vital parts, on the devouring pyre: because I detested the Muses, my accusers, or because the poem was rough and still unfinished. The verses were not totally destroyed: they survive—several copies of the writings, I think, were made—(trans. Kline 2003)]

Two things must be noted here. First, there is a possible allusion to the famous tradition of Virgil and his attempt to burn the *Aeneid* on his deathbed.[73] Although it is uncertain how early that tradition came into being, it is enticing to read this passage against that tradition,[74] for if Ovid is alluding to the Virgilian tradition here, he is co-opting for his *Metamorphoses* the same canonical status by creating a similar tradition (Stok 2010, 111). Moreover, such an adoption of canonical status would place the *Metamorphoses* on the level of immortal poetry, as an *opus quod nec Iovis ira nec ignis nec poterit ferrum nec edax abolere vetustas* (*Met.* 15.871–72), which he professes it to be at the end of the work. Second, the canonical tradition includes a statement that multiple copies survived (*pluribus exemplis scripta fuisse reor*). This means that the work was popular enough to be circulating but also possibly that there may have been multiple editions of revision.[75] In either case, the mention of copies seems to presuppose the exile's activity in a poetic community.

So through the mention of a canonical tradition of the *Metamorphoses*, the exile accomplishes two things: he depicts his previous involvement with a literary group and asserts that his work was good enough to stand beside the *Aeneid*. With this in mind, the exile mentions revision and the new lines to be affixed to the *Metamorphoses* not because the work lacked quality but in an attempt to recover the community of revision, which he has lost.

Such reminiscences of the exile about past communities of revision can also be found throughout the exile literature, and frequently they are deployed to exhort members of those communities to reconnect and to include the exile in their circles in the present, as well. In such instances, the exile first recalls for his addressees a past time in which they had engaged in a community of revision together. In *Epistulae ex Ponto* 2.4, the he reminds Atticus of their poetic connection:

> Ante oculos nostros posita est tua semper imago
>     et videor vultus mente videre tuos.
> Seria multa mihi tecum conlata recordor
>     nec data iucundis tempora pauca iocis.
> Saepe citae longis visae sermonibus horae,
>     saepe fuit breuior quam mea verba dies.
> Saepe tuas venit factum modo carmen ad auris
>     et nova iudicio subdita Musa tuo est.
> Quod tu laudaras, populo placuisse putabam
>     —hoc pretium curae dulce recentis erat—
> utque meus lima rasus liber esset amici,
>     non semel admonitu facta litura tuo est.
>         (*Pont.* 2.4.7–18)

[Your image is always in front of my eyes, and I seem to see your features in my mind. Often I remember discussing my serious productions with you, yet not a small time was given to pleasant jokes. Often, the hours seemed short with long conversations, often the day was shorter than my words. Often a newly composed poem came to your ears and a new Muse was critiqued by your judgment. That which you had praised, I used to think would have been pleasing to the people—this was the sweet reward of fresh critique—that my book would be shaped by a friend's file, and more than once an erasure was made because of your advice.]

Similarly, he enjoins the poet Tuticanus in *Epistulae ex Ponto* 4.12:

> *tibi carmina mittam,*
> *paene mihi puero cognite paene puer,*

> perque tot annorum seriem quot habemus uterque
>     non mihi quam fratri frater amate minus.
> *Tu bonus hortator, tu duxque comesque fuisti,*
>     *cum regerem tenera frena novella manu.*
> *Saepe ego correxi sub te censore libellos,*
>     *saepe tibi admonitu facta litura meo est,*
> *dignam Maeoniis Phaeacida condere chartis*
>     *cum te Pieriae perdocuere deae.*
> Hic tenor, haec viridi concordia coepta iuventa
>     venit ad albentis inlabefacta comas.
> Quae nisi te moveant, duro tibi pectora ferro
>     esse vel invicto clausa adamante putem.
> Sed prius huic desint et bellum et frigora terrae,
>     invisus nobis quae duo Pontus habet,
> et tepidus Boreas et sit praefrigidus Auster,
>     et possit fatum mollius esse meum
> quam tua sint lasso praecordia dura *sodali*.
>         (*Pont.* 4.12.19–37)

[I'll sing you in some measure, send you a song, you, known to me, barely a lad, when you were barely a lad, and, through the ranks of all the many years we've seen, no less beloved by me than brother by brother. When I first controlled the reins, in my weak grasp, you were kind encouragement, my friend and guide. I often revised my works with you acting as critic, I often made changes based on your suggestions, while the Muses, those Pierian goddesses, taught you how to compose a Phaeacis worthy of Homer's pages. This steady path, this harmony begun in green youth, has extended undiminished to white-haired age. If that didn't move you, I'd think you'd a heart encased in hard iron or unbreakable steel. But this land will sooner be free of war and cold, the two things hateful Pontus offers me, sooner might north winds be warm, south winds cold, and my fate have the power to be gentler, than your heart be harsh to your weary friend. (trans. Kline 2003)]

And again, the exile reminds Messallinus of their past engagement in poetic revision, this time in multiple locations but always with the same refrain:

> quo vereare minus ne sim tibi crimen amicus,
>     invidiam, siqua est, auctor habere potest.

nam tuus est primis cultus mihi semper ab annis—
   hoc certe noli dissimulare—pater,
ingeniumque meum (potes hoc meminisse) probabat
   plus etiam quam me iudice dignus eram;
deque meis illo referebat versibus ore,
   in quo pars magnae nobilitatis erat.
     (*Tr.* 4.4.25–32)

[Don't fear lest my friendship with you be a crime, if there's any harm its author can be blamed. I always honoured your father from my earliest days—at least don't wish that fact to be concealed, and (you may remember) he approved my talent even more than, in my judgement, it deserved: he used to speak of my verse with that eloquence which was a part of his great nobility. (trans. Kline 2003)]

Nec tuus est genitor nos infitiatus amicos,
   hortator studii causaque faxque mei,
cui nos et lacrimas, supremum in funere munus,
   et dedimus medio scripta canenda foro.
Adde quod est frater, tanto tibi iunctus amore
   quantus in Atridis Tyndaridisque fuit:
is me nec comitem nec dedignatus amicum est,
   si tamen haec illi non nocitura putas;
     (*Pont.* 1.7.27–34)

[Your father didn't repudiate my friendship, he, the spur, the torch, the reason for my studies: for whom I shed tears, the last gift to the dead, and wrote verses to be sung in the midst of the forum. And there's your brother, joined to you by as great a love as that which joined the sons of Atreus, or the Twins: he didn't disdain me as a friend and companion: if you don't think these words likely to harm him. (trans. Kline 2003)]

In all the above examples, the exile reminds the addressees of their previous engagement in poetic revision. He remembers the multiple times he submitted a new poem for Atticus to criticize and edit (*Saepe tuas uenit factum modo carmen ad auris / et noua iudicio subdita Musa tuo est*). Likewise, the exile reminds Tuticanus of how they used to write epic poetry (*Tu bonus hortator, tu duxque comesque fuisti, / cum regerem tenera frena nouella manu*) and how he plans to continue to write such epic from exile (*tibi carmina mittam*). Both of these individuals are identified by the exile as his *sodales* (Atticus = *Pont.* 2.4.33; Tuticanus = *Pont.* 4.12.37), linking them to the exile in past communities of revision. In Messallinus's case, the relationship is different, but the emphasis on community remains. Messallinus is not a *sodalis* of the exile but the son of his literary patron, Messalla Corvinus. The exile reminds Messallinus of how Messalla Corvinus had nurtured him (*ingeniumque meum probabat*) and encouraged his studies (*hortator studii*), exhorting Messallinus to continue the patronage that his father had begun and to continue to include the exile in his literary circle.

After reminding the addressees of past poetic interaction, the exile then turns to the purpose of his letter: to urge them to continue that same interaction and to foster a community of revision with the newly exiled poet. He proclaims his faith that Tuticanus will never forsake him and will always be a *sodalis* through the use of *adunata* to describe things that would happen before Tuticanus would forget him.[76] Likewise, the same use of *adunata* is employed in regard to Atticus, as the exile states that days would be longer in the winter and Babylon would be colder than Pontus before Atticus would forget that the exile was his *sodalis* (*Pont.* 2.4.25–28). In Messallinus's case, the exile takes a more formal and reserved approach and, while appealing to Messallinus's sense of *officium*, explains logically that there is no danger in continuing to include him (*Tr.* 4.4.35–54).

Yet perhaps the clearest and most vivid example of the exile's use of writing to return to the lost communities of revision comes in *Epistulae ex Ponto* 3.5, a letter to Maximus Cotta. In the epistle, the exile thanks Cotta for sending him a copy of a speech that he had recently delivered in Rome (ll. 5–12). After then bemoaning the fact that he had missed the opportunity to sit and hear the speech delivered in person, the exile bursts into a series of questions punctuated by imperatives and an anaphoric *ecquid*:

Dic tamen, o iuvenis studiorum plene meorum,
    ecquid ab his ipsis admoneare mei.
Ecquid, ubi aut recitas factum modo carmen amicis
    aut, quod saepe soles, exigis ut recitent,
quaeror, ut interdum tua mens, oblita quid absit,
    nescioquid certe sentit abesse sui,
utque loqui multum de me praesente solebas,
    nunc quoque Nasonis nomen in ore tuo est?
        (*Pont.* 3.5.37–44)

[But tell me, O youth, pregnant with my studies, if anything among them reminds you of me when you read your friends a new made poem, or, as you often used to, urge them to recite, do you sometimes think your mind, unsure what's missing, nevertheless feels that something is missing, and as you often used to talk about me, present, is Ovid's name on your lips, even now? (trans. Kline 2003)]

The exile's mind turns to an image of Cotta reciting poetry in a literary group, and he wonders if Cotta remembers the time when the exile was present in the group. The emotional use of *ecquid* and the rambling nature of a sentence pieced together over three couplets emphasize the exile's grief at the image of what he has lost. Instead of being present in a community of poets, the he is left isolated and forced to read transcripts of what was occurring. Yet he concludes with a reminder of how close writing letters to Cotta makes him feel to the community:

Hac ubi perveni nulli cernendus in Urbem,
    saepe loquor tecum, saepe loquente fruor.
Tum mihi difficile est quam sit bene dicere quamque
    candida iudiciis illa sit hora meis.
Tum me, si qua fides, caelesti sede receptum
    cum fortunatis suspicor esse deis.
      (*Pont.* 3.5.48–54)

[When I enter the City in this [letter], unseen by all, I often speak with you, and enjoy your speech. I can't tell you then how blessed I am, and how bright that hour is to my mind. Then, if you can believe it, I dream I've been received in the heavenly realm, to exist among the happy gods. (trans. Kline 2003)]

Although isolated in body from his poetic community, the exile can overcome the isolation through speaking in letter form, *littera pro verbis*. Then he can be a part of his community, and, perhaps Cotta may read some of the exile's poetry in the communal meetings.

    As I hope to have shown, therefore, the use of letters in the exile literature acts as writing through which the exile can overcome the schematic associations of speech loss and reconnect with his lost community, just as Philomela's tapestry or Io's markings did for them. The use of epistles as the means of mediating the distance between the exile and his lost community is especially appropriate because of the theoretical background of epistolography and because of the poetic audience to whom the letters were ostensibly addressed. In epistolographic theory, the letter served as a surrogate voice, as one half of a vocal conversation held at a distance. Letters were also seen as metaphors for the sender's body, as the letter brought actual markings made by the sender's person. In these ways, the letters were the most appropriate means to describe the exile's attempts to regain his voice and to reconnect with his community. Moreover, the poetic audience of the letters fits well when read against the use of literary revision as the creation of a poetic community at the time of Ovid's exile. By making reference to revision and even by sending revisions of previous poetry through his letters, the exile is attempting to reconnect with his community in another manner.

Thus Ovid's manipulation of the speech-loss schema that undergirded so many transformations in the *Metamorphoses* is brought to bear in the exile literature. Just as transformed characters lost the ability to speak, were isolated from their community, and attempted to reconnect with community through writing, so Ovid describes the exile as undergoing a transformation and speech loss in *Tristia* 1.3, struggling to negotiate his identity in the wake of the loss of his community and attempting to reconnect to his lost community through the writing of letters. Yet one final question remains. Philomela and Io, the two characters from the *Metamorphoses* who employ writing to regain community, are successful in doing so and have their voice, identity, and community restored. Was the exile so lucky? Did his plan work?

The answer, it seems to me, is a qualified "yes." Although the exile is never successful in attaining a physical return to his community, he does find a voice through his letters and is successful in communicating with his community. As we have seen, on multiple occasions the exile refers to letters and copies of speeches he has received from members of his community in Rome.[77] Therefore, on some level, there is a connection with his poetic community. Moreover, the emphasis on poetry in the exile literature leads us to the conclusion that perhaps for the exile physical return was only part of the goal of his writing; for the manner in which he could interact with his poetic community was through his poetry itself. And as we saw at the outset of this chapter, the role of the exile and the experiences through which Ovid puts him re-create the manner in which tales of exile are told. For Seneca and Martial, descriptions of exile took part of their cue from the experiences of Ovid's exile. Now one need not push as far as Claassen (1999) does in saying that such allusions were made by Seneca and Martial because Ovid had invented a "genre" of exile in which they were locating themselves. However, Ovid's description of exile did create a reformulation of the exilic experience that was centered to a large extent on the loss of speech, and as Jennifer Ingleheart (2011) and others have shown, the notion of speech loss became a much more dominant method of describing exile after Ovid. So, in this way, Ovid's exile has connected himself to a community of poets much larger than he perhaps intended, for his isolation and speech loss gave rise to a community of exiles described in those same terms. Yet maybe that is exactly what he had in mind, as he always kept an eye to the continuance of his poetry into posterity and how it would be remembered. It is with this concept of poetic memory, therefore, that we will conclude our discussion in the next chapter.

*chapter 4*

# Speech Loss and Memory in the Exile Literature

Sed tamen, qui semel verecundiae fines transierit, eum bene et naviter oportet esse impudentem. Itaque te plane etiam atque etiam rogo, ut et ornes ea vehementius etiam, quam fortasse sentis, et in eo leges historiae negligas gratiamque illam, de qua suavissime quodam in prooemio scripsisti, a qua te flecti non magis potuisse demonstras quam Herculem Xenophontium illum a Voluptate, eam, si me tibi vehementius commendabit, ne aspernere amorique nostro plusculum etiam, quam concedet veritas, largiare. Quod si te adducemus, ut hoc suscipias, erit, ut mihi persuadeo, materies digna facultate et copia tua. . . . Atque hoc praestantius mihi fuerit et ad laetitiam animi et ad memoriae dignitatem, si in tua scripta pervenero, quam si in ceterorum, quod non ingenium mihi solum suppeditatum fuerit tuum . . . sed etiam auctoritas clarissimi et spectatissimi viri et in rei publicae maximis gravissimisque causis cogniti atque in primis probati, ut mihi non solum praeconium . . . sed etiam grave testimonium impertitum clari hominis magnique videatur.[1]

—CICERO, *Epistulae ad Familiares* 5.12.3, 7

felices ornent haec instrumenta libellos:
fortunae memorem te decet esse meae.[2]

—OVID, *Tristia* 1.1.9–10

OVER THE PAST THREE CHAPTERS, we have explored the schematic associations of speech loss, community loss, and writing as a medium of reconnection that Ovid developed in the transformation narratives of the *Metamorphoses* and then employed in the exile literature to describe his exilic persona. Whenever a character undergoes a physical metamorphosis, she or he is rendered speechless, and that speechlessness compromises his or her ability to communicate identity and to connect with community. Two characters, however, are able to overcome this handicap through the written medium: Io and Philomela use the respective media of writing and weaving to reconnect with their communities. In the exile literature, Ovid depicts his exilic persona in similar fashion: as one who loses the ability to speak when he assumes the role of *exul* in *Tristia* 1.3; as one who struggles to come to grips with his speech loss throughout the exile literature; and as one who ultimately overcomes his voicelessness in some fashion through the composition of letters to his lost community at Rome.

We ended the previous chapter with the realization that the community to which Ovid's exilic persona was writing was the poetic community and that one of the reasons for this choice of addressees was the fact that the exile self-identified as a poet. In this chapter, we will push this notion of Ovid's audience further, arguing that the main reason for the exile's focus on poetic circles was his concern with memory and, in particular, his memory. In effect, this chapter explores the "why": Why did Ovid choose to describe his exile through the schema of speech loss? What did he hope to achieve by doing so? Exiled from Rome, Ovid faced the all-too-real prospect of being forgotten not only by his friends and family but also by Rome itself. The exact nature of how Ovid ran the risk of being forgotten, how that forgetting was tied to speech loss, and how Ovid conceived of writing as a means of fending off forgetfulness are the topics of this chapter. First, I will situate Ovid's exile in the broader socio-literary context of memory, or *memoria*, in Rome. *Memoria* can be broadly defined as a "memory not bound by historical fact"; it will be defined more fully at the beginning of the next section. As a society intimately linked with *memoria*, Rome provided Ovid with ample ways of exploring his exile in terms of *memoria*. In the late republic, the principate, and the early empire, writers controlled the manner in which literature transmitted the *memoria* of individuals and of Rome itself. Ovid, as a *vates*, held a position as one of these writers while he was in Rome, but upon his exile, his role as a creator of *memoria* was threatened. Second, I will discuss how Ovid uses the schema of speech loss identified in the previous three chapters to comment on his loss of the ability to create and partake in *memoria*. In particular, I will turn to the modern sociological theories of cultural and communicative memory, first developed by Maurice Halbwachs and later expanded on by Jan Assmann, to show the connection made by Ovid between a loss of *memoria* and a loss of speech. Finally, I will examine how Ovid's attempts to maintain communities of revision with his fellow poets through his letters are tantamount to his attempts to retain his ability to create *memoria*. Through the maintenance of his connection with the poetic community, Ovid is able to continue in his position as *vates*, as a creator of *memoria*. Because he is able to keep this ability intact, Ovid can thus craft a new *memoria* for himself, one that effectively both erases the *memoria* of his exile that was based in historical fact and superimposes upon the "true" *memoria* a new *memoria* crafted by Ovid, one that points to the actions of his exilic persona as the *memoria* that Ovid wishes to be remembered. As such, the schematic associations of speech loss, community loss, and writing as a medium of reconnection become not only a narrative description of the exilic persona's life in exile but also a metaphor for Ovid's larger attempts to fashion a *memoria* of exile for himself.

## Memoria in Rome: Setting the Background for Ovid's Exilic Project

### Theoretical Underpinnings

Before discussing Ovid's manipulation of *memoria* in his exile literature, we first must unpack the term *memoria* and situate ourselves within the world of *memoria* in Ovid's Rome. A logical place to start in exploring *memoria* is the *Oxford Latin Dictionary*, which describes the term with no fewer than ten definitions varying from the basic ability, (1) "the power or faculty of remembering" (*OLD* s.v. 1); to a verbal action, (2) "the action or fact of remembering" (*OLD* s.v. 3); to the ability of an entire society to remember, (3) "the collective memory which men have of the past, tradition, history" (*OLD* s.v. 7); to the highly selective, (4) "what is remembered of a person or thing" (*OLD* s.v. 5); to finally the highly subjective, (5) "the period covered by one's recollection" (*OLD* s.v. 6).[3] The underlying concept of *memoria*, then, is multifaceted, but a few foundational concepts can be identified: (1) the term denotes a remembrance of something in the past; (2) the agent who remembers can be an individual, a group of people, or an entire culture; (3) the remembrance of something is entirely subjective.

The first of these concepts does not need any further explanation, but the other two may. The question of the agency of memory—To whom should memory be attributed? To the individual or to the group?—is one that lies at the heart of memory studies, and there are two clear schools of thought.[4] The first school, termed by Paul Ricoeur (2004, 96–97) as *la tradition du regard intérieur*, argues that memory occurs only on the individual level. This tradition takes its cue from the Aristotelian idea that memories are subjective experiences that belong to the individual and work to create a differentiated sense of identity (Arist. *Parv. nat.* 449b15–450b1). The second school, *le regard extérieur*, argues for the existence of a collective consciousness, an amalgamation of remembrances that provides the identity of a group of individuals (Ricoeur 2004, 120–24). The first scholar to argue for such an idea of a group memory was Halbwachs in his *La Mémoire Collective* (1950).[5] For Halbwachs, memory depended on two things:

(1) the group in which an individual lives, and (2) the status an individual holds in that group. An individual can remember only by placing himself or herself in the frameworks of the group's memory (*cadres sociaux de la mémoire*). Moreover, if an individual is removed from the group's memory framework, the individual forgets and is forgotten. Consequently, Halbwachs concluded that memory was not entirely the construction of an individual, as an individual only has memories if she or he is situated in a larger group.

Halbwachs's original concept of collective memory has since been broken down further into two smaller groupings: cultural and communicative memory. This distinction between communicative and cultural memory was first introduced by Jan Assmann (1992) in order to differentiate different types of collective memory that had been treated more or less in the same fashion (figure 4).[6] Communicative memory is noninstitutional (i.e., not supported by any institutions of learning, transmission, and interpretation) and not formalized by any material symbolization (Assmann 2010, 111), but is instead based exclusively in "everyday communication" and is shared and conveyed within a social group defined by common memories of that communication over a time span of only eighty to one hundred years (Assmann and Czaplicka 1995, 127).[7]

Cultural memory, on the other hand, is more systematized and institutionalized than communicative memory. Whereas communicative memory is a

|  | *Communicative memory* | *Cultural memory* |
|---|---|---|
| Content | history in the frame of autobiographical memory, recent past | mythical history, events in absolute past ("in illo tempore") |
| Forms | informal traditions and genres of everyday communication | high degree of formation, ceremonial communication |
| Media | living, embodied memory, communication in vernacular language | mediated in texts, icons, dances, rituals, and performances of various kinds; "classical" or otherwise formalized language(s) |
| Time structure | 80–100 years, a moving horizon of 3–4 interacting generations | absolute past, mythical primodial time, "3,000 years" |
| Participation structure | diffuse | specialized carriers of memory, hierarchically structured |

FIGURE 4. Description of communicative and cultural memory from Assmann 2010, 117.

short-term, nonstandardized form of memory, cultural memory is a long-term, formalized accumulation of objectified symbols that, unlike forms of communication, are "stable and situation-transcendent," as they can be passed from one generation to another and transferred from one situation to another (Assmann 2010, 110–11). Each society's cultural memory is, therefore, comprised of a store of symbols, a collection of "reusable texts, images, and rituals specific to each society in each epoch, whose 'cultivation' serves to stabilize and convey that society's self-image" (Assmann and Czaplicka 1995, 132).[8]

The third concept regarding *memoria*, the question of its subjectivity, is also an aspect that should be unpacked briefly. Alain Gowing, in his 2005 discussion of the deployment of the *memoria* of the republic in imperial Rome, provides the clearest explanation of the subjectivity of *memoria*, defining *memoria* in relationship to modern conceptions of historicity and the Roman concept of *historia*. For Gowing, *memoria* is inherently subjective, as an individual or a group of individuals may recollect an event in a manner that differs considerably from the "historical facts" of the remembered event, individual, or thing.[9] This distinction between subjectivity and historicity is based on the modern notion of what history ought to be, namely, a "set of 'facts' or 'truths' arrived at not through or exclusively through recollection and remembrance, which are notoriously fallible, but through rigorous inquiry and research" (Gowing 2005, 11). Yet *memoria* is not bound by such historistic constraints, for it presents an experiential viewpoint. Moreover, the Romans themselves did not subscribe to such modern distinctions between *memoria* and history, as can be seen from a comparison of *memoria* to *historia*: *Memoria* could be used to describe any recollection of past experiences, regardless of genre; *historia*, likewise, was linked not to a "historiographical" genre but to *any attempt* to transmit the past.[10] In Roman thought, therefore, the relationship between subjective *memoria* and *historia* was not oppositional, as in modern thought, but rather complementary: "*Historia* is simply a vehicle for *memoria*" (Gowing 2005, 12).

So the conception of *memoria* with which we are left and on which we shall base the entire discussion of Ovid in this chapter is multifaceted and ever changing. *Memoria* is the subjective recollection of individuals, groups, or whole societies, and the process of *memoria* can be both static (as in the case of cultural memory) and a constantly changing reevaluation and renegotiation (as in the case of individual or communicative memory). Now that a theoretical basis of *memoria* has been established, we will turn to the Roman context in order to frame our subsequent discussions of Ovid's manipulation of *memoria* in that context.

## Memoria *in Rome*

Over the past three decades, interest in these theoretical formulations of memory and remembrance has burgeoned, leading some scholars to term the trend a "memory boom" (Galinsky 2014, 3). Driven in part by the progressive loss of the generation of individuals who survived the horrors of the Holocaust, memory studies have used such theories to interpret cultural and individual responses to and recollection of traumatic and culturally defining events. Such a reevaluation of the process of memory has not failed to find root in classical studies, as well. More recently, classicists have attempted to reevaluate ancient conceptions and discussions of memory through the prism of memory studies. In particular, Rome has received the lion's share of scholarly attention because of the profound emphasis that Roman culture placed on *memoria*, a focus summed up best by the opening sentence to a recent collection of studies on *memoria Romana*: "Memory defined Roman civilization" (Galinsky 2014, 1).

Studies of the role of *memoria* in Rome have broadly fallen into two categories: (1) material culture and (2) literature. Taking its cue from theoretical concepts outlined in Pierre Nora's *Les lieux de mémoire* (1984–92), studies of material culture have focused on the use of both certain geographical spaces and the iconography and inscriptions of *monumenta* to evoke and influence *memoria*. However, since our discussion is interested in Ovid's literary construction of exile, we shall focus entirely on literature. Two statements concerning the study of literature and *memoria* must be made at the outset: (1) literature both codifies and communicates collective memory; (2) authors of literature have immense control over that *memoria*.

In the context of ancient Rome, this first point can be demonstrated by Livy and Virgil. Livy's history—and indeed historiographical writing in general—is chiefly concerned with the presentation of *exempla* to the audience. These *exempla* were highlighted in order to communicate certain Roman values and to serve as models for how Romans ought to live their lives. Livy says as much in the *Praefatio* to his history:

> ad illa mihi pro se quisque acriter intendat animum, quae vita, qui mores fuerint, per quos viros quibusque artibus domi militiaeque et partum et auctum imperium sit; labente deinde paulatim disciplina velut desidentes primo mores sequatur animo, deinde ut magis magisque lapsi sint, tum ire coeperint praecipites, donec ad haec tempora quibus nec uitia nostra nec remedia pati possumus perventum est. Hoc illud est praecipue in cognitione rerum salubre ac frugiferum, omnis te exempli documenta in

inlustri posita monumento intueri; inde tibi tuaeque rei publicae quod imitere capias, inde foedum inceptu foedum exitu quod vites. (Livy, *Praefatio* 9–10)

[These are the subjects to which I would ask each earnestly turn his attention: what kind of life, what kind of morals there were; through which men and which arts domestic and foreign power was achieved and increased. Then, as discipline gradually lowers, let him follow the decaying customs, then how at first it slowly sinks, then slips downward more and more rapidly, and finally begins to plunge into headlong ruin, until he reaches these days, in which we can bear neither our vices nor their remedies. This is the exceptionally beneficial and fruitful advantage in considering past affairs: that you see documents of every example placed in a clear monument. Thence you may select for yourself and your country what you are to imitate, and also what, disastrous in inception and completion, you are to avoid.]

Livy is interested not only in communicating the shared cultural history of Rome but also in transmitting the cultural memory of what it meant to be Roman. Values such as *industrias*, *pietas*, *gravitas*, and *honestas*—core Roman values—are handed down to following generations in the traditional stories of Romulus, Camillus, the Horatii, and so on, all of which fit Assmann's criteria stated above: "reusable texts, images, and rituals specific to each society in each epoch, whose 'cultivation' serves to stabilize and convey that society's self-image" (Assmann and Czaplicka 1995, 132).

The sixth book of Virgil's *Aeneid*—a *locus communis* for memory study in antiquity, along with Cicero's *Epistulae ad Familiares* 5.12 (see below) and Augustine's *Confessions*—should also be seen as an effort to codify and communicate Roman collective memory. As Anchises shows his son Aeneas the famous Romans who will be his offspring, the external audience is presented with a "history" of Rome that includes many of the *exempla* whose stories both punctuated Livy's history and demonstrated Roman *mores*. As an example, consider this gnomic statement that caps the end of Anchises's penultimate speech in the book:

excudent alii spirantia mollius aera
(credo equidem), vivos ducent de marmore vultus,
orabunt causas melius, caelique meatus
describent radio et surgentia sidera dicent:

tu regere imperio populos, Romane, memento
(hae tibi erunt artes), pacique imponere morem,
parcere subiectis et debellare superbos.
  (Verg. Aen. 6.847–53)

[Others will beat out bronzes breathing so softly (indeed, I believe it), will lead forth living likenesses out of marble, will argue cases better, will describe the measure of the heavens with the rod and will name the surging stars: You, Roman, remember to rule people with power (these will be your arts), and to place custom on peace, to spare the downtrodden and to beat down the proud.]

Again, as can be seen here through the strong imperative *memento* the simultaneously calls to Aeneas and to the external Roman audience, the force of Virgil's and Livy's "recollection" of *exempla* is to communicate a codified version of Roman cultural memory to their audiences.

As to the second point regarding literature and *memoria*, we can remain with *Aeneid* 6. Included in Virgil's rehearsal of Roman cultural memory are members of Augustus's family, both natural and adoptive: Julius Caesar, Marcellus, and Augustus himself (ll. 788ff.; 855ff.). In addition to demonstrating the mores of Roman cultural *memoria* through *exempla*, Virgil weaves the members of Augustus's family into that *memoria*, effectively codifying them as individuals to be held on par with Romulus, Camillus, and other traditional Roman *exempla*. In so doing, Virgil shows the authorial ability to exert control over *memoria* and, to a certain extent, to shape the development of such *memoria*, for here Virgil stakes a claim for Augustus within Roman *memoria* through Augustus's connection to the *gens Iulia* and their descent from Venus and Anchises, a claim providing the *princeps* a portion of divine nature for himself.

Virgil was not the only writer interested in effecting *memoria* for the benefits of the ruling family in Rome. Statius too has been shown to have done similar things for the Flavians in his works. Gianpiero Rosati, in his recent essay on Statius and *memoria* (2014), argues that at various points, Statius helps a *memoria* for the Flavians who otherwise had no claim to imperial power through lineage.[11] In particular, Rosati focuses on the fact that in literature of the principate, the emperor drew power from the celebration of the *memoria* of his triumphs in literature, as their introduction into literature provided the vehicle for their inclusion in the Roman collective consciousness.[12] In the particular instance of the Flavians and Statius, Rosati points to the recollection of the Flavian victory in the war of Jupiter (i.e., the civil war between two "emperors"

Vespasian and Vitellius in 69 CE) in both the opening to his *Thebaid* (*aut defensa prius vix pubescentibus annis / bella Iovis*, 1.21–22) and in the first poem of his *Silvae* (*tu bella Iovis, tu proelia Rheni, / tu civile nefas, tu tardum in foedera montem / longo Marte domas*, 1.1.79–81). The placement of this triumph in a literary context introduces the event into the Roman collective *memoria* and provides a means for the Flavians to legitimate their power in a manner similar to how the *Aeneid* solidified the Julio-Claudian claim.

Beyond Virgil and Statius, one of the most-examined passages in the study of *memoria* in Rome is the Ciceronian passage with which I opened this chapter. In it, Cicero writes to the historian Lucceius regarding a history of Cicero's consulship that Cicero wants Lucceius to write. Cicero's chief concern is that Lucceius write the history in a manner flattering to Cicero (*Itaque te plane etiam atque etiam rogo, ut et ornes ea vehementius etiam, quam fortasse senis*). The goal of doing so would be to present a more dignified *memoria* (*ad memoriae dignitatem*) for Cicero. Although this passage has typically been used to describe the lack of modern historicity in *memoria*, it can also speak to the idea that authors had a great amount of control over how they shaped a *memoria* that could ultimately inform Roman tradition.

As we turn our attention to Ovid, therefore, we need to keep this concept of *memoria* in mind. Ovid, just as Virgil and Statius, was the author of an epic poem that helped define Roman cultural memory: the *Metamorphoses*. Ovid's work created a type of repository of Graeco-Roman mythology, traditional stories that helped the Romans decipher who they were and how to approach their world. Part of this mythology espoused by Ovid was a type of teleological outlook tracing the history of the world from its first seeds (*semina*, 1.9) to the rule of Rome in Ovid's day:

In nova fert animus mutatas dicere formas
corpora; di, coeptis (nam vos mutastis et illas)
adspirate meis primaque ab origine mundi
ad mea perpetuum deducite tempora carmen!
  (*Met.* 1.1–4)

[My mind moves me to speak of forms changed into new bodies; gods, inspire my beginnings (for you have changed even those) and lead an everlasting song from the first beginning of the world to my times.]

Moreover, the last third of the *Metamorphoses* picks up strands of Virgil and Livy, showing traditional *exempla* from Roman cultural memory and incorporating both Julius Caesar and Augustus. Although Ovid's motives for including these sections have been debated, the points regarding *memoria* are clear: Ovid, as a producer of literature, both engages in Roman collective *memoria* and manipulates that *memoria* with the topics he includes.

However, as we saw in chapter 3, when Ovid is exiled, his status is transformed. He is physically removed from his community, and, more importantly, his status as producer of literature is threated. In Halbwachsian terms, he is taken outside the social frameworks of both his physical, Roman society and his literary society. He even shows the particularly Halbwachsian indication of removal from society: speech loss. Most importantly, as a speechless exile, he runs the risk of forgetting and being forgotten.

## Performing *Memoria*

Ovid describes his exile in the schematic terms of speech loss and community loss because both concepts are bound up in the idea of memory. According to communicative memory theory, one must be an active participant in a society in order to take part in that society's memory and, more importantly for Ovid, to be remembered by the society. When he is exiled, Ovid loses his place in communal memory and loses the voice with which he can interact with that memory. Moreover, the loss of his poetic community is especially painful for Ovid because—as just mentioned—poets in ancient Rome had the ability to fashion memory. Thus, in exile, Ovid not only loses his place in communicative memory but also his ability to create memory itself.

Yet, as we discussed in chapter 3, Ovid turns to writing in an effort to mediate his loss of voice and to reintegrate himself in his community. Whereas our previous discussion dealt mostly with *the form* of Ovid's writings back to Rome and the role epistolography played in creating a voice, this section will deal with *the content* of those letters. In particular, it will explore the interplay between community, speech, and memory in the exile literature. Three poems—*Epistulae ex Ponto* 1.9, 2.4, and *Tristia* 1.1—will form the heart of our discussion, as each focuses on issues of speech and community in the explicit context of memory. In the first two of these poems, the exile writes to a friend within the typical conventions of *amicitia*: *Epistulae ex Ponto* 1.9 and 2.4 both address friends, Maximus Cotta and Atticus, who are described as unsure and hesitant about helping or even interacting with the exile.[13] Then the exile urges his addressees to fulfill the duties of *amicitia* by rehearsing a memory of the exile's identity: he reminds each of them of the activities that each had performed with him before his exile. The exile's hope is that his rehearsal will remind the addressees of his identity so that they will be inspired to carry on the same activities with him while he is in exile and, in effect, will re-create the community that the exile has lost. In terms of the memory theory outlined at the beginning of this chapter, through rehearsing his own *memoria* for his addressees, the exile is attempting to place himself back within the social framework of his lost community, allowing himself to be remembered and to remember; in terms of the literary models of this topos, the exile is writing his *memoria* into letters to his lost community in the same manner that Philomela wrote her *memoria* of Tereus's rape into a tapestry for her lost community: in both cases, the writers attempt to gain control over *memoria* and to write a *memoria* that will cause the recipients of that *memoria* to remember the writers and to reconnect with them.

In Ovid's exilic context, *Epistulae ex Ponto* 1.9 and 2.4 aim to effect such a reconnection *via memoria* in the same manner, following a similar narrative sequence that can be broken into three portions. First, the exile broaches the topic of *memoria* by describing how a vision, an *imago*, of the addressee comes before his eyes and causes him to recall times that he and the addressee shared together before exile. Second, he recalls the specifically literary relationship that existed between himself and his addressee, describing how they used to write poetry of various types. Third, he continues his recollection of literary production, pointing out how he and the addressee used to be in a community of poetic revision and how the addressee used to edit the exile's poetic productions before they were performed for the public. The exile closes this final section with an allusion to one of Ovid's prior poetic works, referencing the *Tristia* and *Ars Amatoria*.

*Invoking Memoria*

Starting with the exile's invocation of *memoria* first, we turn our attention to the beginning of two of these poems:

> Ante meos oculos tamquam praesentis imago
>   haeret et extinctum vivere fingit amor.
>     (*Pont.* 1.9.7–8)

[Before my eyes, his image just as if
he were present clung and love made the dead one come alive.]

> Ante oculos nostros posita est tua semper imago
>   et videor vultus mente videre tuos.
>     (*Pont.* 2.4.7–8)

[Your image is always in front of my eyes, and I seem to see your features in my mind.]

In each of these openings, both placed as the fourth couplet of their respective poems, the exile describes how he sees the *imagines* of Celsus and Atticus before his eyes. Such a use of *imago* serves two purposes in this context: (1) to introduce the fact that this is the exile's *memoria* and (2) to depict the exile as an epic hero seeing a vision of a member of his lost community.

The use of *imago* to describe the act of remembering was a prevalent one in Roman literature.[14] In an epistolary context, Cicero uses the term to describe a recollection of his past experiences: *me consolatur recordatio meorum temporum, quorum imaginem video in rebus tuis* (*Fam.* 1.6.2). Likewise, Virgil, another major influence on Ovid's exile literature, uses the term multiple times in the *Aeneid* to refer to memory: Aeneas, having watched the brutal death of Priam at the hands of Neoptolemus, recalls the dangers that his own family faces without him to guard them in the form of an *imago* of his loved ones: *subiit cari genitoris imago, / ut regem aequaeuum crudeli uulnere uidi / uitam exhalantem, subiit deserta Creusa / et direpta domus et parui casus Iuli* (2.560–63); the Sibyl tells Charon to recall the golden bough in his mind as a token that allows Aeneas to cross to the underworld: *"si te nulla mouet tantae pietatis imago, / at ramum hunc" (aperit ramum qui ueste latebat) / "agnoscas"* (6.405–7).[15] Finally, Ovid himself uses the term to describe his memory of the night of his exile in *Tristia* 1.3, introducing the poem-long description of his exile as an *imago*:

> Cum subit illius tristissima noctis *imago*,
>     quae mihi supremum tempus in Urbe fuit,
> cum repeto noctem, qua tot mihi cara reliqui,
>     labitur ex oculis nunc quoque gutta meis.
>         (*Tr.* 1.3.1–4)

[Whenever comes to mind the image, most grievous, of that well-known night, on which was my final time in the city, when I think back to the night on which I left so many things dear to me, there falls even now from these eyes of mine a tear.]

Against this background, the use of *imago* in the context of *Epistulae ex Ponto* 1.9 and 2.4 can be taken as a means of introducing the idea that the descriptions to follow are the exile's rehearsal of *memoria*, his recollections of his lost identity and community.

In addition to the more straightforward interpretation of *imago* as a mental image of recollection, the term also carries markedly epic resonances.[16] In the *Aeneid*, the term *imago* is consistently used to describe the appearance of Aeneas's dead family members to the hero.[17] Moreover, this use of *imago* is sometimes paired with the phrase *ante oculos*:

in somnis, ecce, *ante oculos* maestissimus Hector
visus adesse mihi largosque effundere fletus,
raptatus bigis ut quondam, aterque cruento
puluere perque pedes traiectus lora tumentis.
     (Verg. *Aen.* 2.270–73)

[In my sleep, behold, before my eyes the most sorrowful Hector seemed to be present and to pour out huge tears, as once seized by the chariot, black with gory dirt and dragged with straps through his swollen feet.]

       ipsius umbra Creusae
visa mihi *ante oculos* et nota maior *imago*.
obstipui, steteruntque comae et vox faucibus haesit.

. . .

ter conatus ibi collo dare bracchia circum;
ter frustra comprensa manus effugit imago,
par levibus ventis volucrique simillima somno.
     (Verg. *Aen.* 2.772–74, 792–94)

[The shade of Creusa herself seemed to be present before my eyes and an image, known but somewhat larger. I gaped in astonishment; my hair stood on end and my voice clung to my throat.

. . .

Thrice I tried to throw my arms about her neck; thrice the image, pressed by my hands in vain, fled, equal to the light breeze and most similar to a fleeting dream.]

ille autem: "tua me, genitor, tua tristis *imago*
saepius occurrens haec limina tendere adegit";

. . .

ter conatus ibi collo dare bracchia circum;
ter frustra comprensa manus effugit *imago*,
par levibus ventis volucrique simillima somno.
  (Verg. *Aen.* 6.695–96, 699–701)

[However, [Aeneas] said: "Your sad image, father, your sad image, coming so often to me, drove me to touch these shores;

. . .

thrice I tried to throw my arms about her neck; thrice the image, pressed by my hands in vain, fled, equal to the light breeze and most similar to a fleeting dream.]

In these three passages, Aeneas is visited by Hector, Creusa, and Anchises, all members of his family who have died. Moreover, these specific members of Aeneas's family represent members of his lost Trojan community who continuously guide him until he reestablishes the Trojan community in Italy: Hector warns Aeneas about the Greek raid and instructs him to take the Trojan Penates, symbols of the community, to safety in Italy; Creusa informs Aeneas of her death and tells him that another wife is fated for him, a wife through whom he will solidify the new foundation of the Trojan community; and Anchises is a constant advisor to Aeneas who pushes him ever toward his fate, but here in book 6 his appearance is especially bound up in community, as he rehearses for Aeneas the lineage of the new Trojan community that he will found in Italy.

If the exile's use of *imago* to describe the appearance of Celsus and Atticus before his eyes is read as an allusion to these Virgilian uses, the force of the term changes from only a method of describing a recollection to a more expansive means of depicting the exile as an epic hero who is experiencing visions of members from his own lost community. The exile's situation is fairly analogous to that of Aeneas: the images of Atticus and Celsus, members of his lost poetic community, are always before the exile's eyes, and he hopes that, like Hector, Creusa, and Anchises, both Atticus and Celsus will fulfill their duties as *amici* and will help effect the exile's own refoundation back within his lost community.

## Memoria loquendi: *Recalling a Literary Community*

After having initiated his rehearsal of *memoria* and having drawn a close parallel between his relationship with the addressees and an epic hero's relationship with members of his lost community, the exile expands on his *memoria* and brings it into a markedly literary dimension. For the lost community in which the exile wants to be remembered is not Aeneas's Trojan one but a community of poetic revision (see chapter 3). Therefore, the excerpts of *memoria* on which the exile focuses are instances in which he and the addressees engaged in literary production and revision:

> *Saepe* refert animus *lusus gravitate carentes,*
>     *seria* cum liquida *saepe peracta* fide.
>         (*Pont.* 1.9.9–10)

[Often the mind recalls *lusus* lacking seriousness, often it recalls serious productions acted out with pure faith.]

> *Seria multa* mihi tecum conlata recordor
>     nec data *iucundis* tempora pauca *iocis.*
> *Saepe* citae longis visae sermonibus horae,
>     saepe fuit breuior quam mea verba dies.
> *Saepe* tuas venit factum modo carmen ad auris
>     et nova iudicio subdita Musa tuo est.
> Quod tu laudaras, populo placuisse putabam
>     —hoc pretium curae dulce recentis erat—
> utque meus lima rasus liber esset amici,
>     non semel admonitu facta litura tuo est.
>         (*Pont.* 2.4.9–18)

[Often I remember discussing my serious productions with you, yet not a small time was given to pleasant jokes. Often, the hours seemed short with long conversations, often the day was shorter than my words. Often a newly composed poem came to your ears and a new Muse was critiqued by your judgment. That which you had praised, I used to think would have been pleasing to the people—this was the sweet reward of fresh critique—that my book would be shaped by a friend's file, and more than once an erasure was made because of your advice.]

In both of these passages, the exile continues the theme of *memoria* and reminds the audience that the events he is describing are his recollections (*animus refert*; *recordor*), keeping the following descriptions of literary production within the context of the exile's *memoria*; they are his constructions of his identity, the identity that he wishes to project to his addressees (cf. again Philomela and her construction of her own rape as depicted in her tapestry).[18] Moreover, the literary nature of his *memoria* is highlighted in *Epistulae ex Ponto* 1.9 by the description of his recollection as *refert animus*, which through its metrical position and vocabulary provides an oblique allusion to the opening of the *Metamorphoses*, which uses a version of this phrase to describe the impetus to Ovid's literary production of the epic:

> In nova *fert animus* mutatas dicere formas
> corpora;
> (*Met.* 1.1–2)

[My mind moves me to speak of forms changed into new bodies;]

In the exilic context, the point of such an allusion is that the main theme of the exile's *memoria* is literary in nature, and the exile refers to the fact that he and his addressees engaged in literary production of both the "serious" and the "lighter" variety.

In *Epistulae ex Ponto* 1.9, this antithesis is described in terms of *seria peracta* and *lusus gravitate carentes*. Although one reading of these terms allows for them to be general and not literary-specific, the generically charged nature of the terms lends itself to a literary reading. If cast in terms of literary production, this antithesis would indicate the exile's participation in the production of both serious (e.g., tragic, epic) and more playful (e.g., elegy, epigram, comedy) works. The term *peracta* was commonly used to describe the completion of poetic endeavors but more frequently to describe the act of theatrical performance, as in the following examples from Cicero's *de Senectute*:

> Quibus qui splendide usi sunt, ei mihi videntur *fabulam* aetatis *peregisse* nec tamquam inexercitati histriones in extremo actu corruisse. (Cic. *Sen.* 18.64)

[The men who have put these distinctions to noble use are, it seems to me, like skillful actors who have played well their parts in the drama of life to the end, and not like untrained players who have broken down in the last act.]

> Neque enim histrioni, ut placeat, *peragenda fabula* est, modo, in quocumque fuerit actu, probetur, neque sapientibus usque ad "Plaudite" veniendum est. (Cic. *Sen.* 19.70)

[The actor, for instance, to please his audience need not appear in every act to the very end; it is enough if he is approved in the parts in which he plays; and so it is not necessary for the wise man to stay on this mortal stage to the last fall of the curtain.]

Senectus autem aetatis est *peractio* tamquam *fabulae*, cuius defatigationem fugere debemus, praesertim adiuncta satietate. (Cic. *Sen.* 23.85)

[Moreover, old age is the final scene, as it were, in life's drama, from which we ought to escape when it grows wearisome and certainly when we have had our fill.]

In all these passages, Cicero uses the metaphor of acting on the stage to describe life, using the terms *peragere* and *fabula* to portray the theatricality of it. Thus, in the Ovidian context, it is acceptable to understand the term *peracta* as referring to such theatricality, and the modification of it by *seria* as referring to theatrical or artistic productions of a more serious nature, such as tragedy or epic.

Moreover, the connection between *seria peracta* and the *gravitas* that its opposite generic styles lack adds an even further literary dimension. *Gravitas*—like *lusus* below—had strong generic connotations and often referred to the serious nature of epic and tragedy. Although numerous instances of the term's connotations can be found, two examples suffice to make the point here. First, Quintilian, in his description of the tragic style, chooses the term *gravitas* as indicative of the genre and in contrast to the *elegantia* of comedy: *in tragoediis gravitas, in comoediis elegantia et quidam velut atticismos inveniri potest* (*Inst.* 1.8.8). Second, Ovid, in his famous opening to the *Amores*, juxtaposes the serious style of an epic that he had been planning to compose with the slightly lower tenor of the elegies that he actually composed: *Arma gravi numero violentaque bella parabam / edere, materia conveniente modis. / par erat inferior versus— risisse Cupido / dicitur atque unum surripuisse pedem* (*Am.* 1.1.1).

Juxtaposed against the *seria peracta* and their attendant *gravitas* are the *lusus* that lack *gravitas*. Again, as with *seria peracta*, this phrase too is charged with literary resonances. In particular, the term *lusus* is of interest to us, for by Ovid's time the term already had a long association with more subversive or playful genres such as elegy or epigram. Ovid himself makes this connection throughout the exile literature, frequently using *lusus* to describe the earlier amatory works, and the *Ars Amatoria* in particular.[19] In *Tristia* 2, the exile makes perhaps the most pointed reference in the exile literature to the *Ars* as a *lusus*:

non ea te moles Romani nominis urget,
   inque tuis umeris tam leve fertur onus,
*lusibus* ut possis advertere numen *ineptis*,
   excutiasque oculis otia nostra tuis.
      . . .
Mirer in hoc igitur tantarum pondere rerum
   te numquam nostros evoluisse *iocos*?
At si, quod mallem, vacuum tibi forte fuisset,
   nullum legisses crimen in *Arte mea*.
         (*Tr.* 2.221–24, 239–42)

[The weight of Rome's name is not so light, pressing its burden on your shoulders, that you can turn your power to foolish games, examining my idle things with your own eyes.

. . .

So, should I wonder if, weighed down by such great things, you've never unrolled my witticisms? Yet if, by chance, as I wish, you'd had the time you'd have read nothing criminal in my "Art."]

Here the exile identifies the *Ars* (*Arte mea*) as an example of a *lusus*, using the same vocabulary (*lusus, iocus*) that describes the types of literary productions undertaken by the exile and his addressees in *Epistulae ex Ponto* 1.9 and 2.4. Moreover, the light and playful nature of these *lusus* is juxtaposed against the weight (*pondere*) of the domestic and foreign affairs that should have been at the forefront of Augustus's mind, an antithesis that is reworked in strictly literary terms in *Epistulae ex Ponto* 1.9 and 2.4 through the comparison of the exile's *lusus* to the *gravitas* of the *seria peracta*.

Returning to the context of *Epistulae ex Ponto* 1.9, then, the exile is clearly describing his *memoria* of the interactions between himself and Celsus in terms of literary production: not only is his depiction of his act of remembering (*refert animus*) an allusion to the impetus that drove him to compose the *Metamorphoses*, but the actions in which he remembers engaging with Celsus are literary, both of the serious (*seria*) and the more playful (*lusus gravitate carentes*) in nature. Moreover, the *lusus* he describes come with associations not only to poetry of the neoteric variety in general but also to his own *Ars Amatoria* in particular.

The situation the exile recalls in *Epistulae ex Ponto* 2.4 is similar to that of 1.9 in its literary dimension, but it goes farther than 1.9 in its explicit description of the exile's interaction with his poetic community, especially in regard to his verbal involvement in the act of poetic revision. The recollection starts in the same fashion as *Epistulae ex Ponto* 1.9: a verb of remembering and the description of a lost literary relationship: *Seria multa mihi tecum conlata recordor / nec data iucundis tempora pauca iocis.* What the exile recalls are nearly the same actions of *Epistulae ex Ponto* 1.9, as he remembers the production of serious (*seria*) and less serious poetry (*iucundis iocis*). *Seria* brings with it all of the literary resonances that it did in *Epistulae ex Ponto* 1.9 (see above discussion), but here the *lusus* of 1.9 have been replaced by *iocis*. Although there is a change in vocabulary, the use of *iocis* should be read not as providing an entirely new reading but as an instance of Ovidian *variatio*. In fact, in the present context, *iocis* and *lusus* are near synonyms, for as we shall see below in Catullus 50, both terms are used to describe the same neoteric poetry (*lusibus, ludebat, iocis*). Moreover, in the above passage from *Tristia* 2, the exile himself refers to the *Ars Amatoria* as both a *lusus* and a *iocum*. Therefore, the opening couplet of the exile's *memoria* in *Epistulae ex Ponto* 2.4 should be read as a *variatio* on that in 1.9 and as an attempt to emphasize the same aspect: the literary nature of the exile's lost community.

At this point, however, *Epistulae ex Ponto* 2.4 diverges from 1.9 and turns its attention to the specifics of that literary production and introducing another key schematic aspect of the exile's lost community: speech.

> Saepe citae longis visae *sermonibus* horae,
>    saepe fuit breuior quam mea *verba* dies.
>       (*Pont.* 2.4.11–12)

[Often, the hours seemed short with long conversations, often the day was shorter than my words.]

As he recalls the literary nature of his relationship with Atticus, the exile makes an explicit mention of how he had the ability to speak when he was involved in the poetic community.[20] Moreover, he states that he used to speak so much that he filled the entire day with his words and conversations (*sermonibus, verba*). Such a reference to his old ability to speak contrasts with the speech loss that the exile initially suffered on the night of his exile in *Tristia* 1.3 and continued to grapple with throughout the rest of the exile literature, eventually attempting to overcome it through the use of letters (see chapter 3). This contrast is made more poignant by the selection of *sermonibus* to describe the verbal interactions of the exile; for, as discussed in chapter 3, *sermo* was the conventional term used by the exile to describe the character of his letters. They were, in essence, conversations in absentia. By using the same terminology to describe his actual, oral conversations with Atticus, the exile draws attention to the changed nature of his conversations (i.e., from oral to written), a transformation marking his metamorphosis into an exile and his removal from the poetic community.

Having called attention to his transformed, exilic state through his rehearsal of a *memoria* in which he was a voiced, active participant in poetic production, the exile makes a final statement about his previous relationship with the poetic community in the third of the three anaphoric couplets:

> Saepe tuas uenit factum modo carmen ad auris
> et noua iudicio subdita Musa tuo est.
> Quod tu laudaras, populo placuisse putabam
> —hoc pretium curae dulce recentis erat—
> utque meus lima rasus liber esset amici,
> non semel admonitu facta litura tuo est.
> Nos fora viderunt pariter, nos porticus omnis,
> nos via, nos iunctis curua theatra locis.
> (*Pont.* 2.4.13–20)

[Often a newly composed poem came to your ears and a new Muse was critiqued by your judgment. That which you had praised, I used to think would have been pleasing to the people—this was the sweet reward of fresh critique—that my book would be shaped by a friend's file, and more than once an erasure was made because of your advice. The fora, porticos, road, and curved theatre—in adjoining seats!—saw us all the same.]

Here the exile describes the relationship between himself and Atticus as one of mutual poetic revision, again providing a picture of the exile's life when he was a full-fledged member of a poetic community. According to the exile, he used to bring his poetry to Atticus for the sake of revision, for he valued Atticus's opinion as one that would lead to public praise (*Quod tu laudaras, populo placuisse putabam*). Moreover, the exile seems to give Atticus partial credit for the success of his own poetry, stating that the approval of the people was the sweet reward of having Atticus review the work (*hoc pretium curae dulce recentis erat*).

However, both the connection drawn between the exile and Atticus and the attribution of responsibility to Atticus are not simply positive in nature. After giving Atticus "credit" for the success of his poetry, the exile makes an explicit allusion to one of his poems in particular: the *Ars Amatoria*. The locations identified as the regular haunts of Atticus and the exile are the same places that Ovid notes as his prime areas to seduce women in the *Ars Amatoria* (*fora*: *Ars Am.* 1.79–88; *porticus*: *Ars Am.* 1.67–74; *viae*: *Ars Am.* 1.585ff.; *theatra*: *Ars Am.* 1.89–134). The specific reference to the *curvis locis* of the theater confirms the allusion to the *Ars*, as Ovid uses similar phrasing when advising how to get close to a woman during a performance:

> Proximus a domina, nullo prohibente, sedeto,
>   Iunge tuum lateri qua potes usque latus;
> Et bene, quod cogit, si nolis, linea iungi,
>   Quod tibi tangenda est lege puella loci.
>     (*Ars Am.* 1.139–42)

[Let him sit next to the lady, with no one keeping him back; join your side to hers as far as possible; and even if you don't like it, it is a good thing that the rows push you close because the girl must be touched by you due to the nature of the place.]

Such allusion to the *Ars* leads one to believe that the exile is implying Atticus's editorial involvement with the *Ars*. Moreover, such an involvement would entitle Atticus not only to the fame acquired by the work's success but also to the anger of Augustus that the exile has said the work caused. The exile thus implies that Atticus should be suffering the same face as he, or at least should be working to effect the exile's return. The desire for such loyalty is hinted at in the couplet following the allusions to the *Ars*:

> Denique tantus *amor* nobis, carissime, semper
>   quantus in Aeacide Nestorideque fuit.
>     (*Pont.* 2.4.21–22)

[In sum, such a love was always for us, dearest Atticus, as was in Achilles and Antilochus.]

The exile states that there was such a love between them that it rivaled the love of Achilles and Antilochus. This statement clearly lays out to Atticus what the exile is after. First, the *amor* referenced in the first line of the couplet should be read not so much as a "true" love but rather as a more literary *amor*, specifically a work of *amor*: the *Ars Amatoria*. Second, the myth of Achilles and

Antilochus is especially apt for the desire of the exile, as Achilles avenged the death of his close friend Antilochus. Although multiple traditions of this myth exist and the reason for Antilochus's death is different in each, Hyginus's version—roughly contemporary to Ovid—of the tale tells that Antilochus, like Patroclus, was killed by Hector.[21]

If the exile has this version in mind, the meaning of this couplet gains another dimension in keeping with the general argument put forth in both *Epistulae ex Ponto* 1.9 and 2.4: because of Atticus's involvement in the *Ars*, the work for which the exile was relegated by Augustus (= Hector), Atticus should play the role of Achilles to the exile's Antilochus and should avenge his exile, thereby effecting his return to his lost community. Thus, the exile points to the literary nature of his lost community not only to rehearse his identity as a prior member of it but also to show that it is partially due to a failure of that community that he finds himself in exile. As a result, he expects members of his community to remember their prior literary relationship and the responsibility that entailed, and he urges them to fulfill their obligations and effect his return to the community.

Yet in addition to the clear literary resonances made by the use of generically charged vocabulary such as *gravitas* and *lusus* and the literary relationship with its attendant responsibilities, in both *Epistulae ex Ponto* 1.9 and 2.4 the focus of the exile's recollection of his literary production with a fellow poet to whom he is writing creates an allusion to two particular models—both rooted in the tradition of epigram/elegy—that focus on a poet's *memoria* of such literary production.[22] The first of these models is Catullus's famous poem to C. Licinius Macer Calvus, in which he recalls the literary production and revision shared by the two poets:[23]

> Hesterno, Licini, die otiosi
> multum *lusimus* in meis tabellis,
> ut convenerat esse delicatos:
> scribens *versiculos* uterque nostrum
> *ludebat* numero modo hoc modo illoc,
> reddens mutua per *iocum* atque vinum.
>     (Catull. 50.1–6)

[Yesterday, Licinius, at leisure we played much on my tablets, as had been the custom to please us: writing little verselets, both of us kept playing in this meter and that meter, handing back the tablets with changes while joking and drinking.]

Catullus recounts for his fellow poet Licinius how they spent the previous day engaging in the playful (*ludere*) literary production of jocular poetry (*versiculos, iocum*). The poem's specific vocabulary and its focus on poetic production and revision have led many commentators to point to Catullus 50 as the model for *Epistulae ex Ponto* 1.9 and 2.4.[24] Indeed, the exilic condition provides situations analogous to the Catullan one, as the exile too recalls his literary relationship with both Celsus and Atticus. In particular, the exile encourages both addressees to help him re-create such a close literary relationship with his lost poetic community by rehearsing his *memoria* of his previous role in the poetic community through an allusion to the ideal poetic relationship of Catullus and Calvus, a type of relationship that the exile had previously enjoyed with Celsus, Cotta Maximus, and Atticus.

In addition to the allusion to Catullus, the exile also can be seen looking further back to that poem's supposed model, Callimachus's second epigram on Heraclitus of Halicarnassus:

εἶπέ τις Ἡράκλειτε τεὸν μόρον, ἐς δέ με δάκρυ
ἤγαγεν, ἐμνήσθην δ' ὁσσάκις ἀμφότεροι
ἥλιον ἐν λέσχηι κατεδύσαμεν: ἀλλὰ σὺ μέν που
ξεῖν' Ἁλικαρνησεῦ τετράπαλαι σποδιή:
αἱ δὲ τεαὶ ζώουσιν ἀηδόνες, ἧισιν ὁ πάντων
ἁρπακτὴς Ἀίδης οὐκ ἐπὶ χεῖρα βαλεῖ.
(Callim. *Epigr.* 2.1–4, Pf.)

[Someone told me, Heraclitus, of your fate and drove me to tears; I remembered how we both often caused the sun to set in conversation; yet although, you, my Halicarnassean friend, have been ash for quite some time, those nightingales of yours still live, on which Hades, the snatcher of all, will never lay a hand.]

In this epigram, Callimachus writes to a certain Heraclitus about his own reaction upon hearing of his fate. Typically, the Heraclitus mentioned here has been identified as the same Heraclitus that Strabo (14.556) refers to as ὁ ποιητής and Diogenes Laertius (9.17) as ἐλεγείας ποιητής. One of his major poetic compositions was a collection of elegiac poems called the Nightingales, in Greek the Ἀηδόνες. In addition, *Antholigia Palatina* 7.465 is generally ascribed to him. At the opening of the epigram, Callimachus states that when someone mentions Heraclitus, he recalls (ἐμνήσθην) the many times (ὁσσάκις) he had spent with Heraclitus in conversation (ἐν λέσχηι).[25] Callimachus then goes on to make a statement about the immortality of poetry, saying that although Heraclitus has died, his "Nightingales" (ἀηδόνες) will live on, going beyond the reach of mortal death.[26]

This situation described in the epigram is markedly similar to that of both *Epistulae ex Ponto* 1.9 and 2.4, forming an allusive background unique to each. *Epistulae ex Ponto* 2.4 re-creates both the dimensions of literary production and the focus on verbal conversation between the poets: as Heraclitus and Callimachus cause the sun to set with their conversation (ἥλιον ἐν λέσχηι κατεδύσαμεν), the exile and Atticus engage in so many *sermones* (λέσχη) that the day (*dies* ≈ ἥλιον) was made shorter than the exile's words. Likewise, *Epistulae ex Ponto* 1.9 re-creates the exact situation of the epigram, as the exile hears from someone else (Maximus Cotta ≈ τις) that a poet friend has died, causing him to cry (*lacrimis umida facta meis* ≈ ἐς δέ με δάκρυ) and to remember (*saepe refert animus* ≈ ἐμνήσθην) the literary relationship he had with Celsus.

Yet, unlike *Epistulae ex Ponto* 2.4, 1.9 also plays off the latter portion of the Callimachean epigram, as it moves from the recollection of literary production to the discussion of the exile's death through exile (more on this below). Immediately after recalling his relationship with Celsus, the exile recalls how Celsus was present on his day of relegation, a day described in terms of death:

cum domus ingenti subito mea lapsa *ruina*
    concidit in domini procubuitque caput.
Adfuit ille mihi, cum me pars magna reliquit,
    Maxime, Fortunae nec fuit ipse comes.
Illum ego non aliter *flentem mea funera* vidi
    *ponendus* quam si frater *in igne foret*.
(*Pont.* 1.9.13–18)

[When suddenly my house, collapsed in a great ruin, fell on the head of its master. He was there with me, when a great part left me, Maximus, and Fortune herself was not my companion. That one I saw crying over my funeral as if a brother had been placed on the pyre.]

In these lines, the exile plays not the role of Callimachus, writing about the death of a friend, but the role of Heraclitus, the poet who has died. Like Heraclitus, who is nothing but ash (σποδιή), the exile himself is mourned as if he had been cremated and turned to ash (*ponendus . . . in igne foret*). Moreover, now Celsus becomes the Callimachus figure and cries (*flentem*) over the death of the exile.

With the exile playing the role of Heraclitus, the latter lines of the epigram, which focus on poetic immortality, carry an increased weight. Callimachus states that Heraclitus's poetry, the Ἀηδόνες, would be able to help him conquer death and avoid Hades, the snatcher of all (ὁ πάντων ἁρπακτὴς). If these lines are read against the exile's situation, the point would be that the exile's own poetry would help him conquer his exilic death. Moreover, the Callimachean terminology of nightingales (ἀηδόνες) and snatchers (ἁρπάζω) recall a particularly formative story from the exile's own poetry: the Philomela narrative. As mentioned in chapter 2, Philomela was taken away from her homeland by Tereus, dragged into a remote hut, and brutally raped (ἁρπάζω). To prevent her from telling of the deed, Tereus cut out her tongue and told her family members that she had died, creating a false *memoria* of Philomela's demise. However, through her weaving, described in terms of poetic composition, she was able to reconnect with her family and tell her own version of her *memoria*. Then she, along with her family, was transformed into a bird, specifically into a nightingale (ἀηδόνη). Tereus, on the other hand, was transformed into either a hawk or a hoopoe depending on the narrative version, but in all cases into a bird of prey (ἅρπη). In the exilic poetry, this narrative served as a model for the exile's speech loss and his attempts to reconnect with community through writing (chapter 3). Therefore, by closely aligning the exile with Philomela, Ovid points to the fact that not only will poetry provide the means of escaping the death of exile but Philomela's style of poetry in particular, namely, writing one's identity and sending it to one's lost community in order to effect reconnection with that community and to replace the *memoria* imposed on one by another with one's own version.

## Memoria Exsilii: *Creating False Memories*

So far, I have analyzed *Epistulae ex Ponto* 1.9 and 2.4 to show that the idea of *memoria* is placed at the thematic forefront. In particular, I have shown that the theme of *memoria* is presented in a tripartite structure. First, the exile broaches the topic by describing how a vision of the addressee comes before his eyes and causes him to recall times that he and the addressee shared before exile. Second, he recalls the specifically literary relationship that existed between him and his addressee, describing how they used to write poetry of various types. Third, he continues his recollection of literary production, noting how he and the addressee used to be in a community of poetic revision and how the addressee used to edit the exile's poetic productions before they were performed for the public. Moreover, I have shown that such a *memoria* of a community of poetic revision can be understood as an allusion to Catullus and Callimachus, poems that act to amplify the idea that participation in a literary community was bound up in the idea of *memoria*.

In this final section, I will turn to the self-allusions made by the exile in *Epistulae ex Ponto* 1.9. In *Epistulae ex Ponto* 2.4, the exile concludes his discussion of *memoria* with an allusion to the *Ars Amatoria* and the fact that Atticus, as an editor of that work, should bear part of the responsibility for the effects of that work: namely, the exile being sent away to Tomis. In *Epistulae ex Ponto* 1.9, another allusion is made by the exile, but this time the focus of it is not simply to cause the addressee to remember but to create a *memoria* and to place it in the addressee's mind as fact. In essence, the exile attempts to replace one *memoria* of his exile with another "false" *memoria*, one that he has created. The *memoria* that the exile selects as his topic is the night of his exile, which he first described in *Tristia* 1.3.

Again, we return to *Epistulae ex Ponto* 1.9:

Ante meos oculos tamquam praesentis imago
    haeret et extinctum vivere fingit amor.
Saepe refert animus lusus gravitate carentes,
    seria cum liquida saepe peracta fide.
Nulla tamen subeunt mihi tempora densius illis
    quae vellem vitae summa fuisse meae,
cum domus ingenti subito mea lapsa ruina
    concidit in domini procubuitque caput.
Adfuit ille mihi, cum me pars magna reliquit,
    Maxime, Fortunae nec fuit ipse comes.
Illum ego non aliter flentem mea funera vidi
    ponendus quam si frater in igne foret.
Haesit in amplexu consolatusque iacentem est
    cumque meis lacrimis miscuit usque suas.
O quotiens vitae custos invisus amarae
    continuit promptas in mea fata manus!
O quotiens dixit: "Placabilis ira deorum est:
    vive nec ignosci tu tibi posse nega!"
       (*Pont.* 1.9.7–24)

[Before my eyes, his image just as if he were present clung, and love made the dead one come alive. Often the mind recalls *lusus* lacking seriousness; often it recalls serious productions acted out with pure faith. Still, no times come to mind more often than those, which I wish were the last of my life: When suddenly my house, collapsed in a great ruin, fell on the head of its master. He was there with me, when a great part left me, Maximus, and Fortune herself was not my companion. That one I saw crying over my funeral as if a brother had been placed on the pyre. He clung to me in embrace, consoled the one lying dead, and mixed his tears together with my own. Oh how many times, that hated guard of my bitter life restrained my hands, which were ready to cause my own death! Oh how many times he said: "The anger of the gods is placable: live and do not deny that you can be forgiven."]

As we have discussed in this chapter, *Epistulae ex Ponto* 1.9 opens with a reference to *memoria*, as the exile remembers Celsus and the literary relationship they shared. After these lines, the exile introduces another memory (*nulla subeunt mihi tempora*), one that he describes as more poignant (*densius illis*) than his recollection of literary production: the memory of the night of his exile.[27] In his *memoria*, the exile focuses on the loyalty of Celsus: how he continued to stand by his friend although many other friends had deserted the exile (*Adfuit ille mihi, cum me pars magna reliquit*); how he mourned for the exile as if for a brother (*Illum ego non aliter flentem mea funera uidi / ponendus quam si frater in igne foret*); how he kept him from committing suicide, offering advice for how the exile could keep living in hope rather than in despair (*O quotiens . . . O quotiens*). Celsus, in effect, is held up as an ideal friend and a model whose actions Cotta Maximus is encouraged to follow. Because of such emphasis on ideal *amicitia*, much of the scholarship on *Epistulae ex Ponto* 1.9 has focused on that aspect (Evans 1983, 116–17).

However, underpinning all these same references to friendship is an extensive allusion to *Tristia* 1.3, the poem in which the exile describes his actual night of relegation. On a basic level, the situation described in *Epistulae ex Ponto* 1.9 is identical to that described in *Tristia* 1.3: on the night of his banishment, the exile was surrounded by a small group of friends and family, for many of his other friends had forsaken him (*adloquor extremum maestos abiturus amicos, qui modo de multis unus et alter erat*, Tr. 1.3.15–16); the exile is described as a corpse, having suffered the "death" of exile (*egredior—sive illud erat sine funere ferri? / squalidus inmissis hirta per ora comis*, Tr. 1.3.87–88); and all around the exile tears and weeping abounded (*quocumque aspiceres, luctus gemitusque sonabant, / formaque non taciti funeris intus erat*, Tr. 1.3.21–22).

In addition to the basic situation, much the same vocabulary is employed in both poems. As mentioned above, both begin with the same image of an *imago* coming to the exile's mind:

Cum subit illius tristissima noctis *imago*,
    quae mihi supremum tempus in urbe fuit,
        (*Tr.* 1.3.1–2)

[Whenever comes to mind the image, most grievous, of that well-known night, on which was my final time in the city . . .]

Ante meos oculos tamquam praesentis *imago*
    haeret et extinctum vivere fingit amor.
        (*Pont.* 1.9.7–8)

[Before my eyes, his image just as if he were present clung, and love made the dead one come alive.]

Likewise, the same idiomatic verb for remembering used *Tristia* 1.3 (*subit*) is also employed in *Epistulae ex Ponto* 1.9 to describe the specific recollection of the same night of exile (*nulla tamen subeunt mihi tempora*). Beyond the use of the same descriptors for the memory of that night, the same anaphoric *quotiens . . . quotiens* appears in both poems:[28]

*a! quotiens* aliquo dixi properante "quid urges?
    vel quo festinas ire, vel unde, vide."
*a! quotiens* certam me sum mentitus habere
    horam, propositae quae foret apta viae.
        (*Tr.* 1.3.51–54)

[Ah! How often I spoke as someone hurried by: "Why do you hasten? Consider whither and whence you are hurrying to go." Ah! How often I lied that I had a set time that was appropriate for the intended journey.]

O (a?) *quotiens* vitae custos invisus amarae
    continuit promptas in mea fata manus!
O (a?) *quotiens* dixit: "Placabilis ira deorum est:
    vive nec ignosci tu tibi posse nega!"
        (*Pont.* 1.9.21–24)

[Oh how many times, that hated guard of my bitter life restrained my hands, which were ready to cause my own death! Oh how many times he said: "The anger of the gods is placable: live and do not deny that you can be forgiven."]

Yet the most conspicuous connection between *Tristia* 1.3 and *Epistulae ex Ponto* 1.9 is the similarity between Celsus and the exile's wife. Both are described as mourning for the "dead" exile and clinging to his body as it is taken into exile. Moreover, these actions of theirs are described as nearly identical:

Illum ego non aliter *flentem* mea funera vidi
  ponendus quam si frater in igne foret.
*Haesit* in amplexu consolatusque iacentem est
  cumque meis *lacrimis miscuit* usque *suas*.
    (*Pont*. 1.9.17–20)

[That one I saw crying over my funeral as if a brother had been placed on the pyre. He clung to me in embrace, consoled the one lying dead, and mixed his tears together with my own.]

uxor amans *flentem* flens acrius ipsa tenebat,
  imbre per indignas usque cadente genas.
. . .
tum vero coniunx umeris abeuntis *inhaerens*
  *miscuit* haec *lacrimis* tristia verba *suis*.
    (*Tr*. 1.3.17–18, 79–80)

[My very wife, loving and crying quite bitterly, kept holding me, crying, with a stream of tears falling from both of her cheeks, deserving of more.
. . .
Then indeed my wife, clinging to the shoulders of her departing husband, mixed these sad words with her tears.]

Both Celsus and the exile's wife are shown weeping over the exile's impending "death" and mixing those tears with those of the exile (*miscuit lacrimis*). Moreover, we also see Celsus cling to the exile's corpse just as the exile's wife does (*haesit* / *inhaerens*). The striking similarities drawn between Celsus and the exile's wife continues the portrayal of Celsus as a close friend—one who reacts to his friend's exile not only as his brother would (*Pont.* 1.9.18) but also as a wife would—as a model for Cotta Maximus.

Through such connections to *Tristia* 1.3, it becomes clear that in addition to depicting Celsus as an ideal friend, in *Epistulae ex Ponto* 1.9 the exile is retelling the story of the night of exile from *Tristia* 1.3. In particular, both versions of the story are described in terms of memory, of a recollection of a factual event. In *Tristia* 1.3, the exile remembers his night of relegation (*cum . . . imago*) and tells us what he remembers actually happened that night. In *Epistulae ex Ponto* 1.9, the exile again recalls that night, alluding to the previous story of *Tristia* 1.3 as a factual recollection. Moreover, this recollection is included in a list of other memories of the exile's relationship with Celsus, which seem to have had some modicum of truth behind them.

By drawing attention to the identification of these stories as memories and by placing them in a list of other "true" memories, Ovid can be seen engaging in the type of *memoria* fashioning that we saw with Cicero at the beginning of the chapter. In that instance, Cicero implores Lucceius to manipulate his retelling of Cicero's consulship in order to highlight its positive aspects and to produce a *memoria* that Cicero wanted promulgated. Likewise, Ovid crafts a *memoria* of the night of exile on his terms, one that is a self-referential allusion (*Pont.* 1.9) to a narrative of exile built on literary topoi (*Tr.* 1.3). The point of creating such a *memoria* seems to be that it enables Ovid to gain control over the story of the exile and tell it on his terms.

Therefore, as I have shown in this section, the concept of *memoria* is pervasive throughout the exile literature. In the specific examples given above—*Epistulae ex Ponto* 1.9, 2.4, and *Tristia* 1.3—Ovid engages with *memoria* on multiple levels. First, he has the exile urge his addressees to fulfill the duties of *amicitia* by rehearsing a *memoria* of the exile's identity, reminding each of them of the activities that each had performed with him before his exile. Then Ovid describes the night of exile not as it most likely occurred but as he wants it to be remembered, gaining control over his own *memoria* and creating the *memoria* by which he wants to be remembered.

## Conclusion: Returning to *Tristia* 1.1

Throughout this study, I have attempted to analyze the importance of the schema of speech loss in Ovid's exile literature and the role it played in his overall poetics of exile. In chapter 1, I explored the concept of speech and the schematic associations of speech loss in the Roman world, identifying the salient features surrounding speech loss as the loss of human community and the loss of the ability to communicate ones identity. In chapter 2, I analyzed how speech loss was deployed in Ovid's *Metamorphoses*, arguing for the topos of speech loss that isolated those very concepts: when a character is transformed into a nonhuman entity, she/he loses the ability to speak, a loss that results in the subsequent loss of identity and human community. However, such speech loss can be overcome by use of the written medium to mediate the disconnection, as demonstrated by the examples of Philomela and Io. In chapter 3, I described how Ovid's exilic persona turned to this schematic topos to portray his own exilic condition. Stripped of speech on the night of his exile (*Tr.* 1.3), Ovid's exilic persona struggles to interact with the inhabitants of Tomis and yearns to return and communicate with his lost poetic community in Rome. Following the lead of Philomela and Io, he turns to the written word, to epistolography, a genre traditionally described as creating a oral conversation (*sermo*) through written words (*littera*), as a means of reconnecting with his poetic community. Finally, in the present chapter, I have discussed the significance of why it is the poetic community in which the exile is interested, arguing that the goal of reconnecting with that community centered on the idea of memory, (1) so that the exile would be remembered by and hence reconnected with his poetic community, and (2) so that, having regained his place in that poetic community, he would be able to renegotiate the *memoria* of his exile, recovering control of his life's narrative from the hands of Augustus and replacing it with a *memoria* of his own.

To conclude this study, I now return to the text with which we began our investigation: *Tristia* 1.1. In this poem, programmatic for the entirety of the exile literature, Ovid combines all the concepts considered in this study in an effort to set the foundation for how his exile literature should be read. As we identified at the outset, Ovid tells his readers that the persona he will put forth in the exile literature should be counted among the changed characters of the *Metamorphoses*:

> sunt quoque mutatae, ter quinque volumina, formae,
>     nuper ab exequiis carmina rapta meis.
> *his mando dicas, inter mutata referri*
>     *fortunae vultum corpora posse meae,*
> namque ea dissimilis subito est effecta priori,
>     flendaque nunc, aliquo tempore laeta fuit.
>         (*Tr.* 1.1.117–22)

[Also there are changed bodies—thrice five volumes—songs recently snatched from my ashes. To these I ask you to say that the appearance of my fortune is able to be counted among the changed bodies, for the fortune has suddenly been made different from before: now it is lamentable but was in another time happy.]

If Ovid's exilic persona should be considered thus, it follows that the exilic persona is subject to the same effects of the type of transformation outlined in the *Metamorphoses*: like the characters from Ovid's *magnum opus*, the exilic persona, once changed, undergoes a loss of speech and a schematically associated loss of community. These losses lead to the change in Ovid's outlook: what once was happy (*laeta*) is now lamentable (*flenda*).

Moreover, like the speechless characters Io and Philomela, Ovid has the exile attempt to overcome the speech-loss schema and reconnect with his lost community by turning to the written medium. In *Tristia* 1.1, this takes the form of the famous *parvus liber* that is to go where the exile is not allowed: to his lost community.

> vade, liber, *verbisque meis loca grata saluta*:
>     contingam certe quo licet illa *pede*.
> siquis, ut in populo, *nostri non inmemor* illi,
>     siquis, qui, quid agam, forte requirat, erit:
> vivere me *dices*, saluum tamen esse negabis;
>     id quoque, quod vivam, munus habere dei.
> atque ita tu tacitus, (quaerenti plura legendum)
>     ne, quae non opus est, forte loquare, cave!
> protinus admonitus repetet mea crimina lector,
>     et peragar populi publicus ore reus.
> tu caue defendas, quamuis mordebere dictis:
>     causa patrocinio non bona maior erit.
> invenies aliquem, qui me suspiret ademptum,
>     carmina nec siccis perlegat ista genis,
> et tacitus secum, ne quis malus audiat, optet,
>     sit mea lenito Caesare poena leuis.
>         (*Tr.* 1.1.15–30)

[Go, book, greet places accepting of my words: those places where it is certainly permitted for me to touch with my foot. When you are with the people, if there is anyone who has not forgotten us there, if there is anyone who perhaps will ask how I am doing, you will say that I live, but that I am not safe; that the very fact I'm alive is a gift from a god. But otherwise be silent (the one seeking more ought to read) and beware lest you perhaps say something that isn't needed. Immediately the reader, reminded, will recall my crimes, and I shall be borne on the mouth of the people as a public criminal. Beware of defending me, despite the biting words: *a poor case will prove too much for advocacy.* You will find someone who sighs about my exile, and reads those verses with wet eyes, and wishes, silent, lest he be heard by enemies, that my punishment be lightened by a gentler Caesar.]

Here Ovid describes a personified *liber* that will act as a surrogate for the exile who remains in Tomis. The most often remarked on aspect of this personification is the fact that the poet's physical foot is replaced by the *liber*'s metrical one (*quo . . . pede*). However, there is an equally important replacement of the poet's physical voice with that of the *liber*. The exile, speechless due to his transformation, asks the book go to places receptive to his words (*verbisque meis loca grata*) and to perform the act of salutation typical at the opening of epistles (*saluta*). This line highlights the shift in communicative medium: no longer is the exile able to speak with actual words, but instead he has turned to the written letter (i.e., the *liber*) to achieve communication with his lost community. Moreover, the personified *liber* acts out this shift by truly speaking to various people in Rome, as evidenced by the use of *dicere* to describe the *liber*'s communicative technique. Now not only has the *pes libri* become a surrogate for the *pes poetae*, but the *verba poetae* has transformed into the *verba libri*.

Thus far it should be clear that, in this programmatic poem, Ovid is closely following the schema of speech loss and community loss, and the subsequent manipulation of it through writing, all of which he initiated in his *Metamorphoses*. The instructions the exile gives to the *liber* and the audience to which the *liber* is directed to speak further this schema and follow the general line of argument proposed in this study, for the *liber* is directed to a specific community, and the explicit task of the *liber* is to ensure that the exilic persona is remembered in his lost community; however, the specific *memoria* desired by Ovid is the one he himself has created.

When sending the *liber* back to Rome, the exile gives it explicit instructions regarding whom it should engage in conversation, identifying two groups to which the *liber* should go (see *Tr.* 1.1.17–30 above). The first group of people to whom the exile instructs the *liber* to go is the group of those who remember him and want to know about his situation (*siquis ut in populo . . . forte requirat, erit*). The salient feature of this group of people is that they *remember* the exile.

As we have seen, the individuals who remember the exile in the *Tristia* and *Epistulae ex Ponto*—or at least are called to do so—are members of the poet's lost community. As an example of a general theme, consider such emphasis on memory in *Tristia* 5.13 and *Epistulae ex Ponto* 4.6:

> Di faciant ut sit temeraria nostra querela,
>     teque putem falso non meminisse mei.
> Quod precor, esse liquet: neque enim mutabile robur
>     credere me fas est pectoris esse tui.
> Cana prius gelido desint absinthia Ponto,
>     et careat dulci Trinacris Hybla thymo,
> inmemorem quam te quisquam conuincat amici.
>     Non ita sunt fati stamina nigra mei.
> Tu tamen, ut possis falsae quoque pellere culpae
>     crimina, quod non es, ne videare, cave.
> utque solebamus consumere longa loquendo
>     tempora, sermoni deficiente die,
> sic ferat ac referat tacitas nunc littera voces,
>     et peragant linguae charta manusque vices.
>         (*Tr.* 5.13.17–30)

[The gods make it that my complaint is baseless and that I'm wrong to think you've forgotten me. It's clear what I pray for is so, for it's wrong of me to believe that the strength of your heart would change. Sooner would pale wormwood be absent from icy Pontus and Trinacrian Hybla lack sweet thyme than anyone could convict you of being forgetful of a friend. The threads of my fate are not so dark. Still, take care lest you seem to be what you're not, so that you too can shed the crimes of false guilt. As we used to consume long periods of time with talking, the day eclipsed by conversation, thus now a letter bears tacit voices back and forth, and paper and hands do the work of the tongue.]

> At si quem laedi fortuna cernis iniqua,
>     mollior est animo femina nulla tuo.
> Hoc ego praecipue sensi, cum magna meorum
>     notitiam pars est infitiata mei.
> Inmemor illorum, vestri non inmemor umquam
>     qui mala solliciti nostra levatis ero.

Et prius hic nimium nobis conterminus Hister
    in caput Euxino de mare vertet iter,
utque Thyesteae redeant si tempora mensae,
    Solis ad Eoas currus agetur aquas,
quam quisquam vestrum qui me doluistis ademptum
    arguat ingratum non meminisse sui.
        (*Pont.* 4.6.39–50)

[But if you see anyone wounded by unjust fate, no woman is more tender than your heart. I felt this especially when the larger part of my friends denied knowledge of me. I shall be forgetful of them but never forgetful of you, who relieve my evils of anxiety. The Hister, all too close, will sooner turn its course back into its source from the Euxine Sea, and the chariot of the sun be driven toward the eastern sea, as if the age of the Thyestean banquet were returned, before any one of you who were pained at my exile will prove me to be ungrateful and forgetful of you.]

In the first example, the exile writes a mild reproach to a friend for not writing. This friend, however, is likely to have been a fellow poet, given the use of the topos of closing the day in conversation that we understood earlier in *Epistulae ex Ponto* 1.9 and 2.4 as an allusion to the poetic activity in Callimachus *Epigram* 2 and Catullus 50. This likely poet is identified not only by his previous verbal relationship with the exile but also by his memory of the exile, the salient characteristic marking him as a friend and member of the exile's lost community.

Likewise, in the second example, taken from a letter addressed to a certain Brutus, memory is used to describe the most salient characteristic of the exile's friends. Since Brutus has remembered the exile and continued to support him after many of those associated with the exile had forsaken him, the exile professes that although he will forget those who forsook him, he will always be mindful of Brutus (*vestrii non inmemor umquam*), using a nearly identical phrase to that which he employs in *Tristia* 1.1 (*nostri non inmemor illi*). It is likely, therefore, that the first group to which the exile instructs the *liber* to speak is his poetic community of friends, as they are ever mindful of him.

The second group of people to which the *liber* is allowed to go is also likely to be his lost poetic community, as the exile again touches on a characteristic of the addressees from his community: the desire that the exile's penalty be lightened by Augustus (*at tacitus . . . poena levis*) and the tearful sorrow for their lost friend (*invenies . . . ista genis*). Again, consider an example of these characteristics taken from *Epistulae ex Ponto* 1.9.

cum domus ingenti subito mea lapsa ruina
　　concidit in domini procubuitque caput.
Adfuit ille mihi, cum me pars magna reliquit,
　　Maxime, Fortunae nec fuit ipse comes.
Illum ego non aliter flentem mea funera vidi
　　ponendus quam si frater in igne foret.
Haesit in amplexu consolatusque iacentem est
　　cumque meis lacrimis miscuit usque suas.
O quotiens vitae custos invisus amarae
　　continuit promptas in mea fata manus!
O quotiens dixit: "Placabilis ira deorum est:
　　vive nec ignosci tu tibi posse nega!"
Vox tamen illa fuit celeberrima: "Respice quantum
　　debeat auxilium Maximus esse tibi.
Maximus incumbet, quaque est pietate, rogabit
　　ne sit ad extremum Caesaris ira tenax,
cumque suis fratris vires adhibebit et omnem,
　　quo leuius doleas, experietur opem."
　　　　(*Pont.* 1.9.13–30)

[When suddenly my house, collapsed in a great ruin, fell on the head of its master. He was there with me, when a great part left me, Maximus, and Fortune herself was not my companion. That one I saw crying over my funeral as if a brother had been placed on the pyre. He clung to me in embrace, consoled the one lying dead, and mixed his tears together with my own. Oh how many times, that hated guard of my bitter life restrained my hands, which were ready to cause my own death! Oh how many times he said: "The anger of the gods is placable: live and do not deny that you can be forgiven." However, the most frequent comment was: "Consider how much help Maximus will be for you. Maximus will take the trouble (such is his loyalty) and will ask that the harsh anger of Caesar not be taken to extreme. He, along with his own, will exert his brother's influence, exploring every means by which you may grieve more easily."]

In this passage, we return to *Epistulae ex Ponto* 1.9 and to the relationship between the exile and his poet friend Albinovanus Celsus. The exile relates that because Celsus was such a good friend, he cried as a family member would at his "funeral." Thus, at Celsus's actual funeral, the exile feels an obligation as a friend to shed the same tears for Celsus. Moreover, the friendly action of the exile is described in much the same fashion as the description of the second group to which the *liber* should go in *Tristia* 1.1 (*iure igitur lacrimas Celsi libamus adempto* ≈ *qui me suspiret ademptum carmina nec siccis perlegat ista genis*). Such similarity in vocabulary and theme lends itself to the fact that the group to which the exile is referring in *Tristia* 1.1 is, in fact, the same group to which Celsus belongs: the exile's lost poetic community.

Therefore, as can be seen by the groups to which the *liber* is told to go, the speechless exile turns to the written voice of the *liber* to reconnect with his lost poetic community. The instructions that the *liber* tell the community of the exile's fate serves to call the exile to the collective mind of the community in order that he not be forgotten. Yet in addition to securing the continuance of his *memoria* in the poetic community through the written word, the exile also makes a comment about the nature of the *memoria* he wants to be remembered.

At the beginning of *Tristia* 1.1, the exile makes explicit mention of the specific *memoria* he wants the *liber* to bear to his community at Rome, identifying it through an allusion to his description of the exilic *vultus* with which we started our discussion:

> Parve—nec invideo—sine me, liber, ibis in urbem:
>    ei mihi, quod domino non licet ire tuo!
> vade, sed incultus, qualem decet exulis esse;
>    infelix habitum temporis huius habe.
> nec te purpureo velent vaccinia fuco—
>    non est conveniens luctibus ille color—
> nec titulus minio, nec cedro charta notetur,
>    candida nec nigra cornua fronte geras.
> felices ornent haec instrumenta libellos:
>    *fortunae memorem* te decet esse *meae*.
>       (*Tr.* 1.1.1–10)

[Small book—I do not envy you—you will go without me into the city: alas, because your master is not allowed to go! Go, but unrefined, as is fitting for an exile; unlucky, take up the customs of this time. Neither let berries cover you with purple die—that color is not appropriate for grieving—nor let your title be marked in vermillion, your page in cedar, nor may you bear brilliant horns on your black brow. These decorations adorn happy little books, but you are suitable as a memory of my fortune.]

sunt quoque mutatae, ter quinque volumina, formae,
  nuper ab exequiis carmina rapta meis.
his mando dicas, inter mutata referri
  *fortunae vultum* corpora posse *meae*,
namque ea dissimilis subito est effecta priori,
  flendaque nunc, aliquo tempore laeta fuit.
    (*Tr.* 1.1.117–22)

[Also there are changed bodies—thrice five volumes—songs recently snatched from my ashes. To these I ask you to say that the appearance of my fortune is able to be counted among the changed bodies, for the fortune has suddenly been made different from before: now it is lamentable but was in another time happy.]

Having given the *liber* instructions on how it should present itself to the community to which it will be sent, the exile states that this appearance should match the *memoria* that the *liber* will give regarding the exilic situation. Since the exile's condition is unhappy and unsafe, devoid of the culture of Rome, the *liber* should look worn, unadorned, avoiding all colors and styles that are not appropriate for the grief of an exile (*exulis, luctibus*). However, by calling such attention to a description of the *liber* that highlights its lack of adornment, the exile calls attention to that adornment and makes the portrayal of the *liber* seem all the more artificial. In fact the mention of the smudges (*liturarum*) at the end of the passage quoted above and how they would make whoever saw them think (*sentiat*) that they were made by the exile, calls attention to the very fact that they are, in fact, fake tears. Therefore, *Tristia* 1.1—and the exile literature as a whole—opens with a statement of how artificial the depiction of the exilic situation will be, an artificiality that is to form the foundation for the *memoria* presented by the *liber* to the exile's community.

However, the description of the *memoria* that the *liber* is to tell as that of the exile's fortune (*fortunae memorem . . . meae*) makes an allusion to the end of *Tristia* 1.1 and gives us the final piece of the *memoria* that is to be described. The passage in which we argued for the presence of an exilic persona in chapter 1 contains a pentameter line that is aligned with the *memoria* the exile wants to be told (*fortunae vultum . . . meae*). The placement of the words in these two lines draws *vultus* and *memor* into an extremely close relationship. Against the background of the physical artificiality of the *liber*, the *memoria* that is to be transmitted by the *liber* is equated with something equally artificial: the exilic persona. Just as the *vultus* is a *constructed face*, a poetic depiction of Ovid in exile, the *memoria* told in the *liber* is a *constructed portrayal* of what the exilic persona, the exilic *vultus* does in exile.

In essence, the levels of narrative construction are twofold. On the basic, intranarrative level, Ovid constructs an exilic persona (*vultus*) in terms of the speech loss schema of the *Metamorphoses* and has that exilic persona act out that topos by attempting to communicate with a lost community through the written voice of the *liber*, one by which the exilic persona can effect his return to the *memoria* of his community on the intranarrative level. On a second, extranarrative level, Ovid the poet uses the intranarrative story of the exilic persona to fashion his own *memoria* of exile, his own version based on how he wants to be remembered. This extranarrative level is similar to the desires portrayed in Cicero's letter to Lucceius, which we discussed at the outset of this chapter: that Lucceius create a story of Cicero's consulship on Cicero's own terms, highlighting the aspects that Cicero wants to be prominent, and downplaying those he wishes to consign to oblivion. Like Cicero, Ovid seeks to seize control of his *memoria* from the hands of others and present a story of his exile on his own terms.

Who these others are and what *memoria* of Ovid's exile they might have been promulgating is impossible to recover, not least because evidence of Ovid's exile either independent of Ovid or not dependent on his own description of his exile is not extant; however, an interesting phrase, again in *Tristia* 1.1, does present a possible challenge that Ovid's *memoria* seeks to overcome. Between the descriptions of the two groups to which the *liber* should engage is a warning not to say too much lest the reader recall the exile's crimes:

> atque ita tu tacitus, (quaerenti plura legendum)
>   ne, quae non opus est, forte loquare, caue!
> protinus admonitus repetet mea crimina lector,
>   et peragar populi publicus ore reus.
>       (*Tr.* 1.1.21–24)

[But otherwise be silent (the one seeking more ought to read) and beware lest you perhaps say something that isn't needed. Immediately the reader, reminded, will recall my crimes, and I shall be borne on the mouth of the people as a public criminal.]

The second couplet of this passage, in particular, speaks to the *memoria* that Ovid wishes to be remembered as well as the one that he perhaps is attempting to downplay. This couplet describes the sequence of recollection that will begin for the readers of the exile literature if the *liber* says too much: (1) the reader (*lector*) will be reminded (*admonitus*) of the crimes that led him to be sent into exile (*mea crimina*); (2) consequently, the exile will be remembered (*peragar populi ore*) by the people as a criminal who has been convicted of those crimes (*publicus reus*). As such, the *memoria* that Ovid is attempting to suppress with his own is one in which he has been publicly convicted of *crimina* by Augustus and one in which his *memoria* will be stained by those convictions. As readers of the *Tristia* know, it is these convictions that Ovid attempts to refute in *Tristia* 2, a work-styled defense speech professing that at most Ovid is guilty of an *error* and certainly not deserving of the harsh punishment of exile that a *publicus reus* would deserve.

Ovid professes the competition between his *memoria* and the one offered to the exile at the hands of Augustus by an allusion to the *sphragis* of the *Metamorphoses*, a section that also speak to Ovid's *memoria*:

Iamque opus exegi, quod nec Iovis ira nec ignis
nec poterit ferrum nec edax abolere vetustas.
cum volet, illa dies, quae nil nisi corporis huius
ius habet, incerti spatium mihi finiat aevi:
parte tamen meliore mei super alta perennis
astra ferar, nomenque erit indelebile nostrum,
quaque patet domitis Romana potentia terris,
*ore legar populi*, perque omnia saecula fama,
siquid habent veri vatum praesagia, vivam.
    (*Met.* 15.871–79)

[I have now produced a work that neither the anger of Jove nor fire nor iron nor greedy old age will be able to destroy. Let that day, which has power only over my body, end, when it will, my uncertain span of years: however, I, everlasting, shall be borne beyond the high stars by a greater part of me, and my name will be indelible, and wherever Roman power spreads over conquered lands, I shall be read by the mouth of the people, and I shall live through all ages, if the prophecies of seers have anything of truth.]

In the *sphragis*, Ovid states that he has created a poetic work that is not subject to physical destruction and that will continue to live on beyond the lifespan of the poet. As a result, Ovid will be able to live forever through his poetry as long as Rome holds sway on the earth. Through poetry, Ovid can ensure that his *memoria* will be preserved in the collective memory of Rome.

In addition to being read as a statement of Ovid's *memoria*, this *sphragis* has also been read as a challenge to Augustus. First, the reference to the anger of Jove is often read as an allusion to Augustus because Ovid frequently equates Augustus with Jove throughout his works but especially in the exile literature. Second, the mention of a star has also been thought to refer to Augustus's numismatic iconography, in which he used the symbol of the star of Julius Caesar to link himself to the deified Julius. If both of these aspects of the *sphragis* are read as allusions to Augustus, Ovid should be seen as professing his superiority to the *princeps*: his poetry cannot be destroyed by the wrath of Augustus, and because of the *memoria* provided by his poetry, he himself shall be borne higher than the deified Julius, attaining a higher place of honor than either of the Caesars.

Returning to *Tristia* 1.1., Ovid makes an allusion to the *sphragis* of the *Metamorphoses* through the manner in which he describes the effect of the *liber* on his *memoria*. Just as he can be read by the mouth of the people (*ore legar populi*) through the *Metamorphoses*, he fears that he will be borne on the mouth of people as a criminal (*peragar populi . . . ore*) and that the charges levied against him by Augustus will forever tarnish his *memoria*. However, by alluding to the *sphragis*, Ovid also points to the fact that although Augustus has great power and the ability to exile him, Ovid, through his poetry, can create his own *memoria* of his exile, effectively trumping Augustus and his imperial power.

Perhaps the greatest evidence that Ovid was successful in his attempt can be seen in two regards. First, until very recently, scholars believed much of what Ovid professed in the exile literature to be true (recall the story of Ronald Syme in the introduction). Second, to this day, scholars still debate the historical reasons for Ovid's exile and Augustus's motivations for doing so by teasing out possible hints and clues from Ovid's own exile literature. Augustus's *memoria* of Ovid's exile, the "truth" behind the exile, has vanished; now we are left only with Ovid's *memoria* to go on. Ovid has indeed followed through on his threat: his *memoria* has destroyed that of Augustus.

Moreover, the aspects of that *memoria*—the schematic associations of speech loss, community, transformation—became some of the dominant means of discussing exile after Ovid. Seneca and Martial used speech loss to describe their exiles from their homeland. This practice is also evident among later writers such as Rutilius Namatianus, who looked to the concept of transformation to describe his separation from his native Gaul. Ovidian depictions of exile also came to form part of the basis for early Christian ideas of the itinerant life as manifesting exile from God. All this attests to the power of Ovid's *memoria* and the popularity of his poetry. Yet as stated at the outset of this work, Ovid's description of exile was a persona built on the accretion of exilic topoi that came before him. Ovid's innovation lay in the collection of these topoi into a cohesive metaphor for exile based on the Roman cognitive schema of speech loss, community, and memory. Through that metaphor, Ovid was ultimately successful in overcoming his exilic death and voicelessness. Far from remaining *mutus*, Ovid found his voice through his poetry and the *memoria* described in it, a *memoria* that was carried *ore populi*, ensuring Ovid's place within his community for as long as Rome held sway and beyond.

# Notes

INTRODUCTION

1. The writings on these authors are too numerous to recount here. However, these may act as starting points: Spalek 1976; Bevan 1990; Roth-Souton 1994. For the relationship between these authors—including Rushdie—to Ovid, see Kennedy 2002.

2. The term *exuum trias* is taken from the famous title of Leopold 1904.

3. The major discussion of classical exile from a historical approach is still Grasmück 1978. The large psycho-literary analyses of exile literature are Doblhofer 1987 and Claassen 1999. More particular studies on the legal and historical issues of exile in antiquity include Balogh 1943; Seibert 1979; Cawkwell 1981; Roisman 1982; Crifò 1985; Brown 1988; McKechnie 1989; Sordi 1994; Bearzot 2001; and Forsdyke 2005. More recently, Gaertner 2007 brings together a collection of essays on exile in the ancient world, particularly from a literary viewpoint.

4. Claassen 1999, 2–3: "The main ordering principle of the study hinges, however, on a second and relatively precise meaning of *person: grammatical person*. Discussion will start . . . with the *third grammatical person*, that is, narratives about exiles, 'he' or 'they.' . . . In the *Second Stage*, then, discussion will focus on the *second grammatical person*, that is, on dialogue . . . between the exile and another, a 'you-and-I' situation. . . . By far the longest section of the work, then, will be devoted to the study of utterances in which the *first grammatical person* predominates. Here the isolating effect of exile is prominent—discussion will concentrate on what is essentially monologue."

5. Claassen 2008, which focuses on the exile literature of Ovid, attempts to identify his true emotional state by answering the question "What did our poet feel?" (7); cf. Claassen 2008, 8: "We still need to ask whether this is Ovid the man speaking, or Ovid's first-person narrator as a 'character,' and in what way what the poet depicts is 'true.' We need to deduce emotion behind frequently stylised masks."

6. Solon 24 = fr. 36 West:
ἐγὼ δὲ τῶν μὲν οὕνεκα ξυνήγαγον
δῆμον, τί τούτων πρὶν τυχεῖν ἐπαυσάμην;
συμμαρτυροίη ταῦτ' ἂν ἐν δίκηι Χρόνου
μήτηρ μεγίστη δαιμόνων Ὀλυμπίων

ἄριστα, Γῆ μέλαινα, τῆς ἐγώ ποτε (5)
ὅρους ἀνεῖλον πολλαχῇ πεπηγότας,
πρόσθεν δὲ δουλεύουσα, νῦν ἐλευθέρη.
πολλοὺς δ' Ἀθήνας πατρίδ' ἐς θεόκτιτον
ἀνήγαγον πραθέντας, ἄλλον ἐκδίκως,
ἄλλον δικαίως, τοὺς δ' ἀναγκαίης ὑπὸ (10)
χρειοῦς φυγόντας, γλῶσσαν οὐκέτ' Ἀττικὴν
ἱέντας, ὡς δὴ πολλαχῇ πλανωμένους·
τοὺς δ' ἐνθάδ' αὐτοῦ δουλίην ἀεικέα
ἔχοντας, ἤθη δεσποτ<έω>ν τρομ<εο>μένους,
ἐλευθέρους ἔθηκα.

(ll. 1–15)

And I, of the reasons why I assembled the people, which of them did I halt before I struck upon it? Let the large noble Mother of Olympian gods, black earth, bear witness to these things in the court of time: I myself once tore up the mortgage-stones that pinned her down everywhere, so she who was formerly in bondage is now free. And I led many who were sold away—some justly, others unjustly—into Athens, the divinely founded homeland, and I led those who fled from crushing debt, *never speaking the Attic tongue (so far they wandered)*, some who were right here in shameful slavery, fearing the whims of their masters. I have given these freedom.

7. A good starting point for a handling of the various manners in which recent scholarship has deconstructed historicist arguments is Williams and Walker 1997, a special edition of *Ramus* with articles on multiple methodologies for approaching the exile literature.

8. Stephen Hinds (2006, 428) comes closest to a detailed discussion of the passage. He suggests that the mention of *fortuna* leads readers to read this passage (along with *Tristia* 1.7) with the portion of the *Metamorphoses* that deals explicitly with Ovid's *fortuna*, the *sphragis*: "The instruction at *Trist.* 1.1.119–22 is thus quite pointed. In asking the *Metamorphoses* to take on board the sudden transformation of the *vultus* of his own *fortuna*, Ovid clearly has his eye on that section of the *Metamorphoses* which *already has* his *fortuna* as its theme: viz. the poem's final nine lines. It is here, if anywhere, that the sorry tale of the change in Ovid's *fortuna* will have to be accommodated; and the effect will be, surely, to put something of a damper on the triumphant spirits of the epic's conclusion."

9. All translations are mine, unless otherwise indicated.

10. For more on *vultus*, cf. the discussion of Bettini 2010 in chapter 2.

11. Boillat 1976, 18–19.

12. Galinsky 1975, 42–47. In particular, p. 45: "The physical characteristics of the personages are subject to change, but their quintessential substance lives on." Cf. also de Levita 1965, 77ff.

13. Cf. Forbis 1997, 267: "And like so many transformations in the *Metamorphoses*, this one provides a link between his before and after states; his exile poetry is in essence the *fortunae vultum*."

14. There are forty-four instances of *vultus* in the exile literature: *Tr.* 1.1.120, 1.2.34, 1.2.94, 1.5.27, 1.7.1, 2.88, 2.525, 3.4.37, 3.5.11, 3.8.9, 3.9.21, 4.2.23, 4.2.30, 4.3.9, 4.3.19, 4.3.50, 5.1.40, 5.4.29, 5.4.39, 5.7.17, 5.8.17, 5.8.35, 5.10.47; *Pont.* 1.4.2, 1.10.25, 2.1.28, 2.2.5, 2.2.65, 2.4.8, 2.5.51, 2.8.13, 2.8.21, 2.8.9, 2.8.54, 2.8.60, 3.1.145, 3.1.166, 3.3.13, 3.4.27, 4.1.5, 4.3.7, 4.4.9, 4.4.46, 4.8.13.

15. Tissol 2000, 84; Hinds 2006, 429.

16. Hinds 2006, 429: "Someone at Rome has a portrait of Ovid, an *imago* (1.7.1), in the form of a bust or in the form of a ring: Ovid is grateful for the sign that he is not being forgotten. But for a *better* portrait of him, a *maior imago* (1.7.11), the addressee should turn to the *carmina* of the *Metamorphoses*: this is what Ovid really wants to be remembered by in his absence—even though, as he goes on to explain at some length, he has not had the time to put the finishing touches to the poem."

17. Cf. Hinds 2006, 428ff.

18. See also Richlin 1992; de Luce 1993, 313–15; Segal 1994; Forbis 1997; Hardie 2002.

19. Anderson 1963; Albrecht 1968; Galinsky 1975; Boillat 1976; Solodow 1988, 189–90; Videau-Delibes 1991; Holzberg 1998; Hardie 2002.

20. De Luce 1993, 306: "Of the 250 stories in the *Metamorphoses*, nearly 40 have to do with speech and speech loss." See appendix.

21. Forbis 1997; Natoli 2009; Stevens 2009. For Ovid's proclamations that he is no longer able to compose poetry well, see G. Williams 1994. For Ovid's complete voicelessness, see *Tristia* 1.2.

22. Compare the *poeta dissimulator* of G. Williams 1994.

23. Curran 1978 anticipates later feminist discussions of Ovid (e.g., Richlin 1992; Janan 1994; Keith 2000) and suggests that in the *Metamorphoses* Ovid began to see rape not in terms of sexual gratification but in terms of power and thus focused his depictions of rape on the psychological repercussions for the victims.

24. De Luce 1993, 306–7, identifies that nearly 20 percent of the stories in the *Metamorphoses* have to do with speech and speech loss. Although stories about men outnumber those about women 2:1, women outnumber men in stories of speech loss 3:1. This leads de Luce to conclude that there is a strong correlation between stories of women and those of speech loss, many of which include rape.

25. De Luce 1993, 318: "I will leave to Forbis and others the provocative suggestion that the *Metamorphoses* may have played a part in Ovid's exile."

26. Forbis 1997, 245: "Ovid offsets his vigorous outspokenness with various references to his own voicelessness in the face of imperial disregard and Tomitian illiteracy."

27. Forbis, however, in the last paragraph of her discussion, seems to suggest that the *vultus* from *Tristia* 1.1 is a poetic persona created by Ovid.

28. Ovid on poetic immortality: *Tr.* 1.4, 1.6, 4.8, 4.19, 5.5, 5.14; *Pont.* 2.10, 3.1. For a general discussion of Ovid's claim to immortality in the exile literature, see McGowan 2009, 25ff.

CHAPTER 1. SPEECH AND SPEECH LOSS IN ANCIENT ROME

1. Cf. also to the uses of *taceo*, *quiesco*, *infans*, and *elinguis*. *Elinguis*, in particular, seems to have some connection with *mutus*: it occurred only twenty times in a TLL

search of all Latin literature, and six of those times it was joined to *mutus* by the conjunction *et* (Tac. *Dial*. 36.8.3; Suet. *Vitae* 6.1.9; Apul. *De Deo Soc*. 4.33; Val. Max. *Facta et Dicta Memor*. 5.3.68; Livy 10.19.7.2; Cic. *Red. pop*. 6.9).

2. Discussions of speech, language, and communication are typically difficult to read due to the slippage of definitions between the three. This discussion follows the definitions of Gera 2003, 182–83: "Speech is the vocal expression of language: it involves both the possession of language—a mental system of signs and the relations between them—and the vocal, physical articulation of sounds. One cannot speak without having a language, but one can possess a language without exhibiting it vocally. Communication—more specifically animal communication—is much more limited than speech or language. Communication may be vocal—e.g., a dog barking—but creatures who communicate by means of sound do not necessarily possess language."

3. For the later Roman iteration of this Stoic thought, cf. Cic. *Nat. D*. 2.149: *Ad usum autem orationis incredible est, nisi diligenter adtenderis, quanta opera machinate natura sit. Primum enim a pulmonibus arteria usque ad os intimum pertinent, per quam vox principium a mente ducens percipitur et funditur.* Here the voice proceeds directly from the *mens*, the seat of reason; thus the power of speech, as with that of λόγος, lay in the connection between reason and speech.

4. The question of articulation is the traditional distinction between human and animal communication. For more on articulation, see Ax 1986. For more on the human aspects of speech, reason, and community, see also Lys. *Fun. Or*. 18–19; Xen. *Mem*. 4.3.12; Gorg. *Hel*.; Eur. *Supp*. 201–4; Soph. *Ant*. 354–6; Pl. *Prt*. 322a.

5. For the interpretation of *vocabula* as articulate sounds rather than words, see Cole 1967 and Gera 2003, 158n159.

6. Cf. Vitr. 2.1: *nutu monstrantes ostendebant quas haberent ex eo utilitates*.

7. FGrH 688 F 45.37, 40–3. For more on the Κυνοκέφαλοι, see Karttunen 1989, 180–85; Romm 1992, 78–81; Lenfant 1999, 206–13; Gera 2003, 185–87.

8. FGrH 688 F 45.37. Also FGrH 688 F 45p α = Pliny HN 7.23: *pro voce latratum edere*. See Gera 2003, 186n11.

9. GGM i. 129–41, frr. 31–49. For more on the Ἰχθυοφάγοι, see Burstein 1989, 37–38; Jacob 1991, 133–46; and Gera 2003, 187–90.

10. *De mari Erythraeo*, fr. 41: Ὅθεν (φησὶν ὁ συγγραφεύς) ἔγωγε νομίζω μηδὲ χαρακτῆρα εὔγνωστον ἔχειν αὐτούς, ἐθισμῷ δὲ καὶ νεύματι ἤχοις τε καὶ μιμητικῇ δηλώσει διοικεῖν πάντα τὰ πρὸς τὸν βίον. Cf. Diod. 3.18.6: διὸ καί φασιν αὐτοὺς διαλέκτῳ μὲν μὴ χρῆσθαι, μιμητικῇ δὲ δηλώσει διὰ τῶν χειρῶν διασημαίνειν ἕκαστα τῶν πρὸς τὴν χρείαν ἀνηκόντων.

11. Gera 2003, 189. Agatharchides also describes the Ἰχθυοφάγοι as a herd of cattle, who roar rather than produce articulate speech: ἡ δὲ ὁδοιπορία τούτων παραπλήσιος γίνεται ταῖς ἀγέλαις τῶν βοῶν, πάντων φωνὴν ἀφιέντων οὐκ ἔναρθρον, ἀλλ᾽ ἦχον μόνον ἀποτελοῦσαν (fr. 38). Such a description strengthens Agatharchides's claim that the Ἰχθυοφάγοι lack individuation.

12. A good introduction to the concept of schema theory and its history in scholarship is McVee, Dunsmore, and Gavelek 2005.

13. The concepts underlying schema theory can actually be traced much further back to Plato and Aristotle (Marshall 1995). The work of Kant (1929) also was foundational in the conception of schemata as the organizational building blocks that help us make meaning from our experiences (Johnson 1987).

14. Piaget 1952 passim. Piaget, a social constructivist, argued that development was a continuous process of renegotiation in which an individual either assimilates new information or experience into existing schemata or changes schemata to fit new information or experience. What sets Piaget's conception of schema theory off from others is his focus on sensory motor schemata and how they affect a child's early development.

15. Bartlett (1932) 1995 is perhaps the most often cited work on schema theory (see Saito 1996) and focuses on the interaction between schemata, culture, and memory. "For Bartlett, schemas highlighted the reciprocity between culture and memory. Schemas were necessary to explain the constitutive role of culturally organized experience in individual sense making. This early use of the term suggested a transactional relationship between individual knowledge and cultural practice" (McVee, Dunsmore, and Gavelek 2005, 535).

16. Andersen should be credited with the wholesale introduction of schema theory into the educational setting, especially into the context of reading. Andersen 1977 argues that reading was not simply a static process of symbolic recognition but a dynamic interaction between a reader's prior knowledge (i.e., existing schemata) and the text. If no schemata are present for the reader to interpret the text, it is impossible for meaning to be constructed from the text and the text is of little pedagogical use.

17. The best introduction to the topic is the brief book Stockwell 2002. Other good critical handlings of the use of schema theory and cognitive poetics in the humanities are Sweetser 1999, Turner 2002, Hogan 2003, Evans and Green 2006.

18. Riggsby 2006, 1: "This study has two roughly equal parts. The first, 'external' part looks outward and considers the kind of Roman identity postulated by Caesar's work, particularly how it is constituted in the context of various non-Roman others."

19. See Q. Terentius Scaurus, *De Adverbio et Praepositione* 29.15, 30.4, 30.12, 30.17, 34.9, 51.4, 52.3, 53.5; Fragmenta Bobiensia, *De Littera* 538.30, 539.2, 539.14; Terenianus Maurus, *De Litteris* 91, 94, 104, 188, 720, 781, 806, 815, 826, 883, 859, 870, 883, 890, 912, 949, 970, 1037, 1058, 1078, 1167, 1233, 1244, 1249, 1254, 1258.

20. The majority of the instances of *mutus* in a grammatical sense are accompanied by a comparison to letters described as *semivocales*.

21. See the Ciceronian and Vitruvian passages mentioned earlier in this chapter. In those cases, *vox* was used to describe inarticulate speech. Here Lucretius distinguishes between human and beast by giving both *vox* but bestowing *lingua*, the instrument of articulation, only on humans.

22. Gowers *ad* 1.3.99–124: "The [Horatian] picture owes much to the Epicurean theories of social and linguistic evolution, especially as mediated through Lucretius' adaptation of Democritus at [*Lucr.*] 5.783–1457.

23. Gowers *ad* 1.3.101–2: "Horace implies that articulate speech is a form of expedient invention and an essential precursor to civilization." See also the earlier discussion of the

Ἰχθυοφάγοι and the Κυνοκεφάλοι in this chapter. Like Lucretius, Horace also uses the term *notare* to describe the action of articulate humankind as different from that of inarticulate animals. Gowers *ad* 1.3.103–4 suggests an individual reason for Horace's use of the term in addition to the fact that it carried undertones of civilized action: "This potentially sinister word links the general development of speech with Horace's picture of the development of his own *sermo* from his father's pointing gestures. The word also sets up another *figura etymologica* with *nomina* [line 104]: names are labels for the things we point at. Horace is incidentally shaping a genealogy for satire, which also started from specifically finger-pointing satirical speech with *nomina* 'names' and *notare* 'to label' suggesting outdated *nominatim* abuse." Cf. Hor. *Sat.* 1.4.106 *notando* and 1.4.5 *multa cum libertate notarent*.

24. Similar to the location of the speech impaired at the fringes of civilization in the Greek tradition, Catullus's movement through many peoples (*multas per gentes*) and many waters (*multa per aequora*) can be read as moving from the speaking civilization to the nonspeaking realms, here characterized by the rites of the dead (*has miseras . . . ad inferias*).

25. This expression is found nine times in Latin Literature: Lucr. 1.92; Cic. *Verr.* 2.2.189.4; Verg. *Aen.* 9.341, 12.718; Livy 2.32.5.2; Luc. 1.246; Ann. Flor. *Ep. Bell.* 2.13.51; Tac. *De Or. et situ Germ.* 1.1.2; Servius 9.339.1. *Metus* is also linked with the verb *musso, mussare* (to mutter; stand quiet), a verb of silence etymologically associated with *mutus*. Cf. Plaut. *Aul.* 131 (*per metum mussari*), *Cas.* 665 (*metu mussitant*). On *musso, mussare*, see *Serv. Dan.* 1.152: "MUSSANT modo 'verentur' vel 'timent' significat; alias 'dubitant,' ut mussat rex ipse Latinus quos generos vocet; interdum 'susurrant,' ut de apibus dicit. et proprie 'mussare' est obmurmurare et queribundum tectius velut muto esse vicinum. alias 'tacent,' alias 'quiescunt'" ("Mussant" only signifies "they are fearfully reverent" or "they are terrified'; others "are doubting," as King Latinus himself mutters which races he might call; meanwhile "they whisper," as is said of bees: properly, "to whisper" is to complain under one's breath as if one were almost mute. Some "are silent," others "keep quiet").

26. For the close relationship between *mutus* and *musso*, see above. For the slippage between human and beast, see Wheeler S.M. 1993, 451–52. See Servius on 11.345.

27. Verg. *Aen.* 8.360–61: *passimque armenta videbant / Romanoque foro et lautis mugire Carinis*.

28. Meyer 1987, 63; Turcan 1996, 291ff.; Rüpke 2009, 31.

29. Livy 39.8–19; *ILS* 18; *ILLRP* 511; *IG* ix.12 670. Rüpke 2009, 33: "The year 186 BCE seems to have been the first occasion when the worship of a prestigious and prominent deity was perceived as a real threat to the community." See Beard, North, and Price 1998, 95: "It must have been the power over individuals obtained by the group's leaders that would have seemed so radically new and dangerous to the Roman élite. They had been accustomed to control religious life; now they faced a movement in some sense in opposition to the traditions of state religious life, generated by the personal commitment of individuals. For more on the suppression of the cult, see North 1979 and Gruen 1990, 65–78.

CHAPTER 2. SPEECH LOSS IN THE *METAMORPHOSES*

1. Fränkel 1970, 79–89, provides the foundational discussion of Ovidian metonymic metamorphosis. Cf. Doblhofer 1987, 227–28. More recently scholars have moved away from Fränkel's suggestion that wavering identity was indicative of authors in Ovid's time period who were positioned in a sort of nether region between paganism and Christianity; instead, they have attributed the presence of metonymic metamorphosis to other linguistic and poetic reasons. The most recent and comprehensive treatment of wavering identity is Hardie 2002, 27–29, which gives an informative overview of the scholarly response to Fränkel. For an analysis focused more on poetic aesthetics, see Rosati 1983. For one with a more linguistic bent, see Tissol 2000. For a more psychological, thematic explanation, see Galinsky 1975, 48–61.

2. See Solodow 1988, 190: "Metamorphosis renders statement useless: appearance and action alone tell who a person is. In taking away speech metamorphosis robs [a character] of the power to name himself, to form or change his self, to feign another." See also Altieri 1973, 35: "[The failure of speech] exemplifies the fact that the person transformed can no longer create his own identity or his present reality but becomes captured in the materiality of natural force."

3. Earlier versions of the myth are from Pseudo-Apollodorus, *Bibliotheke* 3.8.1–2; Tzetzes (scholiast on Lycophron 481); Hyg. *Fab.* 176; Nic. Dam. FGH 90 F 38, as reported in the tenth century CE by Suidas; Pseudo-Eratosthenes, *Catasterismoi* 8. Later sources include Pausanias 8.3.1ff. All these sources generally agree on the metamorphosis of Lycaon into a wolf. However, they differ on the victim of his human meal and on the identification of his sons. Bömer 1969–86, *ad loc.*, as well as ancient sources, states that his human meal was the beginning of the Arcadian tradition of human sacrifice. See also Anderson 1997, *ad* 226–27: "Scholars think that the idea may go back to a prehistoric practice of human sacrifice in Arcadia." Nevertheless, *none* of the extant sources make any reference to his speech deprivation. For more on the history of the Lycaon myth, see Forbes-Irving 1992, 216–18.

4. This is consistent with the Ovidian penchant for describing the grotesque, which has typically been seen as a precursor to the focus on the grotesque in early imperial Latin literature (see Conte 1999, 354–55). See also Galinsky 1975, 110–57, esp. 126–27: "For often [Ovid] grotesquely exaggerates the scenes of suffering and takes an almost morbid delight in the varied contortions of agony.... Ovid revels in ever new ways of imagining how bodies can be mangled, maimed, and disintegrated. Death becomes a ludicrous and sensational event, which the poet views without any empathy with its victims."

5. Moreover, Lycaon's removal from his community is amplified by the destruction of his house: *ego vindice flamma / in domino dignos everti tecta penates* (*Met.* 1.230–31). See Cic. *Div.* 2.21 for other ramifications of Jove's thunderbolt and the *relegati*. Many thanks to Jennifer Ebbeler for this reference.

6. *Oxford Latin Dictionary ad* "nanciscor": "'to possess by birth, to have by nature': *maleficam (naturam) nactus est in corpore fingendo*, Nep *Ages*. 8."

7. Galinsky 1975, 42–47, in particular, p. 45: "The physical characteristics of the personages are subject to change, but their quintessential substance lives on." See also de

Levita 1965, 77ff. Anderson 1997, *ad* 232: "The human beast turns into the literal beast that his behavior most suggests: a perfect moral allegory." Barchiesi 2005, *ad* 1.237: "La forma naturale del lupo lascerebbe dunque trasparire la permenenza della forma orginaria" (The natural form of the wolf would leave, then reveal the permanence of the original form). Barchiesi 2005, *ad* 1.198, also notes the foreshadowing of Lycaon's transformation into a fierce wolf through the phrase *feritate Lycaon*: "Il nome proprio merita attenzione: occupa l'ultima posizione nell'intero discorso, secondo una precisa strategia retorica, e l'accostamento con 'feritas' suggerisce, attraverso l'etimologia dela nome da λύκος 'lupo,' una motivazione anticipata della metamorfosi" (Its name deserves attention: it occupies the last position in the entire speech, with a clear rhetorical strategy, and the combination with *feritas* suggests, through the etymology of the name λύκος, "wolf," a motivation anticipating metamorphosis).

8. Barchiesi 2005, *ad* 1.236–38: "L'abbondanza di vocali-*u*- e di semivocali-*v*- fa pensare a una mimesi obliqua del lamento del lupo" (The frequency of the vocalic *u* and the semivocalic *v* suggests a slight imitation of the lament the wolf).

9. Ahl 1985, 72ff., but esp. 72: "LYCaon flees into the silent countryside—*silentia RURis* (1.232); when he tries to speak, he howls, *EXULulat* (1.233). The verb is well chosen, since it carries within it *EXUL*, 'exile': he runs howling into exile, where is transformation into a wolf is completed."

10. The most notable versions are those of Eumelos, Hesiod, Asios, Pherekydes, all whom are cited in Apollod. *Bibl.* 3.8.2ff. Also of note are Hyg. *Fab.* 177 and a somewhat contemporaneous version in Ov. *Fast.* 2.155–92. For more on the tradition of the Callisto myth, see Otis 1970, 116ff. and 350ff., and Forbes-Irving 1992, 202–5.

11. See Anderson 1997, *ad.* 2.401–530: "The detail of Apollodorus permits us to see how wide a choice of incident and of causation Ovid had; and it also suggests that the special emphasis he gives to the act of metamorphosis and the conception of the human consequences inside the animal shape are peculiarly Ovidian realizations of the myth's possibilities."

12. See Cic. *Leg.* 1.9.17: *moderationem vocis, orationis vim, quae conciliatrix est humanae maxime societatis.*

13. For his full analysis, see Bettini 2011, 134–36.

14. For more on *vox* as a marker of articulate speech, see the analysis of the Echo narrative later in this chapter.

15. Cf. the Vitruvian passage on the development of human language in chapter 1. There a distinction is made between inarticulate *voces* and articulate *vocabula* and *sermones*.

16. See *Met.* 1.234ff., 1.710, 3.203, 9.320, 5.224. Anderson 1997, *ad* 2.485–86: "Here is the ingenious theme that Ovid discovered in metamorphosis and made the inspiration for later writers such as Kafka. He had implied it in the case of Io; here he states it to accord with the greater seriousness of his presentation. He will restate it once more to capture the greater tragedy of Actæon. Continuity between new and old form was a traditional topic, and Ovid emphasizes the point not only with this verb [i.e., *mansit*] but also by such words as *servare, nunc quoque, adhuc, etiam, idem*. Continuity of human consciousness is Ovid's innovation." See also Barchiesi 2005, *ad* 2.476–88: "La tradizione

per cui la mente può mantenersi stabile nella metamorfosi da uomo ad animale ha le sue radici in Omero, *Od* X.240 sg., dove i compagni di Ulisse mutati in porci da Cicrce hanno dei porci 'teste, voce, setole, corpo,' ma la mente era 'salda, come quella di prima,' per cui vengono rinchiusi nel porcile 'piangenti,' e anche *Il.* XXIV 67 (Niobe) 'mutata in pietra dagli dei, cova la sua sofferenza'" (The tradition in which the mind is able to remain constant in the metamorphosis of a man into an animal has its roots in Homer, *Od.* 10.240ff., where the companions of Odysseus, changed into pigs by Circe, have the "heads, voice, bristles and body" of pigs, but the mind was "firm as it was before," through which those in the pigsty are "weeping," and also *Il.* 24.67 (Niobe) "having been changed into a rock by the gods, expresses her suffering"). For more, see Bömer 1969-86, *ad loc.*

17. *Ager* here has the force of property (i.e., *ager privatus* or *publicus*). The idea is that the land is not simply a field, but that it belongs to a community, as the reflexive possessive *suis* indicates. Cf. Varr. *Ling.* 7.2.84; Plaut. *Amph.* 1.1.38; Cic. *Leg. Agr.* 3.2; Quint. 4.2.131; Caes. *BGall.* 1.2; Nep. *Paus.* 3; Sall. *Cat.* 36.1; Liv. 2.16. Cf. the contrast in Ovid's second telling of this story in *Fast.* 2.181: *ursa per incultos errabat squalida montes.*

18. The motif of the hunted hunter will be repeated in the story of Actæon. See Barchiesi 2005, *ad* 2.489-90.

19. For more on *mutus metu*, see chapter 1.

20. Most notable are Philo. *De Piet.* 60 Gomperz = Hesiod fr. 346 M-W; *POxy* 30.2509; Diod. Sic. 4.81.4; Eur. *Bacch.* 337-40, Call. 5, Ps.-Apollod. *Bibliotheke* 3.30ff.; Nonnus 5.287ff.; Stesichorus fr. 236 Davies, *PMCG* = Paus. 9.2.3; Acusilaus *FGrH* 1 2 F 33 Jacoby; P. Mich. inv 1447; Aes. *Toxotides* (frr. 417-24 Mette), *Semele* (frr. 354-62 Mette); Hyginus 180. For a more in-depth discussion of the mythological tradition of Actæon, see Bömer 1969-86, *ad loc.*; Renner 1978, 282-87; Forbes-Irving 1992, 197-201; Barchiesi and Rosati 2007, *ad* 3.138-252.

21. Forbes-Irving (1992, 80-90) sees the pre-Ovidian, Greek tradition of the Actæon myth as intensely engaged in both the theme of sexual struggle between male and female and that of the struggle between man and nature, not as one based on speech and community. Forbes-Irving sums up his viewpoint succinctly on 89-90, stating: "The dominant aspect of the transformation and death of Actaeon ... is the reversal of a clearly defined order in which masculine superiority is opposed to women, animals, and the wilds. Actaeon is an extreme example of masculine achievement, bringing in record numbers of dead animals, devastating the countryside, and uncovering forbidden female preserves. Artemis is simultaneously a creature of the wilds, a woman, and a goddess; the combination of these three characters in one mythical figure is the source both of the prurient excitement of the story and of the triple resentment that brings Actaeon down." If we follow Forbes-Irving, the Ovidian departure from this emphasis strengthens the argument for a new, Ovidian focus on speech loss and community.

22. Barchiesi and Rosati 2007, *ad* 3.138-252, recounts the differences between the Ovidian version and the larger mythological tradition of Actæon: "Ovidio elimina, come vedremo subito, qualsiasi traccia di una copla soggettiva di Atteone, non insiste sul tema Greco-arcaico della follia, e recupera la dimensione sessuale solo in una dimensione traslata e simbolica; dà invece grande importanza alla metamorfosi e alla contraddizione

fra identità umana e corpo animale" (Ovid eliminates, as we shall see, any trace of a subjective guilt of Actæon, does not insist on the Greek archaic folly, and recovers the sexual dimension in only one shifted and symbolic dimension; instead he gives great importance to the metamorphosis and the contradiction between human identity and the animal body).

23. Cf. Callisto's roar at *Met.* 2.482–84: *neve preces animos et verba precantia flectant, / posse loqui eripitur: vox iracunda minaxque / plenaque terroris rauco de gutture fertur.*

24. There has been a scholarly debate over the authenticity of these lines (e.g., 3.230–31). See Barchiesi and Rosati 2007, *ad* 3.230: "Il verso è considerate da Tarrant, dopo Heinsius, un'interpolazione, che riempie arbitrariamente lo spazio aperto da *clamare libebat* e da *verba*, ma alla luce dell'importanza del nome di Atteone nella storia, e del nesso con I vv. 243–4 *Actaeona quaerunt . . . Actaeona clamant* penso sia da ritenere genuino" (The verse is considered by Tarrant, after Heinsius, an interpolation, which fills the space arbitrarily opened by *clamare libebat* and by *verba*, but in the light of the importance of the name of Actæon in the narrative, and the link with the vv. 243–4 *Actaeona quaerunt . . . Actaeona clamant*, I think it is to be considered genuine). For more on the issue, see Hardie 2002, 252–53.

25. For more on the use of *sonus* as a marker for inarticulate speech—especially compared to *vox*—see the Echo narrative below and chapter 3.

26. Payne 2010, 129, encapsulates Actæon's crisis of identity in this section: "As Actæon pauses to drink, he is torn between returning home to face his family and remaining in the woods to hide. Shame contends with fear, human emotion with animal affect, and the outcome of the conflict is blockage and death: as he stands rooted to the spot in perplexity, he is spotted by the hounds who give chase."

27. The other extant version is that of Nicander 1, epitomized by Ant. Lib. 32. In that story, after the birth of her son Amphissos, Dryope was transformed into a nymph and granted immortality. A poplar was left to mark the spot of her transformation. See Anderson 1997, *ad* 9.324–93; Kenney 2011, *ad* 9.324–93.

28. Forbes-Irving 1992, 130–31: "It is only in Ovid that we find anything approaching [a tree with a human spirit], in the bleeding tree of Lotus or the one that Erisychthon cuts down, and it is more plausible to consider this an Italian belief, or a literary conceit following on from and going one step further than Virgil's description of the bleeding bush of Polydorus, than a traditional Greek belief."

29. Cf. Actæon, *Met.* 3.148–53; Lycaon, *Met.* 1.221–23.

30. Anderson 1997, *ad* 9.392–93: "Ovid cannot refrain from a witty comment on her mouth: it stops talking and ceases to be a mouth simultaneously."

31. Kenney 2011, *ad* 7.652–53, suggests that when Ovid uses the term *recens* in the context of a metamorphosis, he is calling attention to the distinction between the past and the present form of the character transformed. Cf. *Met.* 9.393 *rami recentes*; *Met.* 11.737: *recentibus alis*; *Met.* 15.846: *recentem animam*.

32. This situation is nearly identical to the one Ovid draws for himself in exile. See chapters 3 and 4 further discussion.

33. Kenney 2011, *ad* 9.390–91: "Un ironico comment finale; sono dispensati dal compiere l'ufficio per i morti: non avranno bisogno di chiuderle gli occhi perché lo farà la

corteccia, avvolgendola" (An ironic final comment; they are exempt from performing the office for the dead: they will not need close her eyes because the bark will make a wrapping). Like Anderson's comment, Kenney seems to miss Dryope's point as well. First, she is not dying in her mind; therefore, she will not need the funeral rites. Second, bark is not a suitable substitute for coins, as bark does not grant one passage into the underworld.

34. Anderson 1997, *ad* 9.390–91: "She is 'dying' inasmuch as she loses her human existence, so the family starts to practice the usual rites for the dead: closing her eyes. But that is not necessary here: bark will cover her eyes anyway." Anderson's comment is contradictory. If her metamorphosis is the end of her human existence and the beginning of a new, nonhuman one—as I argue—than she has no use for the coins. If she is dead, bark would not be an acceptable substitute for the coins, as she would be unable to use it to pay Charon for her passage into the underworld. In essence, the coins are not necessary because Dryope is not dying, not because the bark is an acceptable substitute.

35. There were two mythological traditions regarding Echo in antiquity. The first is found in Longus 2.3.3 and involve Pan, who loved Echo but was spurned by her. In response, he filled shepherds with madness, and they tore her to pieces. The Earth hid the fragments, which still can sing and imitate other sounds. The second began with the Ovidian connection between Echo and Narcissus. Other versions of the story taking their basis from Ovid include Stat. *Theb.* 7.340ff.; Eust. *Il.* 2.498; Paus. 9.31.7.

36. Ovid is the only known poet who pairs Narcissus and Echo together. See Bömer 1969–86, *ad loc.*: "Die Verbindung zwischen Echo und Narcissus findet sich erstmalig bei Ovid." Bömer continues by stating that the reason for Echo's change is unknown ("kennt das Motive nicht") in the older versions of the Echo story.

37. For a complete listing of examples, see Raval 2003, 206n8. A few examples include Ov. *Met.* 5.332, 11.317; *Fast.* 2.91; Prop. 2.34, 37; Tib. 2.5.3; Sen. *Med.* 625; Stat. *Silv.* 2.7, 6.

38. See the similar reading of Raval 2003, 201–17, regarding the terms and their derivatives.

39. The most notable Greek versions are Hesiod *Catalogue* fragments 124–26 and 294–96; Aesch. *PV.* 562ff. and *Supp.* 291ff.; Bacchyl. 19; Soph., *Inachus*; Chaeremon, *Io* (*TGF* 71 F 9). Lesser versions: Soph. *El.* 5; Eur. *IT* 394 ff., *Phoen.* 247 and 1116, *Supp.* 628ff.; Herodotus 1.1ff., 2.41; Pind. *Pyth.* 4.14, *Nem.* 10.5. Latin versions include Val. Fl. 4.350ff.; Paus. 1.251, 3.18.13, 2.16.1; Lucian, *Dia. D.* 3, *D. Mar.* 7, *Salt.* 43; Ps.-Plut. *Fluv.* 18; Nonn. 1.334ff., 3.267ff.; Prop. 2.33; schol. Eur. *Phoen.* 1116; *Suda* s.v. Io; Eust. on Dionys. Per. 92. In addition to its role in these literary sources, the myth of Io was also a popular topic in classical art. For more on the artistic tradition of Io, see; Burkett, *HN* 188–89; Cook, *Zeus* 1:437–57; Wehrli, *AK* Suppl. 4 (1967), 196–200; Otis 1970, 350–60; Forbes-Irving 1992, 215–16.

40. For a brief handling of the differences, see Forbes-Irving 1992, 211–15.

41. See also Reeson 2001, 283, for more examples of parallelism between the two versions.

42. Only Fulkerson 2003 includes Hypermestra's father as a potential reader. Other interpretations of the poem are predicated on the fact that the letter was intended only for Lynceus.

43. Anderson 1997, *ad* 610–11: "Treat *vultus* as synonymous with *formam*"; *ad* 612: "*speciem*: regular synonym for *formam*." Barchiesi 2005, *ad* 1.610–11: "*Vultus* può significare 'aspetto,' ma allude anche alla versione alternativa della vicenda e dell'iconografia in cui la metamorfosi riguarda solo la testa della fanciulla" (*Vultus* can mean "appearance" but also alludes to the alternate version of the story and iconography in which the metamorphosis affects only the head of the maiden).

44. Bettini 2011, chap. 4: "Face to Face in Ancient Rome: The Vocabulary of Physical Appearance in Latin."

45. Ibid., 132. See also Negri 1984, 58ff.; Stramaglia 1998, 29ff.

46. Cf. Cic. *Leg.* 1.9.27: *Nam et oculi nimis argute quem ad modum animo affecti simus, loquuntur et is qui appellatur uultus, qui nullo in animante esse praeter hominem potest, indicat mores, quoius uim Graeci norunt, nomen omnino non habent.*

47. Corbeill 2004, 19–20: "The Romans popularly derived *vultus* ('facial expression') from the verb *volo* ('to want'), since our outward expression voicelessly 'expresses' our inner will." Corbeill goes on to compare this term for one's physical appearance with *facies*, another term that describes the face but focuses on the human physique due to its etymology from *facere*.

48. Cf. Ser. *in Aen.* 1.683: "*faciem*" *pro vultu posuit. nullus enim faciem alterius potest accipere, sed vultum, qui pro mentis qualitate formatur: unde infra est "et notos pueri puer indue vultus."*

49. See the discussion of Verg. *Aen.* 12.715–19 in chapter 1. See also Val. Fl. 4.350; Hor. C. 2.8.21.

50. Feldherr 2010, 17–18, reads Io's inability to complain (*queri*) as an Ovidian reference to the tension between the elegiac and the epic genres: "We can see the self-referential literary game as determining even Io's terror of her own voice. Her discovery that she can only moo offers a parallel for the poet's own witty advertisement of the fact that his elegiac language has been strangely distorted into an epic roar. Io wants to lament, *queri*, the very task of the elegist, in fact the programmatic one, because elegy as a genre was believed to derive from lamentation. So too, the moo that comes out instead recalls the hollow rumblings conventionally used to disparage windy epic utterance."

51. See the section on Echo earlier in this chapter.

52. See Ovid's "earlier" version of Io at *Her.* 14.92: *territaque est forma, territa voce sua*. Tarrant removed *Met.* 1.638 as an interpolation of this line, but there are enough major differences in the sequence of Io's realization to counter his claim. See Barchiesi 2005, *ad* 1.638: "Tarrant espunge il verso come interpolzaione da *Her.* 14,92, ma l'intertestualità con l'*Eroide* 14 è comunque presente nel contest, e il contrasto fra l'esametro e il pentametro complete la somiglianza tra v. 637 e *Her.* 14,91, creando una differenza quasi programmatica tra lo stile continuo dell'epos e quello a *cola* bilanciati e ripetuti del distico elegiaco" (Tarrant deletes the verse as an interpolation of *Her.* 14.92, but the intertextuality with *Heroides* 14 is still present in the contest, and the contrast between the hexameter and pentameter completes the similarity between 1.637 and *Her.* 14.91, creating an almost programmatic difference between continuous epic style and that of balanced cola and the repeated elegiac couplet).

53. In addition to being forced to eat food fit for cattle, Io is also forced to drink from muddy water (*limosa flumina*). The fact that a water nymph like Io is forced to drink from such waters further highlights her removal from her accustomed community. Anderson 1997, *ad* 1.633–34: "The drinking places of cattle strike us as muddy, which does not bother cows, of course, but appalls the girl inside the cow-shape." Bömer 1969–86, *ad loc.*, states the obvious fact that murky water is not liked by either men or cattle: "Es ist bei Menschen und Vieh in gleicher Weise unbeliebt" (It is similarly disliked by men and cattle).

54. R. F. Thomas 2001, *ad G.* 3.219, suggests that Virgil too might be drawing on Calvus's *Io*, as that line states, *"pascitur in magna Sila formorsa iuvenca"* and refers to Sila, a mountain in Bruttium, where Calvus was said to have located Io.

55. Cf. Narcissus (3.339–510). For more on pools and their reflective properties in art, see Hardie 2002, esp. 143–72; Taylor 2008, esp. pp. 56–77.

56. Cf. the Virgilian bull's exile from his *regnis avitis* in *G.* 3.228.

57. Feldherr (2010, 18) argues that the narrative be read along similar "double" lines in his discussion of Io's interaction with Argus: "[The] mirroring within the text reminds us how different things look when viewed from out of the cow's eye, and how disorienting our experience of the narrative becomes when such a possibility enters into it. Io, unlike Argus, does not take her cow form for granted; she acts as though she were human and finds that her form baffles and frightens her and frustrates her intentions." For more on the double nature of external reality and psychological perception, see Rosati 1983, 109–14.

58. In Ovid, animals weeping (e.g., Io, Actæon) is a sign of a human trapped inside an animal form. Whether animals can weep to express emotion is still a debated issue. For more on this topic, see Lateiner 2009, 277–96. For weeping in antiquity, more generally, see Fögen 2009.

59. Barchiesi 2005, *ad* 1.649–54: "Siamo di fronte a una vera 'invenzione' della scrittura, che in questo poema emerge per la prima volta come espressione di un nome e di una identità sommerse e di una assenza di tipo paradossale" (We are faced with a true "invention" of writing, which in this poem emerges for the first time as the expression of a name, of a submerged identity, and of an absence of paradoxical type).

60. Currently, the scholarly consensus regarding what exactly Io wrote in the sand is that it was her name. Bömer 1969–86, *ad* 1.649, posits that Io writes her name IΩ IΩ: "Die Kuh ihren Namen in den Sand schreib[t]" (The cow writes her name in the sand). Anderson 1997, *ad loc.*, agrees: "Ingenious Io finds a way to identify herself: by pawing on the earth the two letters of her name." Barchiesi 2005, *ad* 1.649–54: "Se si immagina che lo scriva il suo nome in lettere greche, si ottiene una forma adatta alle possibilità scrittorie di uno zoccolo nella sabbia: IΩ" (If we imagine that her name is written in Greek letters, we get a form suitable for the possible writings of a hoof in the sand). Hardie 2002, 253, following Barchiesi 2005, *ad* 1.649–54, takes this a step further, arguing for a cross-linguistic pun between the Greek "ιω, ιω," an expression of grief and pain, and the Latin equivalent spoken in response by Inachus: *"me miserum."*

In addition, Ovid's use of *indicium* to describe her symbol of identity foreshadows the similar story of Philomela. Cf. *Met.* 10.215: In the story of Apollo and Hyacinthus,

Apollo draws the letters *AI AI* on the flower as a symbol of grief. Bömer 1969–86, *ad loc.*, sees a link between the *inscriptum* of 10.215 with the *indicium* of I.650.

61. Hardie 2002, 253: "Inachus reads out the letters, translating from Greek to Latin as he does. Translating back into Greek his reduplicated *me miserum* yields a graphic image of the doubling of the person of his daughter through metamorphosis. How different is this Io from that Io!"

62. See Pliny *NH* 35.161; Verg. *Aen.* 6.848, 7.634; Sen. *Ep.* 65.5; Pliny *Letters* 7.125; Tib. 1.3.47–48; Varr. *Sat. Men.* 201.

63. Anderson 1997, *ad* ll. 651–52. The word *gemere* can be used to describe either the groans of humans or the lowing of animals. Likewise, *iuvenca* can be translated as either a young girl or a young cow.

64. Feldherr 2010, 19–20: "But this optimistic reading of reading as a way by which writing literally restores a lost identity is unfortunately only part of the story. For Inachus's subsequent speech reveals that it is very much his own sorrows that are on his mind. Far from empathizing with Io's misfortune, Inachus is interested only in what his daughter's new form means for him."

65. Barchiesi 2005, *ad loc.*, points to the ironic alliteration in this line: "L'allitterazione in *m-* prolunga ironicamente nel linguaggio umano l'eco del muggito da cui Io, incredula, si vede liberata" (The alliteration of the prolonged *m* in human language ironically echoes the mooing from which Io, incredulous, sees herself freed). For the irony of a human mooing as a cow, see also Verg. *Aen.* 12.715–19.

66. An alternate and possibly even earlier version is hinted at in Homer (*Od.* 19.518ff.) and Pherecydes (*FGrH* 2 F 124 Jacoby). In that version, Aedon, a daughter of Pandareos and the wife of Zethus, becomes jealousy of her sister-in-law Niobe's fecundity and attempts to kill the eldest of Niobe's children. However, she accidentally kills her own child instead. As a result, she either becomes a bird immediately after the deed, or she becomes one after being chased by her husband.

67. In all of the Attic versions of the tale, save that of Aeschylus, Tereus is transformed into a hawk. In Aeschylus, however, he is changed into a hoopoe (fr. 581). Forbes-Irving 1992, 248–49, suggests that this may have been because of the "belief that the immature hoopoe is a hawk. [In addition] word-play on the Greek for hoopoe (ἔποψ) which may have been understood to mean the same as Tereus, seems likely to have played a part."

68. For more on the different versions and their roles in Ovid, see Hardie 2002, 265–67.

69. Forbes-Irving 1992, 249. J. Williams 1997, 24ff., attributes this shift to a "confusion between nightingale and swallow in Greek" that filtered down into the Roman tradition (31). Virgil is good example of this: Procne is the nightingale in *Eclogue* 6, but Philomela is in *Georgics* 4.

70. Hardie goes on to equate the scenes of Tereus's rape of Philomela with the woodland consummation of Dido and Aeneas in *Aeneid* 4. For more on this comparison, see Segal 1994, 271.

71. Anderson 1997, *ad* 6.516–18: "The similarity Ovid is stressing exists between the rabbit, helpless and beyond the reach of assistance, about to be destroyed, and Philomela,

helpless and separated from her father, about to be ravished." Ibid., *ad* 6.527–30: "Like the simile in 516–518 this one concentrates on Tereus as beast or bird of prey and on Philomela as his prey; the difference is that now the prey has been hurt."

72. Richlin 1992, 163ff., argues that the dove-hawk and lamb-wolf depictions are often used in Ovidian similes to heighten an erotic or voyeuristic tone. See *Ars Am.* 1.117–18: *ut fugiunt aquilas, timidissima turba, columbae, / utque fugit visos agna novella lupos*; *Ars Am.* 2.363–64: *accipitri timidas credis, furiose, columbas? / plenum montano credis ovile lupo?* Also, see their deployment in the Daphne and Apollo story at *Met.* 1.505–6: *sic agna lupum, sic cerva leonem, / sic aquilam penna fugiunt trepidante columbae*; and in the story of the rape of Lucretia in *Fast.* 2.799–800: *sed tremit, ut quondam stabulis deprensa relictis / parva sub infesto cum iacet agna lupo*. For more on the relationship between Lucretia and Philomela, see Feldherr 2010, 215–23.

73. Cf. *Met.* 2.372, 3.180, 7.114, 7.662, 8.448, 9.165, 12.56, 15.676; *Her.* 5.73, 6.58; *Fast.* 4.482; *Tr.* 3.3.29.

74. Bömer 1969–86, *ad* 6.547: "Beide Intentionen sind ebenso phantastisch, wie sie poetisch das ganze Pathos heroischen Zorns zum Ausdruck bringen. Die Wendung ist sprichwörtlich. Dazu aus Ovid, der das Bild nur gelegentlich auf Orpheus bezieht" (Both intentions are just as fantastic as they poetically bring the whole pathos of heroic scorn to express anger. The phrase is proverbial. Thus it is in Ovid, who only refers to the image occasionally in regard to Orpheus). See *Met.* 9.303ff. (*motura ... duros ... verba ... silices*); 13.48 (*saxa moves gemitu*); *Am.* 3.57ff. (*illa graves potuit quercus adamantaque durum surdaque blanditiis saxa movere suis*); *Ars Am.* 3.321 (*saxa ... lyra movit ... Orpheus*).

75. Rosati 2007, *ad* 6.542–48: "Riempire le selve (di lamenti, anche se qui ambiguamente si lascia intender un grido di denuncia) è l'atto topico dell'usignolo" (Filling the forests (of complaints, even if we set aside the ambiguous intention of a cry of complaint) is the typical act of the nightingale). Cf. Verg. *G.* 4.514–15: *flet noctem ramoque sedens miserabile carmen integrat et maestis late loca questibus implet*.

76. The phrase *conscia saxa*, translated either as "witness" (see Verg. *Aen.* 4.166–68 at the "wedding" of Aeneas and Dido: *prima et Tellus et pronuba Iuno / dant signum; fulsere ignes et conscius aether / conubiis summoque ulularunt uertice Nymphae*) or as "conscious" may include an oblique allusion to the story of Niobe from earlier in *Met.* 6. In that story, Niobe was turned into a *saxum* (*Met.* 6.309) after the murder of her children.

77. Richlin goes on to argue the congruency between speech and gender, especially the phrase of Claudine Hermann, *voleuses de langue*, "women thieves of language." For more on speech and gender, see Joplin 2008 and Ostriker 1985.

78. The participles that build through lines 555–56 deceive the audience because they describe not Philomela's actions but the tongue's, and this revelation does not become clear until the end of the clause and the word *linguam*. Such a delayed and surprising subject of the indirect speech only acts to further emphasize the new narrative focus on the tongue. Moreover, Ovid furthers his emphasis on the tongue through personification, describing the tongue writhing on the dark earth, following the footsteps of its mistress (*terraeque tremens inmurmurat atrae ... dominae vestigia quaerit*), and finally coming to rest and lying on the ground (*ipsa iacet*). Moreover, the tongue's ability to

produce articulate speech is curtailed, as the sound it can make shifts from the articulate *vocare* prior to its removal to the inarticulate *inmurmurare* after that action.

79. Tereus is commonly read as a key narrator in the *Metamorphoses*. For more on his narrating acts—and those of Philomela—see Segal 1994, 262–65.

80. Hardie 2002, 84–91 and 259–72, esp. 86–87, 267. Hardie 2002, 87: "All that the empty tomb contains is one version, Tereus,' of the story of Philomela. But for all his skill as a narrator Tereus will be no match for the true version told by Ovid and retold, within Ovid's fiction, in Philomela's tapestry, the 'piteous poem' that is read by Procne."

81. Bömer 1969–86, *ad loc.*, notes that this is the first instance of this phrase in Latin literature, followed by a repetition at *Fast.* 2.613–14 (*vim parat hic, voltu pro verbis illa precatur, / et frustra muto nititur ore loqui*): "In lateinischer Literatur zuerst hier und fast. II 614 von der ebenfalls verstümmelten Lara."

82. Cf. Cic. *Leg.* 1.9.17: *moderationem vocis, orationis vim, quae conciliatrix est humanae maxime societatis.*

83. See Ov. *Am.* 1.9.32; *Ars. Am.* 1.15.14; *Tr.* 2.424, 2.432, 3.3.73–76; Hor. *Ars P.* 408–18; Prop. 2.24.23. See further Newman 1967, esp. 395ff.; Luck 1977, *ad* 2.423ff.; and Brink 2011, *ad* 408–18.

84. Weaving is often portrayed as an alternate and particularly female form of textuality. Penelope's actions in the *Odyssey* are the Greco-Roman prototype for this conception. For a Roman version, see the depiction of Delia in Tib. 1.3. For more on weaving and the feminine in antiquity, see Klindienst 1984; Keller 1986; Joplin 2008. For weaving as textuality more generally, see Durante 1976, 173–75; in the *Metamorphoses* in particular, see Rosati 1999.

85. Cf. Eisenhut 1961; Deremetz 1995, 289ff.; Rosati 1999. Rosati 1999, 246: "The metaphor of *deducere carmen* seems to take root in the Augustan age to denote both the elaboration of light, refined poetry (in opposition to ambitious and high-sounding genres: Cf. above all the proem of the sixth *Eclogue*), and the composition of poetry in general; even more frequently *deducere Carmen* refers to the composition of narrative texts."

86. In addition to the many Propertian and Horatian examples, see Verg. *Ecl.* 6.4–5 (*pastorem, Tityre, pinguis / pascere oportet ovis, deductum dicere carmen*); Ov. *Met.* 1.3–4 (*adspirate meis primaque ab origine mundi / ad mea perpetuum deducite tempora carmen!*); Ov. *Tr.* 1.1.39 (*carmina proueniunt animo deducta sereno*); Stat. *Achil.* 1.7 (*sed tota iuuenem deducere Troia*).

87. Cf. Ov. *Am.* 1.2 (*an subit et tecta callidus arte nocet?*); Ov. *Her.* 20.25–28 (*non ego natura nec sum tam callidus usu; / sollertem tu me, crede, puella, facis. / te mihi compositis, siquid tamen egimus, arte / adstrinxit verbis ingeniosus Amor*).

88. R. E. Thomas 1983, 106–11; Rosati 1999, 247: "Metaphors derived from the crafts of spinning and weaving are, in sum, ancient and widespread in literary contexts; an entire semantic field is constructed around the idea of the text (written or verbal) as an interlacement, as *textus*."

89. Rosati 2007, *ad* 6.579: "Oltre al nuovo linguaggio 'testuale' per comunicare a distanza con Procne, Filomela deve ricorrere a un altro linguaggio alternative alla lingua, quallo gestuale, per poter comunicare all'ancella la richiesta di consegnare il messaggio" (In addition to the new "textual" language to communicate with Procne from a distance,

Philomela must resort to another alternative language to the spoken word, to gestures, in order to communicate to the slave girl the request to deliver the message). The phrase *gestu rogat* is also an expression applied to pantomime. For the connection of pantomime to the Philomela narrative, see Feldherr 2010, 210n16.

90. For a detailed analysis of the bacchantic imagery in the narrative, see Segal 1994, 273–79.

91. See Forbes-Irving 1992, 233–60, which describes avian metamorphosis as a class of transformation in which the transformed individual never returns to his or her pre-metamorphosis form but instead exhibits characteristics from before metamorphosis in his or her transformed state. See also Payne 2010, 87ff., on Aristophanes's *Birds* and select fragments of Aeschylus.

92. Special thanks to the audience at the Boston University Graduate Conference, especially Mark Payne and Steven Scully, for their advice on this argument.

93. Dierauer 1977; Tabarroni 1988; Sorabji 1993, 80–86; Glidden 1994; Gera 2003, 208–11; Heath 2005; Alexandridis, Wild, and Winkler-Horaček 2008.

94. *De partibus animalium* 660a35–660b2: Καὶ χρῶνται τῇ γλώττῃ καὶ πρὸς ἑρμηνείαν ἀλλήλοις πάντες μέν, ἕτεροι δὲ τῶν ἑτέρων μᾶλλον, ὥστ' ἐπ' ἐνίων καὶ μάθησιν εἶναι δοκεῖν παρ' ἀλλήλων· εἴρηται δὲ περὶ αὐτῶν ἐν ταῖς ἱστορίαις ταῖς περὶ τῶν ζῴων (*All [birds] use their tongues for communication with one another, some more so than others, so that it is likely that there is some information conveyed by some of them to the others. I have spoken of these in my books on animals*. [trans. S. Newmyer 2011, 61]). Aristotle's distinction of νοῦς in terms of speech (λόγος) is discussed at *Eth. Nic.* 1177b27–78a2 and *De An.* 429a22–27. For further discussion, see Zirin 1980; Kullman 1991; Lennox 1999.

95. Cf. Arist. *Hist. An.* 504b1–3, 535a28–536a22; *Int.* 16a28–29; and *Pol.* 1253a10–14. Payne 2010, 84–88, provides a good, concise overview of Aristotle's biology of language, following closely Zirin 1980 and his analysis of Aristotle. For a more detailed analysis of the difference between animal and human speech, see Dierauer 1977, esp. 126–28.

96. *ac ne quis dubitet artis esse, plures singulis sunt cantus, nec iidem omnibus, sed sui cuique* (We may here remark that every bird has a number of notes peculiar to itself; for they do not, all of them, have the same, but each, certain melodies of its own [trans. Bostock 1856, *ad loc.*]).

97. *deinde in una perfecta musica scientia: modulatus editur sonus et nunc continuo spiritu trahitur in longum, nunc variatur inflexo, nunc distinguitur conciso, copulatur intorto, promittitur revocato, infuscatur ex inopinato, interdum et secum ipse murmurat, plenus, gravis, acutus, creber, extentus, ubi visum est, vibrans, summus, medius, imus* (And then, too, it is the only bird the notes of which are modulated in accordance with the strict rules of musical science. At one moment, as it sustains its breath, it will prolong its note, and then at another, will vary it with different inflexions; then, again, it will break into distinct chirrups, or pour forth an endless series of roulades [trans. Bostock 1856, *ad loc.*]).

98. *audit discipula intentione magna et reddit, vicibusque reticent: intelligitur emendatae correptio et in docente quaedam reprehensio* (The younger birds are listening in the meantime, and receive the lesson in song from which they are to profit. The learner hearkens with the greatest attention, and repeats what it has heard, and then they are silent by turns; this is understood to be the correction of an error on the part of the

scholar, and a sort of reproof, as it were, on the part of the teacher [trans. Bostock 1856, ad loc.]).

Fögen 2007, 189–91, reads this description as an instance of Pliny's "tendency towards anthropomorphisation," as Pliny gives the nightingale an ability equal to an *ars*. For the relationship between the descriptions of the nightingale in Pliny and Ovid, see J. Williams 1997, 33.

## Chapter 3. Speech Loss in the Exile Literature

Special thanks to Stephen Hinds for his comments on an earlier version of this chapter.

1. "These things, as best as I am able, I have composed now in an obscure location, far away, and with a dull mind. If, therefore, they seem beneath the consideration of a person of your intelligence incapable of consoling you in your grief, remember how impossible it is for one who is full of his own sorrows to find time to be concerned with those of others, and how hard it is to express oneself in the Latin language, when all around one hears nothing but a foreign words, which even more civilized barbarians regard with disgust."

2. "If anything can be seen, reader, in these pages, whether it be too obscure or not Latin enough, the error is not mine: the copyist harmed those things while he was hurrying to sell it to you."

3. For discussions of Ovid's linguistic decline, see de Luce 1993; G. Williams 1994, 91–99; Casali 1997, 92–96; Forbis 1997; Stevens 2009.

4. Beyond infrequent, the extant mentions of Ovid's exile in the ancient world are so few and far between that the relative absence of accounts of his exile has led to several scholars casting doubts about the reality of Ovid's exile at all. The only literary references to Ovid's exile are Pliny, *NH* 32.152 (*His adiciemus ab Ovidio posita <a>nim<ali>a, quae apud neminem alium reperiuntur, sed fortassis in Ponto nascentia, ubi id volumen supremis suis temporibus inchoavit*); Stat. *Silv.* 1.2.252–55 (*hunc ipse Coo plaudente Philitas / Callimachusque senex Umbroque Propertius antro / ambissent laudare diem, nec tristis in ipsis / Naso Tomis divesque foco lucente Tibullus*); Jerome *Chronicle* 2020.4 (*Ovidius poeta in exilio diem obiit, et juxta oppidum Tomos sepelitur*). In addition to the literary references, Hollis 1996, 26, identifies a graffito from Herculaneum referencing Ovid's exile: *CIL* 4.10595, "*morieris Tomi*." For more on Ovidian allusions in graffiti and other Roman art, see Simon 2007; Knox 2012.

5. Ziolkowski 2005 describes Ovid as the "Ur-Exile" against which subsequent exile literature judged itself. For the effect Ovid has had on subsequent exile literature, see Claassen 1999, 2008; Gaertner 2007; Ingleheart 2011; Fantham 2013; Newlands 2014.

6. These two passages are handled in detail in Hinds 2007 and 2011b.

7. Cf. chapter 1 for the opposite claim made by Doblhofer 1987 regarding *Exilkrankheit*, a type of universal condition affecting all exiles in all times, one aspect of which was the exile's loss of ability to speak in the mother tongue.

8. See Roman 2001, 124: "In general, Martial adapts motifs formed in the context of 'poetry in exile,' and rewrites them in terms of 'poetry as usual.'"

9. Hinds 2011b, 64: "Martial presents himself throughout his career as a low-status writer working in a low-status genre (i.e., epigram): and this gives rise to a distinctive

pattern of engagement with the *Tristia*'s peculiar anxieties about the maintenance of poetic quality and prestige in adverse circumstances. . . . In other words, some Martialian allusions to the *Tristia* do the job of suggesting that the marginalization of the exiled poet and the debasement of his art offer an apt model for the *literary* marginalization of the low-prestige epigrammatist—who encounters *his* professed disadvantages without even leaving Rome."

10. As discussed in chapter 1, the "Ovid" who is the subject of the exile literature is a persona and should not be equated with the historical Ovid, the real person born in Sulmo in 42 BCE. In an effort to keep these multiple "Ovids" separate, this chapter will use the following terminology set forth by Claassen: "I shall refer to the creative poet [i.e., the historical author] as '*Ovid*' or '*the poet*,' to the implicit letter-writer [i.e., Ovid's exilic persona] as '*the exile*'" (1999, 112).

11. Wilamowitz-Moellendorf first suggested the term: "Ich möchte darauf hinweisen, daß Ovid in den Tristien auf diesem Wege so glücklich fortgeschritten ist, daß sein erstes Buch ganz wohl den Titel 'Reise in die Verbannung' tragen könnte" (1926, 298). (I would like to point out that Ovid has so fortunately progressed in this way in the *Tristia* that his first book might very well bear the title "Journey into Exile.") Froesch, writing much later, picks up on Wilamowitz-Moellendorf's theme, calling *Tristia* 1 a "Journey into Exile" as well: "Das erste Tristienbuch enthält u.a. Elegien, die uns Ovids Reise ins Exil miterleben lassen, besser gesagt, un seine 'Reise ins Exil' verführen" (The first book of Tristia contains, among other things, elegies that allow us to witness Ovid's journey into exile, or rather, show us his "Journey into Exile") (1976, 23). Likewise, Luck 1977, 3: "Die Dichtungen, die [das erstes Tristienbuch] enthält, sind alle während der Reise ins Exil geschrieben worden und sind daher thematisch mannigfaltiger, was die Stationen der Reise betrifft" (The poems that [the first book of *Tristia*] contains have all been written during the journey into exile and are therefore thematically varied in terms of the stages of the journey). Cf. Hermann 1924, 13–38; Kenney 1965, 39ff.; Dickinson 1973, 161–63; Evans 1983, 31–32, 45–49; Claassen 2008, 13–15.

12. Froesch 1976 suggests the pattern centers on three groups of three poems: 1.2–4, 1.5–7, and 1.8–10. Hermann 1924, in contrast, favors a strict, chiastic arrangement with poem 1.6 as the centerpiece. Dickinson 1973 argues for a similar structure to that of Evans with only minor variation: level 1 on the prologue and epilogue (1.1 and 1.11), level 2 on the storm and journey (1.2–4 and 1.10), level 3 on friendship (1.5 and 1.7–9), and level 4 on Ovid's wife (1.6). Evans 1983, 185n31, however, misconstrues Dickinson's arrangement as one based on four main themes given equal treatment: "Prologue and Epilogue," "Travel and Storm," "Friendship," and "the Remainder." This misconception is most likely due to the confusing nature of Dickinson's explanation on p. 161, which features a diagram and a list of themes, each of which presents an arrangement different from those of the other scholars. However, of all these arrangements, Evans's seems to make the most sense. Hermann's scheme pairs poems with extremely divergent themes (e.g., 1.4 and 1.9) and Froesch's places poems with divergent themes into the same groups (e.g., 1.8–1.10 as a group).

13. For a more detailed discussion of Evans's arrangement of *Tristia* 1, see Evans 1983, 45–49.

14. Videau-Delibes 1991, 67, notes that continuity in the narration of the exile's journey must be configured by the reader, as it is the reader who must complete any "gaps" or "holes" in the narrative from other poems.

15. Dickinson 1973, 163: "*Imago* means 'ghost,' as well as 'memory-image.'" Dickinson goes on to analyze the poem in terms of its "ghostliness" (163–67). For more on these lines, see Doblhofer 1987, 87–90. In addition, the use of *imago* to describe memory is discussed in detail in chapter 4.

16. Luck 1977, 36: "Der Zeitablauf wird in vier Abschnitte gegliedert" (The passage of time is divided into four acts).

17. In addition to Froesch and Luck, see Della Corte 1973, 218; Posch 1983, 124–25n281; Bonvicini 1991, 231. See also Doblhofer 1987, 86: "Die Elegie trist. 1,3 [ist] Abbild eines Dramas mit Ovid als Protagonisten, seiner Frau als Deuteragonistin und den Frunden als Chor, so könnte man in den fünf Abschnitten die klassischen fünf Akte wiederfinden" (The elegy [is] the image of a drama with Ovid as protagonist, his wife as supporting actor, and his friends as a choir; in such a way, one could find the classic five acts in the five sections).

18. Froesch 1976, 26–27; Eur. *Hipp.* 1091ff. and 1143ff.

19. "The elegy . . . is clearly a drama with Ovid as protagonist; his wife plays the supporting role; his friends and servants make up the tragic chorus, which accompanies the dramatic action with its complaints."

20. Mack 1988, 43: "Ovid's wife is his real wife who stayed behind in Rome at her husband's insistence even though she wanted to join him in exile; she is also Penelope of epic and the beloved mistress of elegy." However, as I discuss later, there is current debate over the historicity of the exile's wife. See Petersen 2005 and Reeber 2014 for more on the literary construction of the exile's wife.

21. Luck 1977, *ad* 1.3.15–16: "Da er die Freunde anspricht, nicht die Freunde ihn" (Here he speaks to his friends, but his friends don't speak to him).

22. Fugier 1976 analyzes the distribution of personal pronouns to show that the exile is writing in isolation, writing to individuals who never reply and leave the exile speaking to himself.

23. *Tr.* 4.7, 5.7, 5.11, 5.12, 5.13; *Pont.* 4.9

24. Cf. Io, Actæon, Callisto.

25. *OLD ad loc.* See Plaut. *Cas.* prol. 19; Ter. *Phorm.* 5.9.30; Cic. *Tusc.* 1.30.74.

26. *Met.* 1.236, 2.674.

27. Cf. Io (*Met.* 1.635–37, 731–33); Callisto (*Met.* 2.485–88); Actæon to his dogs/comrades (*Met.* 3.240–41); Philomela (*Met.* 6.521–26).

28. *Met.* 6.525–26: *vi superat frusta clamato saepe parente / saepe sorore sua, magnis super omnia divis*.

29. See *Tr.* 2.207ff.

30. *Tr.* 2.103–10: *Cur aliquid uidi? Cur noxia lumina feci? / Cur imprudenti cognita culpa mihi? / Inscius Actaeon uidit sine ueste Dianam: / praeda fuit canibus non minus ille suis. / Scilicet in superis etiam fortuna luenda est, / nec ueniam laeso numine casus habet. / Illa nostra die, qua me malus abstulit error, / parua quidem periit, sed sine labe domus.*

*Notes to Pages 94–105*

The connection between Ovid's depiction of the exile and the tale of Actæon has been long noted; see Owen 1924, *ad loc.*; Drucker 1977, 149; Goold 1983, 100; Rosiello 2002, 446–52; McGowan 2009, 195–97; Ingleheart 2011, 124–31. Pohlenz even went as far as to suggest that Ovid wrote the Actæon tale from the *Metamorphoses* in exile because of the allusions of the tale in *Tristia* 2: "Ovid hat III 141–142 erst nach der Verbannung eingefügt, weil ihn sein eigenes Vergehen an Actaeon erinnert hatte" (1913, 11).
For the myth in the *Metamorphoses*, see chapter 2, as well as Pohlenz 1913, 10–13; Otis 1970, 128–37; Galinsky 1975, 66–67, 102–3.

31. *Met.* 3.253–255: *Rumor in ambiguo est; aliis violentior aequo / visa dea est, alii laudant dignamque severa / virginitate vocant: pars invenit utraque causas.*

32. Bonvicini 1991, *ad loc.*: "I due eroi si muovono sulla scena in sintonia" (The two heroes move in harmony on the stage). Della Corte 1972, trans. of *Tr.* 1.3.41–42: "Con questa preghiera invocai gli dèi del Cielo: e ancora di più mentre i singhiozzi troncavano a mezzo le voci. Pregava la mia consorte" (With this prayer, I called upon the gods of heaven: and even more while sobs broke half-spoken words. My wife prayed).

33. See the debate over Verg. *Aen.* 4.449: *mens immota manet, lacrimae volvuntur inanes.* Are these Aeneas's tears or Dido's? The ambiguous nature of the line allows for the tears to come from both, heightening the pathos of the scene.

34. See *Met.* 2.401ff. and *Fast.* 2.153ff. Bonvicini 1991, *ad loc.*: "l'Orsa Maggiore Parrasia, cioè dell'Arcadia, dove sorge il monte Parrasio. Il mito narra che la ninfa Callisto, figlia del re arcade Licaone, conquistò l'amore di Giove e, a causa di ciò, Giunone, gelosa, la trasformò in un'orsa. Giove poi l'assunse in cielo dove splende col nome di Orsa Maggiore" (The Great Parrhasian Bear, that of Arcadia, where the Parrhasian mountain rises. According to the myth, the nymph Callisto, daughter of the Arcadian king Lycaon won the love of Jupiter, and because of this, Juno, jealous, turned her into a bear. Jupiter then took her into heaven, where she shines with the name of Ursa Major). For further discussion, see Bömer 1969–86, *ad* 2.276ff.; Luck 1977, *ad* 1.3.47ff.

35. Bonvicini 1991, *ad* 1.3.48: "[l'Orsa Maggiore Parrasia], visibile tutta la note, ruota intorno al suo asse così che al mattino occupa la posizione opposta a quella della sera" ([The Great Parrhasian Bear], visible throughout the night, rotates around its axis so that in the morning it occupies the position opposite to that of the evening).

36. See Actæon's inner monologue, *Met.* 3.204–5: *quid faciat? repetatne domum et regalia tecta, / an lateat silvis? pudor hoc, timor impedit illud.*

37. For a more detailed analysis of these lines, see chapter 2.

38. Huskey 2002, 100–101, reads this as an allusion to the fall of Troy at *Aen.* 2.801–3: *iamque iugis summae surgebat / Lucifer Idea / ducebatque diem, Danaique obsessa tenebant / limina portarum, nec spes opis ulla dabatur.* He argues that Ovid describes the exile's movement into relegation in the same manner in which Virgil portrays Aeneas leading the Trojans into exile (*matresque uirosque, / collectam exsilio pubem, miserabile uulgus,* 2.797–98).

39. "The act of separation is expressed by three different verbs: *dividior, membra relinquam,* and *abrumpi.*"

40. The perils of sea travel were a common theme in both epic and elegy. For epic, see Ovid *Met.* 11.748ff.; Hom. *Od.* 5.291ff. and 12.403ff.; Verg. *Aen.* 1.81ff. and 3.192ff. For elegy, see Tib. 1.5.35ff.; *Cul.* 383. See also Hor. *Carm.* 1.3, his *propemptikon* for Virgil.

41. The emphasis on speech is a slight modification of the traditional complaints of the epic hero stranded on the sea. Cf. Verg. *Aen.* 1.94-96: *O terque quaterque beati, / quis ante ora patrum Troiae sub moenibus altis / contigit oppetere!*

42. See *Tr.* 1.11.24, *Am.* 2.19.5, *Met.* 14.215; Hom. *Od.* 15.480.

43. Many of these eventually become the topoi of exilic literature identified by Doblhofer 1987 and Gaertner 2007. For further discussion, see chapter 1.

44. For loneliness, see Stevens 2009, 169-70; for lack of poetic inspiration, see 170-73; and for the inability to communicate, see 165-69, 173-76.

45. See also *Fast.* 5.221: *prima per inmensas sparsi nova semina gentes*; and *Tr.* 4.2.59: *ille per inmensas spatiatur libera terras*.

46. Paullus Fabius Maximus is probably the best-known person in Ovid's exilic corpus and is the addressee of at least three of the *Epistulae ex Ponto* (1.2, 3.3, 3.8). Maximus held the consulship in 11 BCE, was a pontifex, and a member of the *fratres Arvales*. Maximus's wife, Marcia, was a cousin of Augustus, and it is thought that Maximus himself exerted some modicum of influence on the *princeps* (Tac. *Ann.* 1.5; Quin. *Inst.* 6.3.52). In addition to Ovid, Maximus appears in Hor. *Carm.* 4. For more on the historical significance of Paullus Fabius Maximus, see Syme 1978, 135-55.

47. For the Scythian arrow as a threat to the exile, see. *Tr.* 3.10.64-65, 4.10.110ff; *Pont.* 1.8.6.

48. See also Frécaut 1972, 315ff.

49. For a detailed analysis of gesture in the exilic corpus, see Stevens 2009, 176-80.

50. Cornelius Severus, like Ovid, was a poet under Augustus who wrote an epic poem on the Sicilian Wars (*Bellum Siculum*) and a poem on the kings of Rome (see Sen. *Suas.* 6.26). Both of these works have come down to us only in fragments. For a more detailed historical sketch, see Syme 1978, 88-89. For fragments of his work, see Morel 1963, 116-19.

51. See Evans 1983, 172ff., for the concept of increasing despair in the exile literature.

52. *Tr.* 2.357, 2.379, 3.4.71, 4.10.100, 5.14.18; *Pont.* 1.5.76, 3.2.104. *Indicium* also has a legal flavor to its meaning: see idioms such as *indicium postulare* (to seek pardon by informing) and *indicium profiteri* and *indicium offerre* (to offer information). See OLD s.v. *indicium* 2b. For more on *indicium* in the exile literature, see Gibson 1999, esp. 27-28, 30, 36.

53. See Conte's integrative allusion (1986 passim).

54. Gaertner 2005, ad 1.3.39-40: "The comparison with a nightingale shut up in a cage suits the exiled poet, as the bird is often associated not only with poetry (Hes. *Op.* 202-12, B. 3.97, Call. *Epigr.* 2.5 (Pfeiffer)) but also with lament." For more on the association of the nightingale with Philomela and her narrative, see chapter 2.

55. This concept in Statius's Silvae, a work that was designed to have the appearance of an unpolished collection of occasional poems. Cf. Coleman 1988, xxii-xxiii; Hinds 1998, 12.

56. For more on *aemulatio* in Latin poetry, see Pasquali 1942 passim; Conte 1986, 24-26; Hinds 1998, 10-16. In addition, Giangrande (1967, 85) forms his concept of *oppositio in imitando* on the back of *aemulatio*, likewise for R. F. Thomas (1986, 171) and the type of reference he terms "correction."

57. See Rosati 2007, *ad Met*. 6.521: "*in stabula . . . vetustis*: il luogo scelto da Tereo per lo stupor evoca risonanze sinistre, legate al bosco che precede la discesa infernale di Enea [Virgilio, *Aen*. VI 179 *itur in antiquam silvam, stabula alta ferarum*], e risulta quasi l'emblema del mondo 'selvaggio,' di quanto di più remote dalla luce della civiltà [una sorta anti-Atene, come suggerisce il contrasto con *Pandione natam*], nonché figura degli obscuri abissi psichici di Tereo" (The place chosen by Tereus for rape evokes sinister resonances, related to the forest before the infernal descent of Aeneas [Virgil, *Aen*. 179 VI *itur in antiquam silvam, stabula high ferarum*], and is nearly the emblem of the "wild" world, how much more remote from the light of civilization [a sort anti-Athens, as suggested by the contrast with *Pandione natam*] and figure of the dark depths of Tereus's psyche).

58. R. F. Thomas 1986, 190, defines an apparent reference as "a context which seems clearly to recall a specific model but which on closer investigation frustrates that expectation."

59. For Virgil: Putnam 1975; R. F. Thomas 1982, 38–50; 1999, 18–24; Ross 1987, 115–19. For the Philomela narrative: Gildenhard and Zissos 2007; Rosati 2007, 316–22.

60. *OLD ad cavea*: "'The part of the theatre in which spectators sat, spectators' seats or benches,' Plaut. Am. prol. 66; Cic. Lael. 7, 24; Lucr. 4, 78; Verg. A. 5, 340; 8, 636; on account of the ascending rows of benches, *ima* or *prima*, 'the seat of the nobility, media and summa or ultima, the seat of the lower classes,' Cic. Sen. 14, 48; Suet. Aug. 44; id. Claud. 21; Sen. Tranq. 11: CAV. II., Inscr. Orell. 2539." See also *Dictionary of Antiquity*, "The theatre in gen.," Plaut. Truc. 5, 1. 39; Cic. Leg. 2, 15, 38; "The spectators," Stat. Th. 1, 423.

61. *Tr*. 3.14.48; *Pont*. 4.13.19–22.

62. Forbis 1997, 261: "Compare *littera pro verbis* in the same metrical position at *Metamorphoses* 1.649, when Io traces her name in the dust to identify herself to her father Inachus. Both Inachus and Messalinus from their civilized perspectives read words from uncivilized sources: Io trapped in a beast's body, and Ovid trapped among the *saevi Getae*."

63. For Io writing her name, see Bömer 1969–86, *ad Met*. 1.649; Barchiesi 2005, *ad Met*. 1.649–52; Hardie 2002, 253.

64. Cherbuliez 2005, 110ff.: "It is through Ovid that 'carmen' is forever linked to 'crimen'; literature cannot be other than contestatory no matter what the protestations of innocence and pledges of submission it contains. Henceforth, and often through Ovid explicitly, the act of writing is always associated with a marginal and therefore a priviledged position for the critique of authority. The attendant fantasy of the lone writer, indeed the lover-writer, remains an anchor for how we understand the contours of state authority as they conflict with conventions of individual human rights. Tracing the edges of the polis, the writer either as person or as producer of texts, designates, describes, and defines the limits of state sovereignty. In a cultural environment where state sovereignty has not yet butted up against the concept of individual sovereignty, let alone the idea of human rights, the status of the marginal poet is especially critical to cultural confrontations with authority."

65. On epistolary markers in the exile poetry, see Stroh 1981, 2640–44. Kennedy 2002 gives an excellent overview of Ovidian epistolarity in general.

66. The notable exception to this scheme is *Tristia* 2, a literary epistle addressed to Augustus. Likewise, the nature of *Epistulae ex Ponto* 4 and the manner in which it would have fit into this scheme is unknown, as that book is merely a collection of exilic poems in no discernible order that were left by Ovid upon his death.

67. Cugusi 1970–79, 32–34; Stowers 1986, 60, 62, 68–69, 157; Malherbe 1988, 12. See also Cic. *Phil.* 2.7; *Q. fr.* 2.10.1; Ambr. *Epist.* 47.4; Synesius *Epist.* 138; Quin. *Inst.* 9.4.19; Jul. Vict. p. 447, 36 Halm; Demetrius 5; Nicol. *Progym.* 11.3; Q. Cic. *Fam.* 16.16.2; Sid. Apoll. *Epist.* 7.18.2.

68. Cugusi 1983, 33–34; Stowers 1986, 29, 35, 38, 58–60, 65–69, 78, 144.

69. For more on the stock nature of the good and the bad friend, as well as the enemy in literary letters, see G. Williams 1994; Rosenmeyer 2006.

70. Nugent 1990, 248–53; Barchiesi 1993; Gibson 1999; Fulkerson 2005, 149ff.

71. Perilla may also be a literary creation to some extent, for she shares the name of a famous elegiac mistress (see *Tr.* 2.437–38). The *communis opinio* is that she was Ovid's stepdaughter (see A. L. Wheeler 1925; Harrison 2002). However, other explanations have been put forward (see Luck 1977, 199).

72. Reeber 2014: "Ovid's third wife is a prominent figure throughout the *Tristia*, as the addressee of seven poems and the subject of long passages in many others. In this paper I argue that 1.6, the first of Ovid's poetic epistles to his wife, makes use of specific generic markers to invite an identification of the woman with the work: *just as the elegiac mistress of his earlier work came to represent both a physical and literary corpus (Wyke), so too does Ovid's wife ultimately amount to a metaliterary stand-in for Ovid's poetry. What appears to be a straightforward poetic tribute to his wife's loyalty thus becomes a hyper-elegiac exploration of the poet's contradictory feelings about his own earlier work, the carmen that came to be an* error" (emphasis added).

73. This was first pointed out by Hinds 1985. The tradition is most clearly articulated by Aelius Donatus, *Vita Vergilii* 39–41: *Egerat cum Vario, priusquam Italia decederet, ut siquid sibi accidisset, Aeneida combureret; at is facturum se pernegarat; igitur in extrema valetudine assidue scrinia desideravit, crematurus ipse; verum nemine offerente nihil quidem nominatim de ea cavit. Ceterum eidem Vario ac simul Tuccae scripta sua sub ea condicione legavit, ne quid ederent, quod non a se editum esset. Edidit autem auctore Augusto Varius, sed summatim emendata, ut qui versus etiam inperfectos sicut erant reliquerit.*

74. The earliest extant text with the traditional story is Pliny the Elder (77–78 CE): *carmina Vergilii cremari contra testament eius verecundiam vetuit* (*NH* 7.11). The most famous account of this is that of Donatus from the mid-fourth century CE. There is a debate over whether Donatus took the story from a lost work of Suetonius (69?–130? CE). Moreover, there is even more debate about what Suetonius's sources may have been. Suggestions include Asconius Pedianus (9 BCE–76 CE) and Varius Rufus (74 BCE–14 BCE), who was intimately involved in the traditional story. For a more detailed discussion, see Stok 2010, 107–20.

75. The term *exemplum* is regularly employed by Cicero in his letters. See Cic. *Fam.* 3.3.2, 6.8.3, 6.18.2, 8.1.1, 9.14.8, 9.26.1; *Att.* 3.8.4, 5.11.6, 7.23.3, 8.2.2, 8.6.1–3, 8.11.3, 8.12.6, 8.15.3, 9.7.1, 9.9.3, 9.11.2–4, 9.12.1, 9.13.1, 9.14.1, 10.3.2, 10.9.3, 11.7.2, 12.18.2, 12.37.1, 12.44.3,

13.6.3, 13.26.2, 13.46.5, 13.50.1, 13.51.1, 14.13.6, 14.17.8, 14.19.1, 14.21.1, 15.14.1, 15.26.2, 15.28.1, 16.4.1, 16.12.1, 16.15.3, 16.16.1.

76. The use of *adunata* is frequent in the exile literature. In fact, similar *adunata* are employed in a similar context in *Tr.* 1.8 and *Pont.* 2.4, both of which are addressed to Atticus. For more, see G. Williams 1994, 119–22.

77. *Tr.* 4.7; 5.7, 5.11, 5.12, 5.13; *Pont.* 4.9.

CHAPTER 4. SPEECH LOSS AND MEMORY IN THE EXILE LITERATURE

1. "But anyhow, if a man has once transgressed the bounds of modesty, the best he can do is to be shameless out and out. So I frankly ask you again and again to eulogize my actions with even more warmth than perhaps you feel, and in that respect to disregard the canons of history; and—to remind you of that personal partiality, of which you have written most charmingly in a certain prefatory essay, clearly showing that you could have been as little swayed by it as Xenophon's famous Hercules by Pleasure,— if you find that such personal partiality enhances my merits even to exaggeration in your eyes, I ask you not to disdain it, and of your bounty to bestow on our love even a little more than may be allowed by truth. And if I can induce you to undertake what I suggest, you will, I assure myself, find a theme worthy even of your able and flowing pen. . . . Again, it will more effectually conduce both to my happiness of mind and the dignity of my memory to have won a place in your history than in that of others, for this reason, that not only shall I have enjoyed the advantage of your literary talent, but also the moral authority of a man highly distinguished and of established reputation, one, moreover, recognized and approved as a leader of men in the greatest and gravest issues of public life so that it will appear that I have had vouchsafed me not only the celebrity but also the weighty testimony of a great and distinguished man" (trans. Williams 1965).

2. "These decorations adorn happy little books, but you are suitable as a memory of my fortune."

3. Beyond the *Oxford Latin Dictionary*, other concise discussions of *memoria* are Walter 2004, 26–35; Heusch 2011, 23–47; Galinsky 2014, 1–4.

4. Assmann 2010, 109–10; Erll 2010, 3–7.

5. Before *La Mémorie Collective*, however, Halbwachs, following in the footsteps of Emile Durkheim and Henri Bergson, had already sketched out the "social frameworks" of memory in his *Les Cadres sociaux de la mémorie* (1925). As Ricoeur notes, the most significant difference between the works is that in *La Mémorie Collective* Halbwachs "was to draw the reference to collective memory out of the very work of personal memory engaged in recalling its memories" (2004, 120).

Olick and Robbins 1998 provides a good sketch of the history of collective memory as well as a useful discussion of how to define the field of social memory. In addition, Olick, Vinitzky-Seroussi, and Levy 2011, 3–29, gives a useful background the development of collective memory and current trajectories in the scholarship on collective memory.

6. Assmann 2010, 110: "Halbwachs, however, the inventor of the term 'collective memory', was careful to keep his concept of collective memory apart from the realm of traditions, transmissions, and transferences which we propose to subsume under the term 'cultural memory.' We [i.e., Jan and Aleida Assmann] preserve Halbwachs's distinction

by breaking up his concept of collective memory into 'communicative' and 'cultural memory,' but we insist on including the cultural sphere, which he excluded, in the study of memory. We are, therefore, not arguing for replacing his idea of 'collective memory' with 'cultural memory'; rather, we distinguish between both forms as two different modi memorandi, ways of remembering."

7. The number of eighty to one hundred years was arrived at because of its identification as a *saeculum*, the timespan of three of four generations. Gladigow 1983, basing his arguments on Herodotus and Tac. *Ann*. 3.75, states that a *saeculum* is the maximum amount of time that a generation can be remembered. Cf. Cat. 1: *quod, <o> patrona virgo, / plus uno maneat perenne saeclo*.

8. Assmann 2010 makes a distinction regarding this store of symbolic objects, describing the storage of institutions of active memory that preserve the "past as present" (i.e., keep past memories relevant in the present) as a canon and the storage of institutions of passive memory that preserve the "past as past" as an archive.

9. Gowing 2005, 10: "But that is to question whether the memory is 'true' or 'false,' 'transmitted' or 'lived,' not whether it is in fact a memory at all. Regardless of origins, such memories become part of the individual's experience and understanding of the past, and, to the extent that such memories are shared, part of the culture's 'collective memory.'"

10. Gowing 2005, 11: "For the Romans *historia* is less a genre than a definition of subject matter. Poetry is therefore not excluded, nor monuments and inscriptions."

11. Rosati 2014, 77: "The Flavians too need their 'foundation myth,' a glorious past that legitimates their leadership. And we know that this 'need of a past' was a serious political problem for the family that, at the end of the civil war of the 'year of the four emperors,' had succeeded the glorious Julio-Claudian dynasty (which the myth of Aeneas traced back to divine origins)." Cf. also Suet. *Vesp*. 1.1: *obscura . . . quidem ac sine ullis maiorum imaginibus*.

12. Rosati 2014, 76: "The *memoria* of his own triumph, entrusted in the world of myth to the Muses (who are the daughters of Memory) and in concrete earthly reality to poets, who are inspired by them, is the foundation on which Jupiter (and his counterpart on earth, the emperor) legitimates his right to command."

13. Maximus Cotta is traditionally considered the adopted son of Messalla Corvinus, Ovid's former patron. He assumed the name Messallinus at the death of his elder brother M. Valerius Messalla Messallinus. Multiple letters in the *Epistulae ex Ponto* are addressed to Cotta: *Pont*. 1.5, 1.9, 2.3, 3.2, and 3.5. For a general overview of these poems, including major themes, see Evans 1983, 114–19. For a discussion of the historical Maximus Cotta, see Syme 1978, 117–31.

In contrast to Maximus Cotta, little is known about Atticus. Evans 1983 postulates that he is the same Atticus whom Ovid addresses at *Am*. 1.9.2 and perhaps the same *eques* Curtius Atticus who is mentioned as a friend of Emperor Tiberius in Tac. *Ann*. 4.58.1 and 6.10.2. Two letters in the *Epistulae ex Ponto* are addressed to Atticus: *Pont*. 2.4 and 2.7. For a general overview of these poems, including major themes, see Evans 1983, 134–35. For a discussion of the historical Atticus, see Froesch 1976, 102–3, 217n386; Syme 1978, 72.

14. See also Tac. *Ann.* 1: *tua, dive Auguste, caelo recepta mens, tua, pater Druse, imago, tui memoria isdem istis cum militibus, quos iam pudor et gloria intrat, eluant hanc maculam irasque civilis in exitium hostibus vertant*; Tac. *Ann.* 2.53: *magna illic imago tristium laetorumque.* For the motif in the exile literature, see Nagle 1980, 92–98a.

15. This use of *imago* to refer to the recollection of the appearance of dead people is also common: see *TLL* s.v. 409-26-47; Cic. *Div.* 1.63; V.Fl. 3.363. Gaertner 2005, *ad Pont.* 1.9.7, also notes the similarly common combination of *imago* and *haerere*: see also *TLL* s.v. 2494.7–38).

16. See Hom. *Od.* 1.115: ὀσσόμενος πατέρ' ἐσθλὸν ἐνὶ φρεσίν.

17. Helzle 2003, *ad Pont.* 1.9.7–8, mentions the use of *imago* to describe Dido as well, linking the use of the motif in Apollodorus, Virgil, and Ovid's later rendition in *Heroides* 7: "Das Motiv *ante meos oculos imago haeret* erinnert besonders an Dido bei Verg. *Aen.* IV 4 *haerent infixi pectore vultus* (vgl. Apoll. Rhod. III 453), Ov. *Epist.* 7,25 *Aeneas oculos vigilantis semper inhaeret, / coniugis ante oculos deceptae stabit imago*."

18. On the use of *referre* as a synonym for *meminisse*, see *OLD* 17; in Ovid, see *Rem. am.* 299; *Met.* 14.451; *Tr.* 5.4.39.

19. See *Tr.* 1.9.61–62: *scis vetus hoc iuveni lusum mihi carmen, et istos, / ut non laudandos, sic tamen esse iocos*; *Tr.* 3.1.5–10: *haec domini fortuna mei est, ut debeat illam / infelix nullis dissimulare iocis. / id quoque, quod viridi quondam male lusit in aevo, / heu nimium sero damnat et odit opus. / inspice quid portem: nihil hic nisi triste videbis, / carmine temporibus conveniente suis.*

20. See *Tr.* 5.13.27: *utque solebamus consumere longa loquendo / tempora, sermoni deficient die.*

21. Hom. *Od.* 11.468; 24.72; Pind. *Pyth.* 6.28; Strabo 13; Dares, *Phrygius* 34; Paus. 2.18.7–9; 3.19; Hyg. 113–14.

22. The "lament" of a friend's death and the recollection of times spent together were traditional topoi of *laudationes funebres*, or poetic epicedia/epitaphioi. Cf. Kierdorf 1980, 64–71, 75–80. In these cases, however, greater emphasis is placed on the literary production undertaken by the exile and his friends than in the straightforward obituaries of such *laudationes*.

23. This Licinius is traditionally identified as C. Licinius Macer Calvus, the son of the annalist C. Licinius Macer and one the *poetae novi*. He is mentioned elsewhere in Catullus 14 and 53. Although few fragments of his poetry are extent (cf. Hollis 2007, fr. 20–42), his *Io* was a fundamental work in the neoteric movement on the same level as Cinna's *Symrna*. Ovid makes direct mention of Calvus and his relationship to Catullus at *Tr.* 2.431–2: *par* [*Catulli licentiae*] *fuit exigui similisque licentia Calvi / detexit variis qui sua furta modis.*

24. Luck 1977, *ad Tr.* 1.9.61–62: "Das Verbum [*lusus*] steht entweder absolut oder hat *carmen, amores, ignes* als Objekt. Die Dichtungen heißen *lusus, blanditiae, ineptiae, ioci, nugae*, der Dichter *lusor*. Die etwas gezierte Selbstverkleinerung scheint ein neoterisches Erbstück zu sein" (The word [*lusus*] is either stands by itself or takes *carmen, amores* or *ignes* as object. The poems are called *lusus, blanditiae, ineptiae, ioci, nugae*, the poet *lusor*. The somewhat fake self-deprication seems to be a neoteric inheritance).

25. This line is also alluded to in Verg. *Ecl.* 9.51-51 (*saepe ego longos / cantando puerum memini me condere soles*) and Hor. *Carm.* 2.7.6–7 (*cum quo morantem saepe*

*diem mero / fregi*). G. Williams 1991, 169n3, argues that Virgil's translation of ἐν λέσχηι as *cantando* "indicates that [he] understood λέσχηι in the sense of 'conversation.'"

26. G. Williams 1991, 171n11: "But Callimachus may term Heraclitus' poetry 'nightingales' for symbolic reasons. Firstly, Swinnen, op. cit. 42 takes to be typological on the analogy of ἀ[ηδονίδες] (Aet. fr. 1.16][Pf.]). The latter term characterizes Callimachus' own poetry in contrast to the poetic ideal of the Telchines; so, by terming Heraclitus' poetry ἀηδόνες, Callimachus gives it an aesthetic value, based on his own ideals. Secondly, nightingales sing after dark, so that in the words of MacQueen, op. cit. 52–3, 'the voice of Heraclitus has in his nightingales conquered darkness and death.' Thirdly, as noted by N. Hopkinson, A Hellenistic Anthology (Cambridge, 1988), p. 249, 'the nightingale's song was proverbially a lament; Heraclitus' ἀηδόνες can be imagined as bewailing their own poet's death.'"

27. The choice of *subire* as the term for his recollection of the night on which the exile's house was destroyed and he was forced to leave his community is reminiscent of a similar use in *Met.* 11. In that setting, the sailors on Ceyx's ship, having been terrified by a storm that was tearing apart their ship, think back on the families that they left behind, an act of recollection that is also described with *subire*: *subeunt illi fraterque parensque, / huic cum pignoribus domus et quodcunque relictum est* (*Met.* 11.542–43).

28. The exclamatory vowels in *Pont.* 1.9 are uncertain. Helzle 2003, *ad Pont.* 1.9.21–22, makes the conjecture that the *o quotiens* should be changed to *a quotiens* in order to match the other allusions to *Tr.* 1.3. Moreover, Gaertner 2005, *ad Pont.* 1.9.21/23, following Tränkle 1960, 149–50, notes that the exclamatory *o* seems to be used mostly for an expression of delight or joy, and an exclamatory *a* tends to indicate pain or sorrow.

# Works Cited

Ahl, F. 1985. *Metaformations: Soundplay and Wordplay in Ovid and Other Classical Poets.* Ithaca, NY.

Albrecht, M. von. 1968. *Ovid.* Darmstadt.

Alexandridis, A., M. Wild, and L. Winkler-Horaček, eds. 2008. *Mensch und Tier in der Antike: Grenzziehung und Grenzüberschreitung.* Wiesbaden.

Altieri, C. 1973. "Ovid and the New Mythologists." *NOVEL: A Forum on Fiction* 7, no. 1: 31–40.

Andersen, R. 1977. "The Notion of Schemata and the Educational Enterprise: General Discussion of the Conference." In *Schooling and the Acquisition of Knowledge*, edited by R. C. Andersen and R. J. Spiro, 415–31. Hillsdale, NJ.

Anderson, W. S. 1963. "Multiple Change in the Metamorphoses." *Transactions of the APA* 94:1–27.

———. 1997. *Commentary and Text*, Ovid's Metamorphoses: *Books 1–10.* Norman, OK.

Assmann, J. 1992. *Das kulturelle Gedächtnis: Schrift, Erinnerung und politische Identität in frühen Hochkulturen.* Munich.

———. 2010. "Communicative and Cultural Memory." In *A Companion to Cultural Memory Studies*, edited by A. Erll and A Nünning, 109–25. Berlin.

Assmann, J., and J. Czaplica. 1995. "Collective Memory and Cultural Identity." *New German Critique* 65:125–33.

Ax, W. 1986. "Quadripartita ratio: Bemerkugen zur Geschichte eines aktuellen Kategoriensystems (adiecto-detractio-transmutio-immutatio). *Historiographia Linguistica* 13:191–214.

Balogh, E. 1943. *Political Refugees in Ancient Greece: From the Period of the Tyrants to Alexander the Great.* Johannesburg.

Barchiesi, A. 1993. "Future Reflexive: Two Modes of Allusion in Ovid's *Heroides*." *HSCP* 37:1–21.

———. 2001. *Speaking Volumes: Narrative and Intertext in Ovid and Other Latin poets.* London.

———. 2005. *Commentary and Text*, Metamorfosi: *Libri I–II.* Milan.

Barchiesi, A., and G. Rosati. 2007. *Commentary and Text*, Metamorfosi: *Libri III–IV.* Milan.

Bartlett, F. (1932) 1995. *Remembering*. New York.
Beard, M., J. North, and S. Price. 1998. *Religions of Rome*. Vol. 1, *A History*. Vol. 2, *A Sourcebook*. Cambridge.
Bearzot, C. 2001. "Xenoi e profughi nell'Europa di Isocrate." In *Integrazione, mescolanza, rifuto, Incontri di populi, lingue e culture in Europa dall'antichità all'umanismo: Atti del convegno internazionale*, edited by G. Urso, 47–63. Rome.
Bettini, M. 2011. *The Ears of Hermes: Communication, Images, and Identity in the Classical World*. Columbus, OH.
Bevan, D., ed. 1990. *Literature and Exile*. Amsterdam.
Boillat, M. 1976. *Les Métamorphoses d'Ovide: Thèmes majeurs et problèmes de composition*. Bern.
Boldor, A. 2005. "Exile as Severance." PhD diss, Louisiana State University.
Bömer, F. 1969–86. *Commentary*, Metamorphosen. 7 vols. Heidelberg.
Bonvicini, M., ed. 1991. *Ovidio, Tristia*. Milan.
Bostock, J. 1856. *The Natural History of Pliny*. London.
Brink, C. O. 2011. *Horace on Poetry: The "Ars Poetica."* Cambridge.
Brown, T. S. 1988. "The Greek Exiles: Herodotus' Contemporaries." *AncW* 17:17–28.
Burstein, S. M. 1989. *Agatharchides of Cnidus on the Erythraean Sea*. London.
Casali, S. 1997. "*Quaerenti plura legendum*: On the Necessity of 'Reading More' in Ovid's Exile Poetry." *Ramus* 26:80–112.
Casson, R. 1983. "Schemata in Cognitive Anthropology." *Annual Review of Anthropology* 12:429–62.
Cawkwell, G. L. 1981. "The King's Peace." *CQ* 31:69–83.
Cherbuliez, J. 2005. *The Place of Exile: Leisure Literature and the Limits of Absolutism*. Lewisburg, PA.
Claassen, J-M. 1999. *Displaced Persons: The Literature of Exile from Cicero to Boethius*. London.
———. 2008. *Ovid Revisited: The Poet in Exile*. London.
Cole, T. 1967. *Democritus and Sources of Greek Anthropology*. Cleveland, OH.
Coleman, K. 1988. *Statius, Silvae IV: Text, Translation, and Commentary*. Oxford.
Conte, G. B. 1986. *The Rhetoric of Imitation: Genre and Poetic Memory in Virgil and Other Latin Poets*. Ithaca, NY.
———. 1999. *Latin Literature: A History*. Baltimore.
Corbeill, A. 2004. *Nature Embodied: Gesture in Ancient Rome*. Princeton, NJ.
Crifò, G. 1985. *L'esclusione dalla città: Altri studi sull'exilium romano*. Perugia.
Cugusi, P. 1970–79. *Epistolographi Latini Minores*. 2 vols. Turin.
Curran, L. 1978. "Rape and Rape Victims in the Metamorphoses." In *Women in the Ancient World: The Arethus Papers*, edited by J. Peradotto and J. P. Sullivan, 263–86. Albany, NY.
Degl' Innocenti Pierini, R. 1990. *Tra Ovidio e Seneca*. Bologna.
de Levita, D. J. 1965. *The Concept of Identity*. New York.
Della Corta, F., trans. 1972. *I Tristia*. Vol. 1, *Traduzione*. Genoa.
———, comm. 1973. *I Tristia*. Vol. 2, *Commento*. Genoa.

de Luce, J. 1993. "'O for a Thousand Tongues to Sing': A Footnote on *Metamorphosis*, Silence, and Power." In *Woman's Power, Man's Game*, edited by M. DeForst, 305–21. Wauconda, IL.

Deremetz, A. 1995. *Le miroir des Muses: Poétiques de la réflexitvité à Rome*. Villeneuve d'Ascq.

Dickinson, R. J. 1973. "The *Tristia*: Poetry in Exile." In *Ovid*, edited by J. D. Binns, 154–90. London.

Dierauer, U. 1977. *Tier und Mensch im Denken der Antike: Studien zur Tierpsychologie, Anthropologie und Ethik*. Amsterdam.

Doblhofer, E. 1987. *Exil und Emigration: Zum Erlebnis der Heimatferne in der römischen Literatur*. Darmstadt.

Drucker, M. 1977. "Der verbannte Dichter und der Kaiser-Gott: Studien zu Ovids späten Elegien." PhD diss, Universität Heidelberg.

Durante, M. 1976. *Sulla preistoria della tradizione poetica greca*. Part 2, *Risultanze della comparazione indoeuropea*. Rome.

Eisenhut, W. 1961. "Deducere camen: Ein Beitrag zum Problem der literarischen Beziehungen zwischen Horaz und Properz." In *Gedenkschrift für G. Rohde*, edited by W. Eisenhut, 91–104. Tübingen.

Erll, A. 2010. "Cultural Memory Studies: An Introduction." In *A Companion to Cultural Memory Studies*, edited by A. Erll and A. Nünning, 1–18. Berlin.

Evans, H. 1983. *Publica Carmina: Ovid's Books from Exile*. Lincoln, NE.

Evans, V., and M. Green. 2006. *Cognitive Linguistics: An Introduction*. Edinburgh.

Fantham, E. 2007. "Dialogues of Displacement: Seneca's Consolations to Helvia and Polybius." In *Writing Exile: The Discourse of Displacement in Greco-Roman Antiquity and Beyond*, edited by J. F. Gaertner, 173–92. Leiden.

———. 2013. *Roman Literary Culture: From Plautus to Macrobius*. Baltimore.

Feldherr, A. 2010. *Playing Gods: Ovid's* Metamorphoses *and the Politics of Fiction*. Princeton, NJ.

Fögen, T. 2007. "Pliny the Elder's Animals: Some Remarks on the Narrative Structure of *Nat. Hist.* 8–11." *Hermes* 135:184–98.

———. 2009. *Tears in the Graeco-Roman World*. Berlin.

Forbes-Irving, P. M. C. 1992. *Metamorphosis in Greek Myths*. Oxford.

Forbis, E. 1997. "Voice and Voicelessness in Ovid's Exile Poetry." In *Studies in Latin Literature and Roman History*, vol. 8, edited by C. Deroux, 245–67. Brussels.

Forsdyke, S. 2005. *Exile, Ostracism, and Democracy: The Politics of Expulsion in Ancient Greece*. Princeton, NJ.

Fränkel, H. 1970. *Ein Dichter zwischen zwei Welten*. Darmstadt.

Frécaut, J-M. 1972. *L'esprit et l'humour chez Ovide*. Grenoble.

Froesch, H. 1976. *Ovid als Dichter des Exils*. Bonn.

Fugier, H. 1976. "Communication et structures textuelles dans *les Tristes* d'Ovide." *Revue Romane* 11:74–98.

Fulkerson, L. 2003. "Chain(ed) Mail: Hypermestra and the Dual Readership of '*Heroides* 14.'" *TAPA* 133, no. 1: 123–45.

———. 2005. *The Ovidian Heroine as Author: Reading, Writing, and Community in the* Heroides. Cambridge.

Gaertner, J. F. 2005. *Commentary on Ovid,* Epistulae ex Ponto, *Book I*. Oxford Classical Monographs. Oxford.

———. 2007. "The Discourse of Displacement in Greco-Roman Antiquity." In *Writing Exile: The Discourse of Displacement in Greco-Roman Antiquity and Beyond*, edited by J. F. Gaertner, 1–20. Leiden.

Galinsky, K. 1975. *Ovid's Metamorphoses: An Introduction to the Basic Aspects*. Oxford.

———, ed. 2014. *Memoria Romana: Memory in Rome and Rome in Memory*. Ann Arbor, MI.

Gera, D. L. 2003. *Ancient Greek Ideas on Speech, Language, and Civilization*. Oxford.

Giangrande, G. 1967. "'Arte Allusiva' and Alexandrian Epic Poetry." *CQ* 17, no. 1: 85–97.

Gibson, B. 1999. "Ovid on Reading: Reading Ovid. Reception in Ovid *Tristia* II." *JRS* 89:19–37.

Gildenhard, I., and A. Zissos. 2007. "Barbarian Variations: Tereus, Procne, and Philomela in Ovid (*Met*. 6.412–674) and Beyond." *Dictynna* 4:1–25.

Glidden, D. K. 1994. "Parrots, Pyrrhonists and Native Speakers." In *Language*, edited by S. Everson, 129–48. Cambridge.

Goold, G. P. 1983. "The Cause of Ovid's Exile." *ICS* 8:94–107.

Gowers, E., ed. 2012. *Horace: Satires*. Cambridge.

Gowing, A. 2005. *Empire and Memory: The Representation of the Roman Republic in Imperial Culture*. Cambridge.

Grasmück, E. L. 1978. *Exilium: Untersuchungen zur Verbannung in der Antike*. Paderborn.

Green, Peter. 1994. *The Poems of Exile:* Tristia *and the* Black Sea Letters. Berkeley, CA.

Gurd, S. A. 2012. *Work in Progress: Literary Revision as Social Performance in Ancient Rome*. American Classical Studies 57. Oxford.

Halbwachs, M. 1975. *Les cadres sociaux de la mémoire*. New York.

Hallett, J. 2009. "Corpus erat: Sulpicia's Elegiac Text and Body in Ovid's Pygmalion Narrative (*Metamorphoses* 10.238–297)." In *Bodies and Boundaries in Graeco-Roman Antiquity*, edited by T. Fögen and M. Lee, 111–24. Berlin.

Hardie, P. 2002. *Ovid's Poetics of Illusion*. Cambridge.

Harrison, S. 2002. "Ovid and Genre: Evolutions of an Elegist." In *The Cambridge Companion to Ovid*, edited by P. Hardie, 79–94. Cambridge.

Heath, J. 2005. *The Talking Greeks: Speech, Animals, and the Other in Homer, Aeschylus, and Plato*. Cambridge.

Helzle, M. 1989. "Mr and Mrs Ovid." *Greece & Rome* 36, no. 2: 183–93.

———. 2003. *Ovids* Epistulae ex Ponto. *Buch I–II. Kommentar*. Heidelberg.

Hermann, K. 1924. "De Ovidii Tristium libris V." PhD diss. Universität Leipzig.

Heusch, C. 2011. *Die Macht der* Memoria. *Die 'Noctes Atticae' des Aulus Gellius im Licht der Erinnerungskultur des 2. Jahrhunderts n. Chr*. Berlin.

Hinds, S. 1985. "Booking the Return Trip: Ovid and *Tristia* 1." *PCPS* 31:21–32.

———. 1987. *The Metamorphosis of Persephone: Ovid and the Self-Conscious Muse*. Cambridge.

———. 1998. *Allusion and Intertext: Dynamics of Appropriation in Roman Poetry.* Cambridge.
———. 2006. "Booking the Return Trip: Ovid and *Tristia* 1." In *Oxford Readings in Ovid*, edited by P. Knox, 415–40. Oxford.
———. 2007. "Martial's Ovid / Ovid's Martial." *JRS* 97:113–54.
———. 2009. "After Exile: Time and Teleology from *Metamorphoses* to *Ibis*." In *Ovidian Transformations: Essays on the Metamorphoses and its Reception*, edited by P.R. Hardie, A. Barchiesi, and S. Hinds, 48–67. Cambridge Philological Society Suppl. 23. Cambridge.
———. 2011a. "Black-Sea Latin, Du Bellay, and the Barbarian Turn: Tristia, Regrets, Translations." In *Two Thousand Years of Solitude: Exile after Ovid*, edited by J. Ingleheart, 59–83. Oxford.
———. 2011b. "Seneca's Ovidian Loci." *Studi Italiani di Filologia Classica* 9, no. 1: 5–63.
Hogan, P. 2003. *Cognitive Science, Literature, and the Arts: A Guide for Humanists.* New York.
Hollis, A. S. 1996. Review of G. Williams 1994. *CR* 46:26–27.
———, 2007. *Fragments of Latin Poetry c. 60 BC–AD 20.* Oxford.
Holzberg, N. 1998. *Ovid: Dichter und Werk.* Munich.
Huskey, S. 2001a. "The Allusive Exile: Philomela and Palamedes in Ovid's *Tristia* 1.1." Paper delivered at the 132nd Meeting of the American Philological Association, January 4.
———. 2001b. "The Argonautic Exile: Ovid and Jason in *Tristia* 1.10." Paper delivered at the Ninety-Seventh Meeting of the Classical Association of the Middle West and South, April 19.
———. 2002. "Ovid and the Fall of Troy in 'Tristia' 1.3." *Vergilius* 48:88–104.
———. 2009. "Ovid as Palinurus in the *Tristia*." Paper delivered at the 105th Meeting of the Classical Association of the Middle West and South, April 4.
Ingleheart, J., ed. 2011. *Two Thousand Years of Solitude: Exile after Ovid.* Oxford.
Jacob, C. 1991. *Géographie et ethnographie en Grèce ancienne.* Paris.
Janan, M. 1994. *"When the Lamp Is Shattered": Desire and Narrative in Catullus.* Carbondale, IL.
Johnson, M. 1987. *The Body in the Mind: The Bodily Basis of Meaning, Imagination, and Reason.* Chicago
Joplin, P. K. 2008. "The Voice of the Shuttle Is Ours." In *Sexuality and Gender in the Classical World: Readings and Sources*, edited by L. McClure and P. Joplin, 259–86. Oxford.
Kant, I. 1929. *Critique of Pure Reason.* Translated by N. K. Smith. London.
Karttunen, K. 1989. *India in Early Greek Literature.* Studia Orientalia 65. Helsinki.
Kaster, R. 2005. *Emotion, Restraint, and Community in Ancient Rome.* Oxford.
Keith, A. 2000. *Engendering Rome: Women in Latin Epic.* Cambridge.
Keller, C. 1986. *From a Broken Web: Separation, Sexism, and Self.* Boston.
Kennedy, D. 2002. "Epistolarity: The *Heroides*." In *The Cambridge Companion to Ovid*, edited by P. Hardie, 217–32. Cambridge.
Kenney, E. J. 1965. "The Poetry of Ovid's Exile." *PCPS* 11:37–49.
———. 2011. *Commentary and Text*, Metamorfosi: *Libri VIII–IX.* Milan.

Kierdorf, W. 1980. *Laudatio Funebris: Interpretationem und Untersuchungen zur Entwicklung der römischen Leichenrede.* Berkeley, CA.

Klindienst, P. 1984. "The Voice of the Shuttle Is Ours." *Stanford Literature Review* 1:25–53.

Kline, A. S, trans. 2003. *Ovid: Tristia.* http://www.poetryintranslation.com/PITBR/Latin/OvidTristiaBkOne.htm.

Knox, P. 2012. "A Fragment of an Augustan Aetiological Elegy in a Pompeian Fresco." Paper delivered at the Southern Section of the Classical Association of the Middle West and South, November 1.

Kullman, W. 1991. "Man as a Political Animal in Aristotle." In *A Companion to Aristotle's Politics*, edited by D. Keyt and F. D. Miller, 94–117. Oxford.

Lateiner, D. 2009. "Tears in Apuleius' *Metamorphoses*." In *Tears in the Graeco-Roman World*, edited by T. Fögen, 277–96. Berlin.

Lenfant, D. 1999. "Monsters in Greek Ethnography and Society in the Fifth and Fourth Centuries BCE." In *From Myth to Reason? Studies in the Development of Greek Thought*, edited by R. Buxton, 197–214. Oxford.

Lennox, J. G. 1999. "The Place of Mankind in Aristotle's Zoology." *Philosophical Topics* 16:97–108.

Leopold, H. M. R. 1904. "Exulum trias, sive de Cicerone, Ovidio, Seneca exulibus." PhD diss, Utrecht University.

Luck, G., trans. and comm. 1977. *Tristia.* Heidelberg.

Luisi, A. 2001. *Il perdono negato: Ovidio e la corrente filoantoniana.* Bari.

Lundhaug, H. 2006. "Cognitive Poetics and Ancient Texts." In *Complexity: Interdisciplinary Communications 2006/2007*, edited by Willy Østreng, 18–21. Oslo.

Mack, S. 1988. *Ovid.* New Haven, CT.

Malherbe, A. J. 1988. *Ancient Epistolary Theorists.* Atlanta.

Marshall, S. 1995. *Schemas in Problem Solving.* Cambridge.

Mazzanti, R., trans. 1991. *Tristia. Con testo a fronte.* Milan.

McGowan, M. 2009. *Ovid in Exile: Power and Poetic Redress in the* Tristia *and* Epistulae ex Ponto. Leiden.

McKechnie, P. 1989. *Outsiders in the Greek Cities in the Fourth Century BC.* London.

McVee, M., K. Dunsmore, and J. Gavelek. 2005. "Schema Theory Revisited." *Review of Educational Research* 75:531–66.

Melville, A. D. 1992. *Ovid: Sorrows of an Exile.* Oxford.

———, trans. 2009. *Metamorphoses.* Oxford.

Meyer, M. 1987. *The Ancient Mysteries: A Sourcebook of Sacred Texts.* Philadelphia.

Miller, F. J., trans. 1939. *Metamorphoses.* Cambridge, MA.

Morel, W., ed. 1963. *Fragmenta poetarum Latinorum epicorum et lyricorum praeter Ennium et Lucilium,* by Emil Baehrens. Stuttgart.

Nagle, B. R. 1980. *The Poetics of Exile: Program and Polemic in the* Tristia *and* Epistulae ex Ponto *of Ovid.* Brussels.

Negri, A. M. 1984. *Gli psiconimi in Virgilio.* Bologna.

Newlands, C. 2014. "Reclaiming Ovid in Statius' *Silvae*." Paper delivered at the 110th Meeting of the Classical Association of the Middle West and South, April 4.

Newman, J. K. 1967. *Augustus and the New Poetry.* Brussels.

Newmyer, S. 1999. "Speaking of Beasts: The Stoics and Plutarch on Animal Reason and the Modern Case against Animals." *Quarderni Urbinati di Cultura Classica* 63, no. 3: 99–110.
———. 2011. *Animals in Greek and Roman Thought: A Sourcebook*. London.
Nora, P. 1984–92. *Lieux de mémoire*. New York.
Nugent, S. G. 1990. "Tristia 2: Ovid and Augustus." In *Between Republic and Empire: Interpretations of Augustus and His Principate*, edited by K. Raaflaub and M. Toher, 239–57. Berkeley, CA.
Olick, J., and J. Robbins. 1998. "Social Memory Studies: From 'Collective Memory' to the Historical Sociology of Mnemonic Practices." *Annual Review of Sociology* 24:105–40.
Olick, J., V. Vinitzky-Seroussi, and D. Levy, eds. 2011. *The Collective Memory Reader*. Oxford.
Ostriker, A. 1985. "The Thieves of Language: Women Poets and Revisionist Mythmaking." In *The New Feminist Criticism: Essays on Women, Literature, and Theory*, edited by E. Showalter, 314–18. New York.
Otis, B. 1970. *Ovid as an Epic Poet*. Cambridge.
Owen, S. G., trans. and comm. 1924. *Tristium Liber Secundus*. Oxford.
Pasquali, G. 1942. "Arte Allusiva." *Italia che scrive* 25:185–87.
Payne, M. 2010. *The Animal Part: Human and Other Animals in the Poetic Imagination*. Chicago.
Petersen, A. 2005. "Ovid's Wife in the *Tristia* and *Epistulae ex Ponto*: Transforming Erotic Elegy into Conjugal Elegy." Master's thesis, University of Georgia.
Piaget, J. 1952. *The Origins of Intelligence in Children*. Translated by Margaret Cook. New York.
Pohlenz, M. 1913. "Die Abfassungszeit von Ovids Metamorphosen." *Hermes* 48:1–13.
Posch, S. 1983. *P. Ovidius Naso*, Tristia 1.1. *Die Elegien 1–4*. Innsbruck.
Poteat, H. M. 1912. *Repetition in Latin Poetry*. New York.
Putnam, M. 1975. "Italian Virgil and the Idea of Rome." In *Janus: Essays in Ancient and Modern Studies*, edited by L. J. Orlin, 171–99. Ann Arbor, MI.
Rahn, H. 1958. "Ovids elegische Epistel." *A&A* 7:105–20.
Raval, S. 2003. "Stealing the Language: Echo in 'Metamorphoses' 3." In *Being There Together: Essays in Honor of Michael C. J. Putnam on the Occasion of His Seventieth Birthday*, edited by P. Thibodeau and H. Haskell, 204–21. Afton, MN.
Reeber, J. 2014. "The Lady and the Tiger: Generic Play in *Tristia* 1.6." Paper delivered at the 110th Meeting of the Classical Association of the Middle West and South, April 4.
Reeson, J. 2001. *Ovid Heroides 11, 13, and 14: A Commentary*. Leiden.
Renner, T. 1978. "A Papyrus Dictionary of Metamorphoses." *HSCP* 83:277–93.
Richlin, A. 1992. "Reading Ovid's Rapes." In *Pornography and Representation in Greece and Rome*, edited by A. Richlin, 158–79. New York.
Ricoeur, P. 2004. *Memory, History, Forgetting*. Chicago.
Riggsby, A. 2006. *Caesar in Gaul and Rome: War in Words*. Austin, TX.
Roisman, J. 1982. "Some Social Conventions and Deviations in Homeric Society." *Acta Classica* 25:35–41.

Roman, L. 2001. "The Representation of Literary Materiality in Martial's Epigrams." *JRS* 91:113–45.

Romm, J. 1992. *The Edges of the Earth in Ancient Thought*. Princeton, NJ.

Rosati, G. 1983. *Narciso e Pigmalione: Illusione e spettacolo nelle* Metamorfosi *di Ovidio*. Florence.

———. 1999. "Form in Motion: Weaving the Text in the *Metamorphoses*." In *Ovidian Transformations: Essays on Ovid's* Metamorphoses *and Its Reception*, edited by P. Hardie, A. Barchiesi, and S. Hinds, 240–53. Cambridge.

———, ed. 2007. *Metamorfosi: Libri V–VI*. Milan.

———. 2014. "Memory, Myth, and Power in Statius' *Silvae*." In *Memoria Romana: Memory in Rome and Rome in Memory*, edited by K. Galinsky, 71–84. Ann Arbor, MI.

Rosenmeyer, P. 2006. *Ancient Greek Literary Letters: Selections in Translation*. Routledge Classical Translations. London.

Rosiello, F. 2002. "Semantica di *error* in Ovidio." *Bolletino di Studi Latini* 32:424–62.

Ross, D. 1987. *Virgil's Elements: Poetry and Physics in the Georgics*. Princeton, NJ.

Roth-Souton, D., 1994. *Vladimir Nabokov: L'Enchantement de l'exil*. Paris.

Rüpke, J. 2009. *Religions of the Romans*. Cambridge.

Saito, A. 1996. "Social Origins of Cognition: Bartlett, Evolutionary Perspective and Embodied Mind Approach." *Journal for the Theory of Social Behavior* 26, no. 4: 399–421.

Segal, C. P. 1994. "Philomela's Web and the Pleasures of the Text: Reader and Violence in the *Metamorphoses* of Ovid." In *Modern Critical Theory and Classical Literature*, edited by I. J. F. de Jong and J. P. Sullivan, 257–80. Leiden.

Seibert, J. 1979. *Die politischen Flüchtlinge und Verbannten in der griechischen Geschichte: Von den Anfängen bis zur Unterwerfung durch die Römer*. Darmstadt.

Sharrock, A. 1994. *Seduction and Repetition in Ovid's Ars Amatoria II*. Oxford.

Simon, E. 2007. "Ovid und Pompeji." *Thetis* 13/14:149–54.

Solodow, J. 1988. *The World of Ovid's* Metamorphoses. Chapel Hill, NC.

Sorabji, R. 1993. *Animal Minds and Human Morals: The Origins of the Western Debate*. Ithaca, NY.

Sordi, M., ed. 1994. *Emigrazione e immigrazione nel mondo antico*. Milan.

Spalek, J. and J. P. Strelka, eds. 1976. *Die deutschsprachige Exilliteratur seit 1933 in Kalifornien*. Vol. 1. Bern.

Spentzou, E. 2003. *Readers and Writers in Ovid's* Heroides: *Transgressions of Genre and Gender*. Oxford.

Stevens, B. 2009. "Per gestum res est significanda mihi: Ovid and Language in Exile." *CPhil*. 104, no. 2: 162–83.

Stockwell, P. 2002. *Cognitive Poetics: An Introduction*. London.

Stok, F. 2010. "The Life of Vergil before Donatus." In *A Companion to Vergil's Aeneid and Its Tradition*, edited by J. Farrell and M. C. J. Putnam, 107–20. Oxford.

Stowers, S. 1986. *Letter Writing in Greco-Roman Antiquity*. Philadelphia.

Stramaglia, A. 1998. *Res inauditae, incredulae: Storie di fantasmi nel mondo Greco-latino*. Bari.

Stroh, W. 1981. *Tröstende Musen: Zur literarhistorischen Stellung und Bedeutung von Ovids Exilgedichten*. Berlin

Sweetser, E. 1999. "Compositionality and Blending: Semantic Composition in a Cognitively realistic framework." In *Cognitive Linguistics: Foundations, Scope and Methodology*, edited by G. Redeker and T. Janssen, 129–62. Berlin.
———. 1978. *History in Ovid*. Oxford.
Tabarroni, A. 1988. "On Articulation and Animal Language in Ancient Linguistic Theory." *Versus* 50/51:103–21.
Tarrant, R. J., comm. 2004. *Metamorphoses*. Oxford.
Taylor, R. 2008. *The Moral Mirror of Roman Art*. Cambridge.
Thomas, R. E. 1983. *The Latin Masks of Ezra Pound*. Ann Arbor, MI.
Thomas, R. F. 1982. *Lands and Peoples in Roman Poetry: The Ethnographical Tradition*. Cambridge Philological Society Supp. 7. Cambridge.
———. 1986. "Virgil's *Georgics* and the Art of Reference." *HSCP* 90: 171–98.
———. 1999. *Reading Virgil and His Texts: Studies in Intertextuality*. Ann Arbor, MI.
———, ed. 2001. *Virgil: Georgics*. 2 vols. Cambridge.
Tissol, G. 2000. "An Altered Portrait of the Artist: Some Transformed Images in Ovid's *Metamorphoses* and Poetry of Exile." In *From Caligula to Constantine: Tyranny and Transformation in Roman Portraiture*, edited by E. Varner, 81–84. Atlanta.
Tola, E. 2008. "Chronological Segmentation in Ovid's *Tristia*: The Implicit Narrative of Elegy." In *Latin Elegy and Narratology: Fragments of Story*, edited by G. Liveley and P. Salzman-Mitchell, 51–67. Columbus, OH.
Tränkle, H. 1960. *Die Sprachkunst des Properz und die Tradition der Lateinischen Dichersprache*. Weisbaden.
Turcan, R. 1996. *The Cults of the Roman Empire*. Oxford.
Turner, M. 2002. "The Cognitive Study of Art, Language, and Literature." *Poetics Today* 23, no. 1: 9–20.
Videau-Delibes, A. 1991. *Les Tristes d'Ovide et l'élégie romaine: Une poétique de la rupture*. Paris.
Walter, U. 2004. *Memoria und res publica: Zur Geschichtskultur im republikanischen Rom*. Frankfurt.
Wheeler, A. L. 1925. "Topics from the Life of Ovid." *AJP* 46:1–28.
Wickkiser, B. 1999. "Famous Last Words: Putting Ovid's Sphragis Back into the *Metamorphoses*." *Materiali e discussioni per l'analisi dei testi classici* 42:113–42.
Wilamowitz-Moellendorff, U. von. 1926. "Lesefrüchte (Auszug)." *Hermes* 61:298–302.
Williams, G. 1991. "Conversing after Sunset: A Callimachean Echo in Ovid's Exile Poetry." *CQ* 41, no. 1: 169–77.
———. 1994. *Banished Voices: Readings in Ovid's Exile Poetry*. Cambridge.
Williams, G. D., and A. D. Walker, eds. 1997. "Ovid and Exile." Special issue, *Ramus Critical Studies in Greek and Roman Literature* 26, no. 1.
Williams, J. 1997. *Interpreting Nightingales: Gender, Class and Histories*. Sheffield, UK.
Williams, W. G., trans. 1965. *Cicero, Letters to His Friends*. Cambridge.
Wyke, M. 2002. *The Roman Mistress*. Oxford.
Ziolkowski, T. 2005. *Ovid and the Moderns*. Ithaca, NY.
Zirin, R. A. 1980. "Aristotle's Biology of Language." *TAPA* 110:325–47.

*Appendix*

# Instances of Speech Loss in the *Metamorphoses*

The following characters undergo a transformation that subsequently leads to their speech loss. They are listed alphabetically, with their location in the *Metamorphoses*. The characters in bold are discussed in detail in this book and are noted with the pages on which they are discussed.

| *Character* | *Pages* |
|---|---|
| Acmon (14.497–98) | |
| **Actæon** (3.229–39) | 8, 41–45, 94–95 |
| Aglauros (2.829–30) | |
| Apulian Shepherd (14.523–26) | |
| Ascalaphus (5.549–50) | |
| Byblis (9.450–665) | |
| Cadmus (4.586–89) | |
| **Callisto** (2.476–88) | 37–41, 100–101 |
| Cecropians (14.91–100) | |
| Chione (11.324–27) | |
| Cyane (5.465–70) | |
| Cygnus (2.369–73) | |
| **Dryope** (9.388–92) | 45–48, 102–4 |
| **Echo** (3.356–69) | 48–53 |
| Galanthis (9.322–23) | |
| Hecuba (13.567–69) | |
| Heliades (2.363) | |
| Harmonia (4.595–97) | |
| **Io** (1.637–38) | 54–65 |
| **Lycaon** (1.232–3) | 7–8, 35–37 |

Lycians (6.374–78)
Minyeides (4.412–14)
Myrrha (10.506)
Niobe (6.306–7)
Ocyrhoe (2.657–69)
**Philomela** (6.551–60)     10, 65–79, 102, 109–22, 164
Pierides (5.677–78)
Rude Youth (5.451–61)

# Index

Actaeon, the myth of, 8, 41–45, 94–95
Atticus (friend of Ovid), 133–34, 136, 159–64

Callisto, the myth of, 37–41, 100–101
Celsus (friend of Ovid), 165–69, 175–76
cognitive poetics, 20–22
communicative memory, 143; compared to cultural memory, 143
Cornelius Severus (friend of Ovid), 113–14
Cotta Maximus (friend of Ovid), 115, 136–37
cultural memory, 143–44; compared to communicative memory, 143

Dryope, the myth of, 45–48, 102–4

Echo, the myth of, 48–53
exile: as death, 92, 108, 166–69; as sickness, 4; as topos, 5

failed prayers, 40–45, 59–60, 93, 106
false memory, 164–69

gesture as speech, 39–40, 63–65, 73–77, 112–16

*imago* as memory, 151–53
individual memory compared to collective memory, 142
Io, the myth of, 54–65

Kafka, Franz, 33–34

letters: as conversation, 124–26; as self, 126
literature and collective memory, 145–49
Lycaon, 7–8, 35–37

*memoria*: compared to *historia*, 144; defined, 142–44
memory: and the literary community, 153–64; and speech, 158–59
Messala Corvinus, 136
Messallinus (friend of Ovid), 134–35
*Mutus*, 17–20, 22–32, 72–73, 122

*oratio recta* as prelude to speech loss, 36, 42, 46, 48–49, 69–70, 89–90
*Os, oris* as speech, 39, 42, 72–73
Ovidian speech loss as trope in Latin literature, 81–83
Ovid's pose of decline, 81
Ovid's relationship to poetic community, 128–37
Ovid's wife, 90, 95–96, 105, 115, 129, 166–69

Paulus Fabius Maximus (friend of Ovid), 111–13
Perilla (Ovid's niece), 128–29
Philomela, the myth of, 10, 65–79, 102, 109–22, 164

Procne, the myth of, 75–79, 112
progression of metamorphosis to emphasize speech loss, 38–39, 46

Rufinius (friend of Ovid), 116–117

schemata, 20–32
scholarship on exile literature: in antiquity, 4–13; in modernity, 3–4; in Ovid, 6, 11–13
*sonus*: as inarticulate sound, 44, 50–53, 95–96; as opposed to *vox*, 50–53, 59–60, 122
speech of birds, 78–79
speech loss: caused by fear, 23–24, 30–31, 36–37, 40–41, 60, 65; caused by grief, 75–76; defined, 11–13, 22–32; as identity crisis, 40–41, 44–46, 58, 66–67, 71, 90–92, 101, 104
structure of *Tristia* 1, 84–85

Tuticanus (friend of Ovid), 133–34

*vox* as articulate speech, 49–53, 59–60, 122
*vultus*, 7–13, 58, 177–78; as opposed to *species*, 58

weaving as writing (poetry), 74
writing as speech, 53–54, 56, 63–64, 72–79, 109–16, 122–38

# *Index Locorum*

Arist., *Pol.*
    1253a9–10: 18
Callim., *Epigr.*
    2.1–4: 162
Catull.
    50.1–6: 161
    101: 26–27
Cic., *Att.*
    12.39.2: 125
  *Fam.*
    2.4.1: 125
    3.11.2: 127
    15.12.37: 140
  *Sen.*
    18.64: 155
    19.70: 155–56
    23.85: 156
Enn., *Ann.*
    175–79: 118
Hor., *Sat.*
    1.3.99–106: 25–27
Livy
    *Praef.* 9–10: 145–46
Lucr.
    1.87–92: 28–30
    5.1056–61, 1087–90: 25–27
Mart.
    2.8.1–4: 80, 82
Ov., *Ars am.*
    1.39–42: 160
    3.699–714: 29–32

*Her.*
    14.85–92: 55
*Met.*
    1.1–2: 155
    1.1–4: 148
    1.221–23: 36
    1.232–35: 36
    1.236–39: 7–8
    1.610–14: 57
    1.630–38: 59
    1.639–44: 61
    1.646–48: 62–63
    1.646–50: 123
    1.649–63: 63–64
    2.474–95: 38–39
    2.489–92: 101
    3.141–42: 95
    3.148–53: 42
    3.192–205: 43
    3.200–203: 8
    3.229–31: 44
    3.237–39: 44
    3.242–46: 45
    6.515–30: 67
    6.519–26: 117, 119
    6.542–48: 69
    6.546–48: 109
    6.551–660: 70–71
    6.571–75: 72, 102
    6.576–80: 109–10
    6.576–86: 73–74

    6.658–60: 112
    9.356–58: 50
    9.359–62: 104
    9.362–67: 49
    9.367–70: 104
    9.375–79: 47
    9.379–92: 51
    9.382–84: 47
    9.393–401: 52–53
    15.871–872: 132
    15.871–79: 179

*Pont.*
    1.3.35–42: 116, 120–21
    1.5.73–76: 115
    1.7.1–4: 123
    1.7.27–34: 135
    1.9: 150–69
    1.9.7–8: 150, 167
    1.9.7–24: 165–66
    1.9.9–10: 154
    1.9.13–18: 163
    1.9.13–30: 175
    1.9.17–20: 168
    1.9.21–24: 167–68
    2.4: 150–64
    2.4.7–8: 150–51
    2.4.7–18: 133
    2.4.9–18: 154
    2.4.11–12: 158
    2.4.13–20: 159
    2.4.21–22: 160
    2.6.1–4: 122
    3.5.37–44: 136–37
    3.5.48–54: 137
    3.8.19–22: 111
    4.2.23–34: 114
    4.6.39–50: 173–74
    4.12.19–37: 134

*Tr.*
    1.1.1–10: 176
    1.1.9–10: 126
    1.1.15–16: 127
    1.1.15–30: 171–72
    1.1.21–24: 178
    1.1.107–22: 6–7
    1.1.117–22: 170–71, 177
    1.2.13–18: 106
    1.2.33–36: 106
    1.2.53–56: 106–7
    1.3.1–2: 167
    1.3: 85–105
    1.3.1–4: 86, 151
    1.3.5–26: 88–92
    1.3.17–18, 79–80: 168
    1.3.26–46: 92–99
    1.3.31–34: 98
    1.3.37–39: 94
    1.3.41–42: 95
    1.3.45–46: 98
    1.3.47–76: 99–105
    1.3.47–54: 100
    1.3.51–54: 167
    1.3.62–72: 103
    1.3.69–72: 107
    1.4.23–24: 107
    1.5: 9
    1.7.1–4: 9
    1.7.13–24: 132
    1.7.29–40: 131
    2.221–24, 239–42: 157
    3.1.17–18: 82
    3.1.55–56: 127
    3.1.69–70: 128
    3.7.1–6: 128
    3.14.27–30, 43–50: 81
    4.4.25–32: 134–35
    4.9.17–26: 110
    5.8: 9
    5.10.35–42: 113
    5.13.17–30: 173
    5.14.15–18: 115

Ps. Lib., *Epis. Char.*
    2.58: 126

Quint., *Inst.*
    1.4.6: 24

Sen. *Constant.*
    18.9: 80, 82

*Ep.*
    40.1: 127
    75.1: 126

*Serv. Dan.*
    1.3.84: 24
Stat., *Silv.*
    1.1.79–81: 148
  *Theb.*
    1.21–22: 148
Varro, *Rust.*
    1.17.1.7: 27–28
Verg., *Aen.*
    2.270–73: 152
    2.705–20: 97
    2.772–74, 792–94: 152
    3.11–12: 98
    6.179–82: 118–19
    6.695–96, 699–701: 152–53
    6.847–53: 146–47
    12.715–19: 29–31
  *G.*
    3.224–34: 60–61
    4.511–15: 74
Vitr., *De arch.*
    2.1.1: 18–19

# Wisconsin Studies in Classics

LAURA MCCLURE, MARK STANSBURY-O'DONNELL, AND
MATTHEW ROLLER, SERIES EDITORS

*Romans and Barbarians: The Decline of the Western Empire*
    E. A. THOMPSON

*A History of Education in Antiquity*
    H. I. MARROU, translated from the French by GEORGE LAMB

*Accountability in Athenian Government*
    JENNIFER TOLBERT ROBERTS

*Festivals of Attica: An Archaeological Commentary*
    ERIKA SIMON

*Roman Cities: Les villes romaines*
    PIERRE GRIMAL, edited and translated by G. MICHAEL WOLOCH

*Ancient Greek Art and Iconography*
    Edited by WARREN G. MOON

*Greek Footwear and the Dating of Sculpture*
    KATHERINE DOHAN MORROW

*The Classical Epic Tradition*
    JOHN KEVIN NEWMAN

*Ancient Anatolia: Aspects of Change and Cultural Development*
    Edited by JEANNY VORYS CANBY, EDITH PORADA, BRUNILDE
    SISMONDO RIDGWAY, and TAMARA STECH

*Euripides and the Tragic Tradition*
    ANN NORRIS MICHELINI

*Wit and the Writing of History: The Rhetoric of Historiography in Imperial Rome*
    PAUL PLASS

*The Archaeology of the Olympics: The Olympics and Other Festivals in Antiquity*
    Edited by WENDY J. RASCHKE

*Tradition and Innovation in Late Antiquity*
    Edited by F. M. CLOVER and R. S. HUMPHREYS

*The Hellenistic Aesthetic*
    BARBARA HUGHES FOWLER

*Hellenistic Sculpture I: The Styles of ca. 331–200 B.C.*
    BRUNILDE SISMONDO RIDGWAY

*Hellenistic Poetry: An Anthology*
    Selected and translated by BARBARA HUGHES FOWLER

*Theocritus' Pastoral Analogies: The Formation of a Genre*
    KATHRYN J. GUTZWILLER

*Rome and India: The Ancient Sea Trade*
    Edited by VIMALA BEGLEY and RICHARD DANIEL DE PUMA

*Kallimachos: The Alexandrian Library and the Origins of Bibliography*
    RUDOLF BLUM, translated by HANS H. WELLISCH

*Myth, Ethos, and Actuality: Official Art in Fifth Century B.C. Athens*
    DAVID CASTRIOTA

*Archaic Greek Poetry: An Anthology*
    Selected and translated by BARBARA HUGHES FOWLER

*Murlo and the Etruscans: Art and Society in Ancient Etruria*
    Edited by RICHARD DANIEL DE PUMA and JOCELYN PENNY SMALL

*The Wedding in Ancient Athens*
    JOHN H. OAKLEY and REBECCA H. SINOS

*The World of Roman Costume*
    Edited by JUDITH LYNN SEBESTA and LARISSA BONFANTE

*Greek Heroine Cults*
    JENNIFER LARSON

*Flinders Petrie: A Life in Archaeology*
    MARGARET S. DROWER

*Polykleitos, the Doryphoros, and Tradition*
    Edited by WARREN G. MOON

*The Game of Death in Ancient Rome: Arena Sport and Political Suicide*
PAUL PLASS

*Polygnotos and Vase Painting in Classical Athens*
SUSAN B. MATHESON

*Worshipping Athena: Panathenaia and Parthenon*
Edited by JENIFER NEILS

*Hellenistic Architectural Sculpture: Figural Motifs in Western Anatolia and the Aegean Islands*
PAMELA A. WEBB

*Fourth-Century Styles in Greek Sculpture*
BRUNILDE SISMONDO RIDGWAY

*Ancient Goddesses: The Myths and the Evidence*
Edited by LUCY GOODISON and CHRISTINE MORRIS

*Displaced Persons: The Literature of Exile from Cicero to Boethius*
JO-MARIE CLAASSEN

*Hellenistic Sculpture II: The Styles of ca. 200–100 B.C.*
BRUNILDE SISMONDO RIDGWAY

*Personal Styles in Early Cycladic Sculpture*
PAT GETZ-GENTLE

*The Complete Poetry of Catullus*
CATULLUS, translated and with commentary by DAVID MULROY

*Hellenistic Sculpture III: The Styles of ca. 100–31 B.C.*
BRUNILDE SISMONDO RIDGWAY

*The Iconography of Sculptured Statue Bases in the Archaic and Classical Periods*
ANGELIKI KOSMOPOULOU

*Discs of Splendor: The Relief Mirrors of the Etruscans*
ALEXANDRA A. CARPINO

*Mail and Female: Epistolary Narrative and Desire in Ovid's "Heroides"*
SARA H. LINDHEIM

*Modes of Viewing in Hellenistic Poetry and Art*
GRAHAM ZANKER

*Religion in Ancient Etruria*
JEAN-RENÉ JANNOT, translated by JANE K. WHITEHEAD

*A Symposion of Praise: Horace Returns to Lyric in "Odes" IV*
TIMOTHY JOHNSON

*Satire and the Threat of Speech: Horace's "Satires," Book 1*
CATHERINE M. SCHLEGEL

*Prostitutes and Courtesans in the Ancient World*
Edited by CHRISTOPHER A. FARAONE and LAURA K. MCCLURE

*Asinaria: The One about the Asses*
PLAUTUS, translated and with commentary by JOHN HENDERSON

*Ulysses in Black: Ralph Ellison, Classicism, and African American Literature*
PATRICE D. RANKINE

*Imperium and Cosmos: Augustus and the Northern Campus Martius*
PAUL REHAK, edited by JOHN G. YOUNGER

*Ovid before Exile: Art and Punishment in the "Metamorphoses"*
PATRICIA J. JOHNSON

*Pandora's Senses: The Feminine Character of the Ancient Text*
VERED LEV KENAAN

*Nox Philologiae: Aulus Gellius and the Fantasy of the Roman Library*
ERIK GUNDERSON

*New Perspectives on Etruria and Early Rome*
Edited by SINCLAIR BELL and HELEN NAGY

*The Image of the Poet in Ovid's "Metamorphoses"*
BARBARA PAVLOCK

*Responses to Oliver Stone's "Alexander": Film, History, and Cultural Studies*
Edited by PAUL CARTLEDGE and FIONA ROSE GREENLAND

*The Codrus Painter: Iconography and Reception of Athenian Vases in the Age of Pericles*
AMALIA AVRAMIDOU

*The Matter of the Page: Essays in Search of Ancient and Medieval Authors*
SHANE BUTLER

*Greek Prostitutes in the Ancient Mediterranean, 800 BCE–200 CE*
Edited by ALLISON GLAZEBROOK and MADELEINE M. HENRY

*Sophocles' "Philoctetes" and the Great Soul Robbery*
NORMAN AUSTIN

*Oedipus Rex*
    SOPHOCLES, a verse translation by DAVID MULROY, with introduction and notes

*The Slave in Greece and Rome*
    JOHN ANDREAU and RAYMOND DESCAT, translated by MARION LEOPOLD

*Perfidy and Passion: Reintroducing the "Iliad"*
    MARK BUCHAN

*The Gift of Correspondence in Classical Rome: Friendship in Cicero's "Ad Familiares" and Seneca's "Moral Epistles"*
    AMANDA WILCOX

*Antigone*
    SOPHOCLES, a verse translation by DAVID MULROY, with introduction and notes

*Aeschylus's "Suppliant Women": The Tragedy of Immigration*
    GEOFFREY W. BAKEWELL

*Couched in Death: "Klinai" and Identity in Anatolia and Beyond*
    ELIZABETH P. BAUGHAN

*Silence in Catullus*
    BENJAMIN ELDON STEVENS

*Odes*
    HORACE, translated with commentary by DAVID R. SLAVITT

*Shaping Ceremony: Monumental Steps and Greek Architecture*
    MARY B. HOLLINSHEAD

*Selected Epigrams*
    MARTIAL, translated with notes by SUSAN MCLEAN

*The Offense of Love: "Ars Amatoria," "Remedia Amoris," and "Tristia" 2*
    OVID, a verse translation by JULIA DYSON HEJDUK, with introduction and notes

*Oedipus at Colonus*
    SOPHOCLES, a verse translation by DAVID MULROY, with introduction and notes

*Women in Roman Republican Drama*
    Edited by DOROTA DUTSCH, SHARON L. JAMES, and DAVID KONSTAN

*Dream, Fantasy, and Visual Art in Roman Elegy*
  EMMA SCIOLI

*Agamemnon*
  AESCHYLUS, a verse translation by DAVID MULROY, with introduction and notes

*Trojan Women, Helen, Hecuba: Three Plays about Women and the Trojan War*
  EURIPIDES, verse translations by FRANCIS BLESSINGTON, with introduction and notes

*Echoing Hylas: A Study in Hellenistic and Roman Metapoetics*
  MARK HEERINK

*Horace between Freedom and Slavery: The First Book of "Epistles"*
  STEPHANIE MCCARTER

*The Play of Allusion in the "Historia Augusta"*
  DAVID ROHRBACHER

*Repeat Performances: Ovidian Repetition and the "Metamorphoses"*
  Edited by LAUREL FULKERSON and TIM STOVER

*Virgil and Joyce: Nationalism and Imperialism in the "Aeneid" and "Ulysses"*
  RANDALL J. POGORZELSKI

*The Athenian Adonia in Context: The Adonis Festival as Cultural Practice*
  LAURIALAN REITZAMMER

*Ctesias' "Persica" and Its Near Eastern Context*
  MATT WATERS

*Silenced Voices: The Poetics of Speech in Ovid*
  BARTOLO A. NATOLI

www.ingramcontent.com/pod-product-compliance
Lightning Source LLC
Chambersburg PA
CBHW070841160426
43192CB00012B/2264